D1609848

THE MALBIM
ESTHER

THE MALBIM
ESTHER

Translated and annotated by
Rabbi Jonathan Taub

TARGUM/FELDHEIM

First published 1998
Copyright © 1998 by J. Taub
ISBN 1-56871-135-2

Published by:
Targum Press Inc.
22700 W. Eleven Mile Rd.
Southfield, Mich. 48034
E-mail: targum@elronet.co.il

in conjunction with
Mishnas Rishonim

Distributed by:
Feldheim Publishers
200 Airport Executive Park
Nanuet, N.Y. 10954

Distributed in Israel by:
Targum Press Ltd.
POB 43170
Jerusalem 91430
FAX: (972) 2-6510342

Printed in Israel

Letter of Approbation from HaGaon Rav Chaim Kreiswirth, *shlita*, Chief Rabbi of Antwerp, Belgium

RABBINAAT

van de

ISRAELITISCHE ORTHODOXE GEMEENTE

" MACHSIKE HADASS "

JACOB JACOBSSTRAAT 22 - 2018 ANTWERPEN

Antwerpen, de

ב״ה

OPPERRABIJN
CH. KREISWIRTH

Ere-Voorzitter van de vereniging
van de Isr. Orthodoxe gemeenten
In Europa

Tel.: 233.55.67
232.00.21

E. STERNBUCH
Rabbijn

T. WEISS
Rabbijn

N. MALIK
Oppervoorzanger

J.S. GLICK
Voorzanger

HOOFDSYNAGOGE :
Oostenstraat 43

SYNAGOGEN :
Oostenstraat 44
Jacob Jacobsstraat 22
BELZ : Van Spangenstraat 6
BETH JITZHAK : Mercatorstraat 56
BOBOV : Lange Leemstraat 224
EISENMANN : Oostenstraat 29
GUR : Ant. van Dyckstraat 43
KLAUSENBURG : Van Leriusstraat 54
LUBAWITCH : Brialmontlei 58
OR SHRAGAI : Van Leriusstraat 22
SATMAR : Jacob Jacobsstraat 6
TSCHORTKOW : Van Leriusstraat 37
WIZNITZ : Jacob Jacobsstraat 35
WIZNITZ : Brialmontlei 18
ZICHRON BENJAMIN : Breughelstraat 38
GITSCHOTEL : Marsstraat 50

Rabbi Nachman Bulman
Yeshivat Ohr Somayach
Ohr Lagolah

הרב נחמן בולמן
ישיבת אור שמח
אור לגולה

כסלו תשנ״ח פה עיה״ק ת״ו
December 1997

Among the great commentators on Torah, Prophets, and Writings, the Malbim has achieved singular preeminence. He unites the Written and Oral forms of Torah through a matchless insight into the utmost subtleties of Torah grammar and style. All of which poses formidable obstacles to adaptation of Malbim in English translation. Many need such translation, but to date Torah scholars to undertake such a task have not been available.

Rabbi Yonasan Taub has completed the Malbim on Megillas Esther with utter faithfulness and stylistic elegance, in a beautiful English rendition.

Many will be grateful to him.

הכותב למען כבוד התורה — לומדי׳ ומלמדי׳

נחמן בולמן
ישיבת אור שמח פה עיה״ק

RABBI ZEV LEFF
Rav of Moshav Matityahu
Rosh Hayeshiva
Yeshiva Gedola Matisyahu
D.N. Modiin 71917 Israel
08-926-1138 Fax 08-926-5326

כ"ז כסלו תשנ"ח נר ג' של חנוכה

I have seen the manuscript of Rabbi Yonasan Taub's rendition of the Malbim's commentary on Megillas Esther into English. It is needless to say that the commentary of the Malbim needs no approbation. However, I feel compelled to extend my heartfelt congratulations and my sincerest commendation to Rabbi Taub for the masterful job he has done.

There is a special blessing that the prophet Yeshayahu asks for to be able to convey the timeless words of the Torah so as to make the proper impression on a specific audience. (See *Yeshayahu*, chapter 50, verse 4.)

Hashem *Yisborach* has blessed Rabbi Taub with this valuable ability, as is evident from the masterful clarity and charming style with which he has rendered the timeless words of the Malbim into English.

May Hashem grant him the wisdom and strength to produce many similar works, to convey so beautifully the enlightening ideas of our sages to the audience of English speakers who thirst for words of Torah and *yiras Shamayim* in their vernacular.

With Torah blessings,

Zev Leff

This book is dedicated
to the beloved memory of

CHANA BIRNBAUM ע״ה

חנה בת חיים ע״ה

נפטרה י״א אלול תשנ״ו

Like Esther before her,
she always placed the needs
of her fellow Jews
before her own well-being.

She *"found grace in the eyes of all who saw her."*

(Esther 2:15)

ת. נ. צ. ב. ה.

Acknowledgements

First and foremost, I would like to express my gratitude to the Almighty for having granted me the opportunity to both study and to introduce others to the brilliance of the Malbim.

Many thanks are due to the readers who expressed to me their appreciation of the *Malbim Haggadah* and thereby provided the encouragement to produce the *Malbim Esther*.

Rabbi Pinchas Waldman's erudition was continuously available during the writing of this book, obviating recourse to computer search programs in researching sources.

Rabbi Joseph Pearlman gave freely of his time to discuss and clarify many of the points discussed in the footnotes.

Rabbi Yisroel Shaw, with whom I wrote the *Malbim Haggadah*, reviewed the entire work, and his innumerable suggestions considerably improved its style.

Both my brothers, Daniel and Adam Taub, read the manuscript, and the imprint of their flair with the English language greatly enhanced the final product.

It is always a pleasure to work with the staff at Targum Press. They combine a serious professionalism with an infectious enthusiasm for the projects they undertake. Particular thanks are due to Rabbi Moshe Dombey who took the decision to produce this book; to D. Liff and Akiva Atwood for their sensitivity in the design; and to Ita Olesker for her thorough proofreading.

This book is dedicated with gratitude to my wife Rachel, in memory of her mother Chana Birnbaum, *z"l*.

J.T

Jerusalem, Kislev 5758

Introduction

Why the Malbim?

S erious students of Torah have always been interested not only in increasing their Torah knowledge, but also in acquiring a *derech halimud*, a methodology in the techniques of Torah study. The reason for this is simple. Improved skill and technique will benefit all subsequent study, leading to increased depth and clarity. Reading anthologies of commentaries will increase the information one knows, without necessarily advancing one's ability to independently study Torah texts. The commentary of the Malbim (Rav Meir Leibush bn Yechiel Michal, 1809–1879) gives the reader superb training in improving textual analysis. By means of his penetrating questions, the Malbim presents a master class in sensitivity to the most delicate nuances and shades of meaning. For example, he demonstrates that the use of the phrase *"Queen Vashti"* in some verses, and *"Vashti the queen"* in others, indicates a fascinating struggle for power and glory between the king and queen (see chapter 1, verse 9.)

When we read the Malbim's commentary and discover how sometimes slight and subtle inferences can radically alter the narrative and uncover fascinating layers of meaning, we gain both the inspiration and the techniques for deeper and more fulfilling study of Torah.

The Malbim answers the questions that he poses in a run-ning commentary on the Megillah. A certain intellectual effort is sometimes required in order to see how the commentary answers all the questions. In some instances, I have suggested possible interpretations of how the questions are answered where we have felt that the answer was not clearly indicated by the commentary. These suggestions have been included as footnotes, as have questions on certain interpretations of the Malbim and, in some cases, possible resolutions.

In addition, I have indicated in the footnotes where the Malbim translates phrases or explains ideas differently from commonly accepted translations and interpretations, and have attempted to show why the Malbim rejects the standard approach.

WHY THE MALBIM ON MEGILLAS ESTHER?

The first commentary that the Malbim published, which appeared in 1845, was on Megillas Esther. This is not surprising in light of the fact that Megillas Esther is one of the best known and beloved books of the Holy Scriptures. It is the only book which every adult Jew is obligated to hear, in its entirety, twice every year. The affection we have for Megillas Esther even has *halachic* ramifications. If two people are reading the weekly portion of the Torah out loud, the congregation has not fulfilled its obligation to hear the reading. This is based on the principle that the words of two voices together cannot be clearly distinguished. However, in the cases of *Hallel* and Megillas Esther this principle does not apply. Since these are so cherished by Jews, it is presumed that extra effort is made to listen closely and, thus, the words are heard by the congregation.[1]

The familiarity which many already have with the narrative and text of the Megillah makes it an excellent introduction to the style and methodology of the Malbim. Following the Malbim's

---

1. See *Megillah* 21b and *Shulchan Aruch, Orach Chayim* 690:2.

probing questions and breathtaking analysis, we are given a stark contrast between the understanding we may have had since childhood and the new vistas that the Malbim reveals. The Malbim transforms what to many seems a rather simple story into a sophisticated, complex historical event with detailed social, economic, and political implications. He enables us to relate to the Megillah — and consequently to Purim — as a real part of our history and our lives.

Hallel, a prayer thanking the Almighty for His miraculous protection and the salvation of the Jewish people, is read on all festivals other than Purim. One reason given by our Sages[1] is that the recitation of Megillas Esther fulfills the obligation to say *Hallel*. Reading this account of the salvation of the Jewish people brought about by the Almighty is meant to fill us with the same feelings of gratitude and thanks expressed in the *Hallel* prayer. Studying the Malbim's commentary enables us to comprehend remarkable aspects of our miraculous deliverance which we would not have otherwise realized, leading to a more heartfelt gratitude to the Almighty — an even deeper expression of *Hallel*.

May this commentary of the Malbim on Megillas Esther be the inspiration to attain deeper appreciation of the riches of Torah wisdom.

---

1. *Megillah* 14a.

CHAPTER 1

א א   וַיְהִי בִּימֵי אֲחַשְׁוֵרוֹשׁ הוּא אֲחַשְׁוֵרוֹשׁ הַמֹּלֵךְ
מֵהֹדּוּ וְעַד־כּוּשׁ שֶׁבַע וְעֶשְׂרִים וּמֵאָה מְדִינָה:

1 And it came to pass in the days of
Achashverosh, he was the Achashverosh
who ruled from India to Ethiopia, over a
hundred and twenty-seven provinces,

QUESTIONS

GENERALLY, the phrase *"and it came to pass in the days"*[1] is used to
recount an occurrence that took place in the life of the person or
during the period mentioned and is a method of dating that occurrence. Here, though, the usage is self-referential, using the
lifetime of Achashverosh to tell us about Achashverosh himself.

THE phrase *"he was the Achashverosh who ruled from India to Ethio-*

---

1. For example, "And it came to pass in the days when the judges
   ruled that there was a famine in the land" (Ruth 1:1).

pia" seems superfluous. We do not know of any other Achash-verosh that this could be coming to exclude. What does this phrase teach us?

THROUGHOUT the entire Megillah, the name "King Achash-verosh" is used. This verse is the only one to use the name Achashverosh without the appellation "King." Why?

IF the absence of "King" is to tell us that he was not yet the mon-arch, then why are we told that he *"ruled from India to Ethiopia"*?

THE phrase *"who ruled"* is written as המולך — in the present tense, rather than the past tense, אשר מלך, as we would expect. Why?

COMMENTARY

An understanding of Megillas Esther requires a brief intro-duction into how monarchies functioned when Egyptians, Me-des, and Persians controlled the world stage.

There were two types of monarchies. The first was a monar-chy in which the king was elected by the people. The second type of monarchy was rule by force, in which the king conquered the country and became its ruler.

The powers of the king in the first type of monarchy were limited. The limits of his powers were legislated at the time of his election. Upon taking office, the king swore to follow the laws and practices of the country. In the second type of monarchy, however, the powers of the king were unlimited. Though he might seek the advice of ministers, he did what he wanted, changing the laws of the country as he saw fit.

There were five major, practical differences between these two types of monarchies:

1. In the limited monarchy, the king was the head of state who legislated and was responsible for leading the country in its wars. The people, in turn, pledged their allegiance, accepting

their duties to the king and agreeing to pay taxes for the mutual welfare of the entire populace. In the unlimited monarchy, however, the country was totally subservient to the king, and its people were his slaves.

2. The national treasuries in the limited monarchy belonged to the state. In the unlimited monarchy, they belonged to the king himself.

3. The king that ruled in a limited monarchy was not free to make major policy decisions without the approval of the country's ministers. The unlimited monarch had no such restrictions.

4. The limited monarch was bound by the laws of the country. The unlimited monarch could change the laws as he wished.

5. The capital city could not be changed in a limited monarchy; the king had to rule from the same city as his forebears. The unlimited monarch could change his capital city as and when he wanted.

With this introduction we can proceed to the Purim story.

Achashverosh was originally a commoner[1] who, through his wealth, gained control over Media and Persia until he eventually conquered one hundred and twenty-seven countries. These had all been provinces of the Babylonian empire which had Babylon[2] as its capital city, and not Shushan.[3]

In order to consolidate his control, he married Vashti, granddaughter of Nevuchadnetzar, the former emperor of the

---

1. *Megillah* 11a.
2. See Daniel 4:26, "... he was walking in the palace of the kingdom in Babylon."
3. Daniel 8:2 refers to Shushan as being in the province of Elam without mentioning that it was the capital city (Malbim). However, this verse does refer to Shushan as הבירה, commonly understood to mean "the capital city." Presumably the Malbim understood it to mean "citadel," an alternative interpretation of הבירה. Therefore, we have rendered it as such in our translation of the Megillah text. (Ed.)

Babylonian empire, and heiress to the throne. Now his position was doubly assured. His wife was successor to the throne and he, himself, had conquered the empire. If his claim to power rested on his conquest, his dominion would be unlimited; if, however, it was based on his wife's claim to the throne, the monarch's power would be limited. Originally, the provinces of the empire had acceded to Achashverosh's dominion in the belief that his claim to power rested on his wife's inheritance of the throne and that his monarchy was, consequently, limited in power. Achashverosh, though, wanted limitless power, and this was his prime motive in moving the capital city to Shushan, in hosting his huge banquet, and in commanding Vashti to appear before him. As we shall see, all these were cunning strategies to achieve this goal.

The name "Achashverosh" is used without the appellation "King" to tell us that he was not from royal descent and that his rise to power was not gradual, which would have given time for people to forget his humble origins, but **it came to pass in the days of Achashverosh**, when he was still a commoner. In those same days he became **the Achashverosh who ruled from India to Ethiopia** — his conquest happened so quickly that nobody remembered which province he had conquered first. That explains why the present tense is used — people could not recollect what he used to control. It all happened so quickly that people could only remember that Achashverosh the commoner *now* ruled **over a hundred and twenty-seven provinces.**

ב   בַּיָּמִים הָהֵם כְּשֶׁבֶת ׀ הַמֶּלֶךְ אֲחַשְׁוֵרוֹשׁ עַל כִּסֵּא
מַלְכוּתוֹ אֲשֶׁר בְּשׁוּשַׁן הַבִּירָה:

2 **that in those days, when King Achashverosh sat on the throne of his monarchy in Shushan the citadel,**

QUESTIONS

THE phrase *"in those days"* is superfluous. The previous verse already stated that *"it came to pass in the days of Achashverosh."* Why is the phrase used here?

ALSO, *"King Achashverosh"* is unnecessary, for he was mentioned in the previous verse. Would it not have been better to say, *"when he sat on the throne of his monarchy"*?

WHY do we need to be told that he sat on the throne and that it was in Shushan?

COMMENTARY

At the outset of his rule, his power was so strong that he decided to move the royal residence from Babylon to Shushan. This would achieve two aims. First, it would show that he intended to rule with unlimited power and was not afraid of public displeasure at the change of location.[1]

Second, it would demonstrate his "eminent status." Generally, when a commoner accedes to the throne, it is an honor for him to be able to sit on the same throne as his royal predecessors. He would not construct a new one for himself because doing so would deprive him of the honor that the old throne conferred. Achashverosh, however, was so arrogant that he ignored all his predecessors, constructing a new throne and moving the capital city to Shushan. This demonstrated that it was not public consent that gave him dominion over the kingdom, but his conquest.

This did not take place after many years in power, but immediately **in those days** it already seemed that **King Achashverosh**

---

1. See commentary on verse 1, the fifth difference between limited and unlimited monarchies.

sat on the throne of his monarchy as one of royal pedigree, sitting on **the throne of** *his* **monarchy,** without recourse to the honor of his predecessors.

ג   בִּשְׁנַת שָׁלוֹשׁ לְמָלְכוֹ עָשָׂה מִשְׁתֶּה לְכָל־שָׂרָיו
וַעֲבָדָיו חֵיל ׀ פָּרַס וּמָדַי הַפַּרְתְּמִים וְשָׂרֵי הַמְּדִינוֹת
לְפָנָיו:

3 **in the third year of his reign, he made a banquet for all his officials and servants and the army of Poras and Modai; the governors and officials before him,**

QUESTIONS

WHY did Achashverosh host this huge banquet?

WHAT is the need for all the details of the banquet?

THE order of those present is puzzling. First the *"officials and servants"* are mentioned, then the *"army,"* and then the *"governors and officials."* Why are *"officials"* mentioned twice and why are the *"governors and officials"* mentioned after the *"servants"* who are, presumably, of lower status?

WHAT is the need to say *"before him"*?

WHY does it say *"in the third year of his reign,"* whereas when Esther becomes queen, the phrase *"in the seventh year of his kingdom"*[1] is used?

---

1. Ch. 2, v. 16.

COMMENTARY

In order to achieve his ambition of unlimited power, **in the third year of his reign,**[1] **he made a banquet** as a stratagem towards this end. The order of those present at the banquet teaches us Achashverosh's motives.

First, **all his officials and servants,** then **the army of Poras and Modai,** and only after them **the governors and officials before him**[2] who had preceded him, holding office before Achashverosh ever conquered their countries. This clearly demonstrated his conviction that his rule was not dependent on their agreement and appointment because, if so, then the officials of the major states would come before those of the small country he originally controlled and would definitely precede the servants and soldiers of the army. By placing his own servants and the army of conquest first, he showed that he regarded the governors and officials as merely vestiges of the era before his conquest occurred.

ד   בְּהַרְאֹתוֹ אֶת־עֹשֶׁר כְּבוֹד מַלְכוּתוֹ וְאֶת־יְקָר
תִּפְאֶרֶת גְּדוּלָּתוֹ יָמִים רַבִּים שְׁמוֹנִים וּמְאַת יוֹם:

4 **when he displayed the wealth of his glorious kingdom and the honor of his great splendor for many days, a hundred and eighty days.**

---

1. The reason that the phrase *"of his reign"*— למלכו — is used here is that it places the emphasis on the king, the root being the word מלך — "king," in contrast to למלכותו — *"of his kingdom"* (ch. 2, v. 16). This indicates that the underlying motivation was to stengthen the monarch's own power.

2. The word לפניו — *"before him"* is explained by the Malbim not as "in front of him" (physically), as is usually understood, but as "preceding him" (temporally).

QUESTIONS

WHY did Achashverosh feel the need to display his wealth to the assembled nations?

WHAT is the point of the repetitive *"honor of his great splendor"*?

WHY are we told that this display lasted for *"many days"*?

COMMENTARY

We have already explained that in a monarchy of limited power, the national wealth and treasuries belong to the nation, not to the king. He is not free to display them as his own.

In order to rule with absolute power, Achashverosh appropriated them and exhibited them before the assembled nation like a man who flaunts his own personal wealth.

Therefore, **he displayed the wealth of his glorious kingdom** as if it belonged to him, available for his own personal honor through his accession to the throne. Every king requires wealth, but a ruler over an empire of one hundred and twenty-seven nations obviously needs commensurate riches and prestige. So he showed them **the honor of his great splendor,** and not only for one or two days but for **many days, a hundred and eighty days**. This was a clear indication to all that he had commandeered the treasuries as his own.

ה   וּבִמְלוֹאת ׀ הַיָּמִים הָאֵלֶּה עָשָׂה הַמֶּלֶךְ לְכָל־הָעָם
הַנִּמְצְאִים בְּשׁוּשַׁן הַבִּירָה לְמִגָּדוֹל וְעַד־קָטָן מִשְׁתֶּה
שִׁבְעַת יָמִים בַּחֲצַר גִּנַּת בִּיתַן הַמֶּלֶךְ:

5 **When these days were completed, the king made a banquet for all the people found in Shushan the citadel, from the greatest to the smallest, a seven-day banquet in the courtyard of the king's palace garden.**

Questions

WHAT was the purpose of this second banquet?

WHY are we told that the banquet was *"for all the people found in Shushan the citadel"* rather than "for the people of Shushan the citadel"?

NORMALLY, the phrase "from the smallest to the greatest" is used to equate the least with the most important. Here, though, the reverse order is used — *"from the greatest to the smallest,"* equating the most important with the least. Why?

WHY are we told that the banquet was located in *"the courtyard of the king's palace garden"*?

WHY do we need all the details of verses 6 to 8?

Commentary

Another element in Achashverosh's scheme was the banquet for the people of Shushan following the completion of the banquet for the officials and governors. He intended to demonstrate that all were equal in status in his eyes; namely, all were his slaves. Therefore, we are told it was for **from the greatest to the smallest**, bringing all down to the lowest common denominator of rank.

Achashverosh had moved his capital to Shushan, and, therefore, he called all those he **found** there to attend this banquet.[1]

The banquet took place **in the courtyard of the king's palace garden.** According to Persian practice, only officials and governors were allowed access there. Achashverosh thereby showed that the masses were no less important in his view than officials, since all were his slaves. In fact, the inhabitants of Shushan, living in the city of his palace, were deserving of equal honor to officials from elsewhere.

ו   חוּר ׀ כַּרְפַּס וּתְכֵ֫לֶת אָחוּז֙ בְּחַבְלֵי־ב֥וּץ וְאַרְגָּמָ֗ן
עַל־גְּלִ֥ילֵי כֶ֖סֶף וְעַמּ֣וּדֵי שֵׁ֑שׁ מִטּ֣וֹת ׀ זָהָ֣ב וָכֶ֗סֶף עַ֛ל
רִֽצְפַ֥ת בַּהַט־ וָשֵׁ֖שׁ וְדַ֥ר וְסֹחָֽרֶת:

6 There were hangings of white, of fine cotton and blue, fastened with cords of fine linen and purple on marble pillars standing on silver cylinders. The divans were of gold and silver on floors of alabaster and marble, pearl and onyx.

COMMENTARY

Since this banquet was hosted in the courtyard of the king's palace garden, which was a place without a roof or walls, tents **of white, of fine cotton and blue** were spread. These were **fastened with cords of fine linen and purple** onto **marble pillars** which in turn stood on **silver cylinders.**

---

1. Further thought is required to understand how the Malbim would explain the identical phrase *"found in Shushan,"* in ch. 4, v. 16. (Ed.)

The **divans** on which the guests reclined were made **of gold and silver,** and even the floor was paved with **alabaster and marble, pearl and onyx.**

זְ וְהַשְׁקוֹת בִּכְלֵי זָהָב וְכֵלִים מִכֵּלִים שׁוֹנִים וְיֵין
מַלְכוּת רָב כְּיַד הַמֶּלֶךְ:

7 **Drinking was from golden vessels, different types of vessels,** and **the royal wine was in abundance, according to the benevolence of the king.**

COMMENTARY

The guests drank from **golden vessels.** In fact, each guest had a set of **different types of vessels,** a decanter with attached goblets, all of gold. This ensured that nobody needed to borrow any vessel from his neighbor.[1]

One might think that there were sufficient vessels because the wine was not plentiful. This was not the case; the wine was **in abundance.** It was also of excellent quality, being **the royal wine,** its superior vintage encouraging plenty of consumption.

ח וְהַשְׁתִיָּה כַדָּת אֵין אֹנֵס כִּי־כֵן | יִסַּד הַמֶּלֶךְ עַל
כָּל־רַב בֵּיתוֹ לַעֲשׂוֹת כִּרְצוֹן אִישׁ־וָאִישׁ:

---

1. This explanation is attributed to Rav Eliezer Ashkenazy (1513?–1586), whose commentary on Megillas Esther is called *Yosef Lekach.*

8 The drinking was according to the law, without duress, for so had the king instituted for all the chief officers of his house to do according to each man's desire.

COMMENTARY

However, the drinking was **without duress**. When there are not sufficient cups and goblets to go around, guests are required to finish drinking quickly so that others can use their drinking vessel. Here, though, since each person had his own set of decanter and goblets, there was no need for this. Although it was the Persian practice to honor the oldest in attendance to be the first to drink,[1] at this banquet this practice was not followed, everyone drinking how and when he wanted. Nevertheless, in order not to offend the older people present, the king had **instituted for all the chief officers of his house** to forgo the honor due to them, thereby setting the example for all present. This was all in order **to do according to each man's desire.**

ט גַּם וַשְׁתִּי הַמַּלְכָּה עָשְׂתָה מִשְׁתֵּה נָשִׁים בֵּית
הַמַּלְכוּת אֲשֶׁר לַמֶּלֶךְ אֲחַשְׁוֵרוֹשׁ:

9 Also Vashti the queen made a banquet for the women in the royal house which belonged to King Achashverosh.

---

1. See *Brachos* 46b which describes how particular the Persians were with etiquette at mealtimes, insisting on rigorous rules as to the seating of those present according to their status.

QUESTIONS

WHY did Vashti make her own separate banquet?

WHY is it called *"a banquet for the women"*?

WHY are we told that it took place *"in the royal house"*?

WHY is it necessary to write that *"the royal house...belonged to King Achashverosh"* — is this not obvious?

WHY in this verse and in verses 11, 16, and 17 is the appellation *"Vashti the queen"* used, whereas in verses 12 and 15 we find *"Queen Vashti"*?

COMMENTARY

We have already explained[1] that when Achashverosh originally came to the throne, the monarchy was controlled by Babylon and the Chaldeans. Achashverosh married Vashti, the granddaughter of Nevuchadnetzar, the former ruler of the Babylonian empire. As a result, their rule was accepted by the people, Vashti being heiress to the throne.

Achashverosh, though, wanted to rule with absolute power, and to this end he moved the capital to Shushan and hosted an extravagant period of feasting. He wanted all the provinces to acknowledge that his authority was unconditional. Now, however, his marriage to Vashti was a liability. It reminded people that his claim to the throne came through Vashti and was not, therefore, the absolute rule of conquest.

He plotted to show that he had not married Vashti because of her title to the throne, owing his position to his wife, but that following his conquest the Babylonian dynasty ceased to exist, Vashti becoming one of his captives. He had married her, accord-

---

1. Commentary on verse 1.

ing to his historical revisionism, because of her beauty. Far from owing his authority to her, the reverse was true; she became queen only because he had taken her to be his wife.

"Vashti the queen" indicates that she was first and foremost "Vashti." Her name preceded her claim to the throne, which, according to Achashverosh's version of events, came only through her marriage to him.

This was highlighted by the banquet that she hosted. If she was the heiress and Achashverosh ruled only through his marriage to her, we would have expected her to host the governors and officials as befitted her position. Furthermore, we would have expected her banquet to be in her own royal house, for she was queen in her own right.

This was not the case. **Also**[1] **Vashti the queen** — the Megillah describes that Achashverosh showed that her name preceded her title — **made a banquet for the women** and not for the officials and assembled people. In addition, it was hosted **in the royal house which belonged to King Achashverosh**, showing that she did not have her own royal house since the monarchy belonged solely to Achashverosh.

י בַּיּוֹם הַשְּׁבִיעִי כְּטוֹב לֵב־הַמֶּלֶךְ בַּיָּיִן אָמַר לִמְהוּמָן בִּזְּתָא חַרְבוֹנָא בִּגְתָא וַאֲבַגְתָא זֵתַר וְכַרְכַּס שִׁבְעַת הַסָּרִיסִים הַמְשָׁרְתִים אֶת־פְּנֵי הַמֶּלֶךְ אֲחַשְׁוֵרוֹשׁ: יא לְהָבִיא אֶת־וַשְׁתִּי הַמַּלְכָּה לִפְנֵי הַמֶּלֶךְ בְּכֶתֶר מַלְכוּת לְהַרְאוֹת הָעַמִּים וְהַשָּׂרִים אֶת־יָפְיָהּ כִּי־טוֹבַת מַרְאֶה הִיא:

---

1. Perhaps one can add that the use of the word *"also"* generally indicates something subsidiary in importance. See *Ayeles Hashachar* of the Malbim, paragraph 590. Also see the commentary of the Malbim on *Vayikra*, paragraph 160. (Ed.)

1 **On the seventh day, when the king's
heart was merry with wine, he
commanded Mehuman, Bizzetha,
Charvona, Bigtha and Avagtha, Zethar
and Carcas, the seven chamberlains that
ministered to King Achashverosh, 11 to
bring Vashti the queen before the king
wearing the royal crown to show the
people and officials her beauty; for she
was of fair appearance.**

QUESTIONS

WHAT stupidity brought Achashverosh to command that his wife
be put on public display before the assembled masses to show them
her beauty? This is even more difficult to understand in light of the
teaching of our Sages[1] that he demanded that she appear naked.

EVEN more astounding is the manner in which Achashverosh
demanded that she come: to appear immediately, escorted by the
lowly chamberlains. Why would Achashverosh do this?

WHY are we told about the chamberlains?

WHAT is the significance in the information that they *"ministered to King Achashverosh"*?

WHAT is the need to write *"to bring...the queen before the king"*?
Why is *"to bring the queen"* not sufficient?

INSTEAD of writing *"to bring Vashti the queen before the king wearing the royal crown,"* it is more correct to write "to bring Vashti
the queen, wearing the royal crown, before the king"; would she
not be wearing her crown before she came before the king?

---

1. *Megillah* 11b.

COMMENTARY

In order to incontrovertibly prove that Achashverosh's rule was founded on conquest, he cunningly commanded that Vashti be brought before him. He planned to show that he had not married her for her royal lineage, but only for her beauty. He showed this in five different ways:

First, he commanded the **seven chamberlains** to escort her. If she had royal title in her own right, she would be escorted by the most important royal officers and not by the lowly chamberlains.

Second, he did not allow her to be escorted by her own chamberlains. Instead, she was to be brought by the chamberlains **that ministered to King Achashverosh**. This is the type of treatment that one of the king's concubines would receive.

Third, the phrase **to bring** rather than "to summon" or "to call" indicates that she was to be brought even against her will, like one of Achashverosh's maidservants.

Fourth, Achashverosh directed the chamberlains to bring her in a manner that would show everyone that they were bringing **Vashti the queen** and not "Queen Vashti" (which would have implied that she was a queen in her own right).[1] This was to be achieved by bringing her **before the king wearing the royal crown** — she was not permitted to wear the royal crown until after she came before the king. Everyone present would understand that Vashti was not entitled to wear the crown in her own right, but only as the wife of Achashverosh.

Fifth, Achashverosh wanted **to show the people and officials** that he had not married her for any royal connections but for her beauty, **for she was of fair appearance**. If his marriage

---

1. With this distinction of the Malbim we understand why Esther is never called "Queen Esther," but only *"Esther the queen."* Esther's title was not hereditary, but only acquired through marriage to the king. (Ed.)

had been motivated by her lineage, it would be totally inappropriate to publicly display her beauty; whether she was beautiful or ugly would be irrelevant if she was his passport to the throne. Indeed, it would be offensive to the provinces to physically exhibit her, implying that he cared more about her appearance than the monarchy he had acquired by being her husband.

Through the combination of all these indications, Achashverosh intended to prove beyond a doubt that he did not owe his power to his marriage to Vashti, but that it had been acquired through conquest and was, therefore, absolute.

יב וַתְּמָאֵ֞ן הַמַּלְכָּ֣ה וַשְׁתִּ֗י לָבוֹא֙ בִּדְבַ֣ר הַמֶּ֔לֶךְ אֲשֶׁ֖ר
בְּיַ֣ד הַסָּרִיסִ֑ים וַיִּקְצֹ֤ף הַמֶּ֙לֶךְ֙ מְאֹ֔ד וַחֲמָת֖וֹ בָּעֲרָ֥ה בֽוֹ:

12 **But Queen Vashti refused to come at the king's bidding, conveyed by the chamberlains; the king was furious and his anger burned inside him.**

QUESTIONS

THE wording, *"refused to come at the king's bidding, conveyed by the chamberlains,"* implies that the conveyance by the chamberlains was the spur for her refusal. Why should this be so?

WHAT is the difference between *"furious"* and *"his anger burned inside him,"* and what is the need for both?

COMMENTARY

Vashti disobeyed the king's command because she was

aware that his intention was to degrade her in order that no one would think that she had any title as queen in her own right.

Therefore **Queen Vashti refused** — the description *"Queen"* precedes the name *"Vashti,"* indicating that her title came before her name, through her birth into royalty.[1]

This refusal was initiated by two slights to her honor. First, **the king's bidding** itself commanded her to appear as a commoner without her crown. Second, it was **conveyed by the chamberlains**. To be escorted by the lowly chamberlains would be a humiliation.

Vashti was determined to confound Achashverosh's plot to undermine her status and to show that he owed his position to her.

As a result, **the king was furious**. The difference between "fury," קצף, and "anger," חמה, is that the former is an external manifestation while the latter remains inside, not visible to the outside world.[2]

Vashti's disobedience led to both: external fury at his command being held in contempt in public view, and internal anger burning inside him because his plot had been foiled. All Achashverosh's secret machinations and preparations had been confounded. The anger that this caused was, therefore, also secret, indiscernible to the onlooker, **and his anger burned *inside* him**.

---

1. See commentary on verse 9.
2. This distinction is confirmed by a close examination of the two words. קצף also means "foam" or "froth," and, therefore, its use to connote "fury" conjures up the image of a furious man foaming at the mouth, a visible sign. חמה is derived from the word חם, which means "hot," and it refers to the burning sensation one feels inside when becoming angry, which is invisible to others. (Ed.)

יג וַיֹּאמֶר הַמֶּלֶךְ לַחֲכָמִים יֹדְעֵי הָעִתִּים כִּי־כֵן דְּבַר
הַמֶּלֶךְ לִפְנֵי כָּל־יֹדְעֵי דָּת וָדִין:

13 And the king said to the wise men, who knew the times, that this matter of the king should be brought before those who knew practice and law

QUESTIONS

WHO are the *"wise men, who knew the times"* and why is it important that they *"knew the times"*?

WHO are *"those who knew practice and law"*?

WHAT is the difference between *"practice"* and *"law"*?

WHY, in verse 15, does Achashverosh ask what should be done with Vashti *"according to practice"* rather than "according to law"?

COMMENTARY

A close reading of Achashverosh's question and Memuchan's response indicates that, in spite of his anger, the king's love for Vashti inspired a desire to pardon her.

The trial of a servant for a misdemeanor against the king differs from one between two ordinary people.

The former was judged by permanent judges — **the wise men, who knew the times.** They were required to know not only the laws of he land, but also *"the times"*; the verdict had to take into account when the offense took place. If it occurred while the king was sitting on his throne, the punishment would be more severe than if it was committed while the king was not in public view. If it happened when all the nobles of the provinces were present, the penalty would be especially harsh.

To judge a trial between two equals, though, it was sufficient to know **practice and law**.

The king realized that if the case was tried by the *"wise men who knew the times"* it would be considered an offense of a commoner against the king, and the death penalty would be the obvious verdict.

Therefore, the king told *"wise men who knew the times"* that they did not need to judge this case. It would be sufficient to take *"those who knew practice and law."*

Achashverosh maintained that this was not a commoner offending the king, but that Vashti was a queen and his status was not superior to hers, since she was descended from royal lineage. As such, this was a case concerning husband and wife, a dispute between equals. It could be judged by any judge who knew practice and law.

The use of the two words **practice** and **law** indicate that Achashverosh was motivated by a desire to totally acquit Vashti. If judged solely by rule of *"law,"* even as a dispute between husband and wife, the case would end with a guilty verdict for Vashti. Then, as now in many oriental and Middle Eastern countries, the wife was totally subjugated to her husband's will, and disobedience was punished severely.

However, from the standpoint of accepted social *"practice,"* Vashti should be acquitted. Persian and Median women were unusually modest in their demeanor, confining themselves to their chamber and not appearing publicly in front of men.[1] Achashverosh had demanded that Vashti display her beauty before a multitude of men, going against all accepted *"practice"* and social mores of the time.

In this light, her refusal was understandable and justifiable.

---

1. See Mishnah *Shabbos* 6:6, which describes how Median women veiled themselves to hide as much as possible from the view of men.

If the judgment was based on *"practice,"* Vashti could be acquitted. Therefore, in verse 15, Achashverosh asks, **"According to practice what should be done with Queen Vashti?"** He was instructing the judges to give their verdict from the standpoint of *"practice,"* not *"law."*

יד וְהַקָּרֹב אֵלָיו כַּרְשְׁנָא שֵׁתָר אַדְמָתָא תַרְשִׁישׁ מֶרֶס מַרְסְנָא מְמוּכָן שִׁבְעַת שָׂרֵי ׀ פָּרַס וּמָדַי רֹאֵי פְּנֵי הַמֶּלֶךְ הַיֹּשְׁבִים רִאשֹׁנָה בַּמַּלְכוּת:

14 (the closest to him were Carshena, Shethar, Admatha, Tarshish, Meres, Marsena, and Memuchan, the seven officials of Persia and Media who regularly saw the king and who sat first in the kingdom)

QUESTIONS

WHY are we told that these seven were *"the closest to him"*?

WHY are they given three designations — *"officials of Persia and Media," "who regularly saw the king,"* and *"who sat first in the kingdom"*?

COMMENTARY

Having explained that this case was merely a domestic feud between husband and wife, Achashverosh chose these seven officials for four reasons:

First, they were the **closest to him** — Achashverosh did not

want the proceedings of the trial to become public knowledge.[1]
These seven already knew what had happened and could be re-
lied upon to keep the trial a secret.

Second, they were **the seven officials of Persia and Media**
and of appropriate rank to judge such a case.

Third, they **regularly saw the king** and understood his
every gesture and insinuation. They would realize that he wanted
Vashti acquitted.

Finally, they **sat first in the kingdom** — they had been in
their positions for a long time[2] and were seasoned, experienced
judges.

טו כְּדָת֙ מַה־לַּעֲשׂוֹת֙ בַּמַּלְכָּ֣ה וַשְׁתִּ֔י עַ֣ל ׀ אֲשֶׁ֧ר
לֹא־עָשְׂתָ֗ה אֶת־מַאֲמַר֙ הַמֶּ֣לֶךְ אֲחַשְׁוֵר֔וֹשׁ בְּיַ֖ד
הַסָּרִיסִֽים׃

15 **to decide according to practice what
should be done with Queen Vashti for not
performing the bidding of the king,
conveyed by the chamberlains.**

---

1. The rationale for clemency was based on Vashti being of equal
   status with Achashverosh. However, Achashverosh had been planning to demonstrate to his empire that his claim to the throne did
   not come from his marriage to her, but that she was taken captive
   and married merely for her beauty. If the trial proceedings became
   public knowledge, this plan would be thwarted. (Ed.)

2. The Malbim understands *"first"* not as describing their position being in front of others, but that they were the first to take office.
   (Ed.)

QUESTIONS

WHY does Achashverosh mention that his command had been *"conveyed by the chamberlains"*?

COMMENTARY

We have seen that it was Achashverosh's intention that Vashti should be judged as equal in status to himself and, thereby, acquitted.

In order that she should not be regarded as a commoner disobeying the king, Achashverosh made two points. First, she was **Queen Vashti** — royalty in her own right, and the dispute was a marital dispute between equals. Second, her refusal was justifiable since it would have been humiliating for her to be brought by the lowly **chamberlains**.

טז וַיֹּאמֶר מְומֻכָן לִפְנֵי הַמֶּלֶךְ וְהַשָּׂרִים לֹא עַל־
הַמֶּלֶךְ לְבַדּוֹ עָוְתָה וַשְׁתִּי הַמַּלְכָּה כִּי עַל־כָּל־הַשָּׂרִים
וְעַל־כָּל־ הָעַמִּים אֲשֶׁר בְּכָל־מְדִינוֹת הַמֶּלֶךְ
אֲחַשְׁוֵרוֹשׁ:

16 And Memuchan replied in front of the king and the other officials, "Not only has Vashti the queen wronged the king but also all the officials and all the people in all the provinces of King Achashverosh.

QUESTIONS

WHY does Memuchan mention both *"all the officials"* and *"all the people"*? If the concern is that wives will despise their husbands, why is there a need to specify two groups?

COMMENTARY

Memuchan realized that Achashverosh wanted to exonerate Vashti. The king had argued that the case was not one of a commoner offending the king but merely a private domestic quarrel between spouses of equal rank. Memuchan also understood that Achashverosh wanted to keep the matter secret by only involving the officials closest to him.

Memuchan argued that this was incorrect on several counts, and he indicated this by the manner of his response — conspicuously, **in front of the king and the other officials**.

This was not a private matter, but one that affected the entire empire. The honor of the king and the honor of his kingdom were synonymous.

In response to Achashverosh's contention that Vashti was a queen in her own right and his equal, Memuchan responded that she was **Vashti the queen** — her title came not from royal descent but from marriage to King Achashverosh.

It affected not only the king but also **all the officials**. Vashti had degraded the king's honor by attempting to show that Achashverosh had acquired his position only through his marriage to her. If so, his monarchy would be of limited power. This, therefore, also concerned *"the officials"* representing the monarch throughout the empire.

Vashti had also harmed **all the people** by causing wives to despise their husbands **in all the provinces**.

Her crime had ramifications both for the monarchy and all the provinces.

כִּי־ יֵצֵא דְבַר־הַמַּלְכָּה עַל־כָּל־הַנָּשִׁים לְהַבְזוֹת יז
בַּעְלֵיהֶן בְּעֵינֵיהֶן בְּאָמְרָם הַמֶּלֶךְ אֲחַשְׁוֵרוֹשׁ אָמַר
לְהָבִיא אֶת־ וַשְׁתִּי הַמַּלְכָּה לְפָנָיו וְלֹא־בָאָה:

17 **For this deed of the queen will go out to all women and will cause them to hold their husbands in contempt, saying that even King Achashverosh told Vashti the queen to be brought before him but she did not come.**

QUESTIONS

WHY should the queen die merely because wives will not respect their husbands? Why would it not be sufficient to pass a law that husbands should rule in their homes?[1]

WHY are we told that word of the queen's act *"will go out"*?

COMMENTARY

Memuchan proceeded to explain how Vashti's crime would have an adverse effect on *"all the people,"* ruining marriages throughout the empire.

The wives of the officials, who had accompanied their husbands to the banquet and had witnessed the entire episode, realized that Achashverosh was trying to degrade her. They knew that Vashti's refusal to appear before the king was perfectly justifiable, and they would not come to disobey and scorn their husbands as a result.

---

1. The reason why Vashti had to be killed is explained in the commentary on verse 18.

However, women who had not been there and who heard about the incident secondhand would only know the bare facts that Achashveiosh had summoned Vashti and that she had refused to appear. They would infer *a fortiori* that they could act brazenly toward husbands.

Therefore the concern was that the **deed of the queen will go out to all women** who had not been present and were unaware of the background behind Vashti's refusal. This would lead to mass insubordination on the part of the wives, arguing that **King Achashverosh**, the king himself, had commanded that **Vashti the queen** — not queen in her own right but only as the wife of the king — **be brought before him**, a small request. Despite all these considerations, Vashti did not comply.

"How much more so," they would tell their husbands, "do I not need to obey you. You are not a king, and I have not become queen because of you. We are equal in rank. You are not merely asking me to appear before you, but to perform all the hard domestic work."

This would definitely have repercussions throughout all the king's provinces.

יח   וְהַיּ֣וֹם הַזֶּ֗ה תֹּאמַ֣רְנָה ׀ שָׂר֣וֹת פָּֽרַס־וּמָדַ֞י אֲשֶׁ֣ר שָֽׁמְעוּ֙ אֶת־דְּבַ֣ר הַמַּלְכָּ֔ה לְכֹ֖ל שָׂרֵ֣י הַמֶּ֑לֶךְ וּכְדַ֖י בִּזָּי֥וֹן וָקָֽצֶף׃

18 **This very day the wives of the officials of Persia and Media who heard the queen's response will speak to all the king's officials, causing much contempt and fury.**

QUESTIONS

WHAT is the purpose of the phrase *"this very day"*?

WE are told that *"the wives of the officials...will speak."* What will they say?

WHAT is the need to write both *"contempt"* and *"fury"*?

COMMENTARY

Memuchan now explains how Vashti's crime will affect *"all the king's officials."* The **wives of the officials**, who had been present at the banquet and who had directly **heard the queen's response**, will tell their husbands **this very day** — having been present, they could recount what happened the same day it occurred. The officials will know that Vashti asserted that Achashverosh owed his position to his marriage to her. If Achashverosh did not kill her it would be tantamount to an admission that she was correct and all his plans would be thwarted.

The consequence would be that there would be **much contempt** of wives towards their husbands and **fury** on the part of officials against the king's attempt to gain unlimited power.

יט אִם־עַל־הַמֶּלֶךְ טוֹב יֵצֵא דְבַר־מַלְכוּת מִלְּפָנָיו
וְיִכָּתֵב בְּדָתֵי פָרַס־וּמָדַי וְלֹא יַעֲבוֹר אֲשֶׁר לֹא־תָבוֹא
וַשְׁתִּי לִפְנֵי הַמֶּלֶךְ אֲחַשְׁוֵרוֹשׁ וּמַלְכוּתָהּ יִתֵּן הַמֶּלֶךְ
לִרְעוּתָהּ הַטּוֹבָה מִמֶּנָּה:

19 **If it please the king, let a royal edict be issued from him, to be written as one of the permanent rules of Persia and Media, that Vashti never again appear before King Achashverosh and that the king should give her royal estate to another woman better than she.**

QUESTIONS

WHAT is the meaning of the phrase *"let a royal edict be issued from him"*?

WHY was it to be written as one of the *"permanent rules of Persia and Media"* that *"Vashti never again appear before King Achashverosh"*? This implies that it was of permanent relevance; but since Vashti was to be executed, surely it was only of temporary application?

COMMENTARY

Having explained the extent of Vashti's wrongdoing and its disastrous consequences, and having revealed the king's hidden motivation in hosting the banquet and how this had been frustrated by Vashti, Memuchan proposed how the situation could be rectified.

First, he suggested how the king could achieve his ambition of unlimited power. **Let a royal edict be issued from him**; until now, laws were enacted by a legislative body with the king having no right of veto, nor the right to introduce his own laws without the agreement of ministers and government advisors. Memuchan was recommending that a new law be passed, transferring all legislative authority to the king. All edicts were to *be is-sued from him,"* from him alone.

Furthermore, every decision of the king should be written as one of the **rules of Persia and Media** to be used as a precedent in similar cases. Even decisions of the king that only had immediate consequences would, thereby, be **permanent.**

The first edict under the new system (the phrase *"to be writ-ten as one of the permanent rules of Persia and Media"* is parentheti-cal, applying to any and every subsequent royal edict) would be that **Vashti never again appear before King Achashverosh.**

This move was brilliant. If Achashverosh were only to kill Vashti, people would still doubt the king's power and say that the king had been unable to make her appear in front of him. By passing a law prohibiting Vashti from appearing in front of the king, they would now think that she had tried to go in front of the king to make amends but was prevented by this new law.

In addition, **her royal estate should be given to another woman better than she.** Memuchan was expressing two points:

First, in choosing a successor to Vashti the emphasis should not be placed on lineage but on the essential qualities of the woman herself; in comparison to Vashti the successor should be **better than she.**

Second, the king should not be worried that the next queen would also be insubordinate, because she would have a clear un-derstanding of the importance of compliance from Vashti's fate.[1]

---

1. This idea is inferred from a second understanding of the phrase טובה ממנה. The first idea interprets it to mean *"better **than** she"* — the first מ of ממנה is one of comparison.

   The second idea interprets it to mean *"better from her"* — the מ now means "from." The successor will become better *"from her"* — from seeing what happened to Vashti.

כ וְנִשְׁמַע פִּתְגָם הַמֶּלֶךְ אֲשֶׁר־יַעֲשֶׂה בְּכָל־מַלְכוּתוֹ
כִּי רַבָּה הִיא וְכָל־הַנָּשִׁים יִתְּנוּ יְקָר לְבַעְלֵיהֶן
לְמִגָּדוֹל וְעַד־קָטָן:

20 Then, when the king's decree, which he
will proclaim, which is a very great one,
will be known throughout the whole
kingdom, wives will give honor to their
husbands, from the greatest to the
smallest."

QUESTIONS

THE *"king's decree...is a very great one"* — what is so *"great"* about
the decree? Is killing one's wife such a *"great"* action?

IS the aim that *"wives will give honor to their husbands"* really sufficient justification to kill Vashti?

WHY say *"from the greatest to the smallest"* instead of the more
usual "from the smallest to the greatest"?[1]

COMMENTARY

Memuchan then elaborated on the benefits of following his
proposal. When the new system is introduced, that all laws be
the king's decree alone, without the assent of ministers, and
when it **will be known throughout the whole kingdom**, no
one will dare disobey the king's command because it will be **a
very great one**[2] — based on absolute authority.

---

1. See commentary on verse 5.
2. The usual understanding of the phrase כי רבה היא — *"which is a very
   great one"* — is that it describes the entire kingdom: the decree will

Although the primary purpose of this proposal was for Achashverosh to obtain the unlimited power he craved, a secondary benefit would be that **wives will give honor to their husbands,** even if the wife is of higher status than her husband: **from the greatest** (of wives) **to the smallest** (of husbands).[1]

כא וַיִּיטַב הַדָּבָר בְּעֵינֵי הַמֶּלֶךְ וְהַשָּׂרִים וַיַּעַשׂ הַמֶּלֶךְ כִּדְבַר מְמוּכָן:

21 **This reply pleased the king and the officials, and the king followed Memuchan's suggestion.**

---

be known throughout the whole kingdom despite the kingdom being *"a very great one."* The Malbim, though, seems to explain that it describes the decree. (This requires further thought, because the word פתגם [decree] is masculine, while רבה is a feminine adjective. It may be that the Malbim understood the phase כי רבה היא as describing the kingdom, in line with other commentators. Achashverosh's kingdom, i.e., his dominion, would become greater as a result of the new system.) (Ed.)

1. Although the usual interpretation of this phrase is "from the greatest of husbands to the smallest of husbands," the Malbim seems to understand *"greatest"* to refer to the wives. (As in the previous footnote, this also requires further thought, because the word גדול [which refers to the wives] is a masculine adjective. It may be that the Malbim understood that both *"greatest"* and *"smallest"* describe husbands. However, this is not to be understood in relation to other husbands, but as describing the husband's status relative to his wife, some husbands being greater than their wives and others smaller.) (Ed.)

COMMENTARY

Understandably, **this reply pleased the king**, offering him absolute authority. However, in order for the new system of legislation to take effect, the officials had to give their consent and relinquish their share of power. The proposal also pleased **the officials** and they acquiesced.[1]

As a result, **the king**, on his own, **followed Memuchan's suggestion** without requiring the endorsement of the officials.

כב וַיִּשְׁלַח סְפָרִים אֶל־כָּל־מְדִינוֹת הַמֶּלֶךְ אֶל־
מְדִינָה וּמְדִינָה כִּכְתָבָהּ וְאֶל־עַם וָעָם כִּלְשׁוֹנוֹ לִהְיוֹת
כָּל־אִישׁ שֹׂרֵר בְּבֵיתוֹ וּמְדַבֵּר כִּלְשׁוֹן עַמּוֹ:

22 He sent letters to all the king's provinces, to each province in its script and to each people in its language, saying that every man should rule his own home and speak the language of his people.

QUESTIONS

WHY are we told that letters were sent *"to each province in its script"*?

---

1. Why were the officials willing to relinquish their power? If the king's power was limited, and thus the people of the empire believed that Vashti was justified in her refusal to obey him, then the decree would not be respected; women would continue making their *a fortiori* argument. To ensure marital stability in the empire (or, more specifically, husbands' supremacy), the decree had to be issued in such a way that it would remove this argument. Therefore, Achashverosh had to be perceived as an absolute monarch. To be the undisputed heads of their homes, the officials agreed to relinquish their political power of veto. (Ed.)

THE idea of sending out letters instructing that every husband should be the master of his own home seems ridiculous. How could this be achieved?

WHY should each man have to *"speak the language of his people"*?

COMMENTARY

Until now, one of the Persian ordinances had been that all vassal nations, when writing to the king, had to use the Persian language, the language of the king's nation. Similarly, all letters from the king to the vassal nations were written in Persian. Everyone had to be conversant in Persian.

Achashverosh, though, considered that it was not the Persian nation that ruled over the empire with him as its representative, but that he alone, in his own right, was the unfettered monarch.

If so, the Persian nation should have no special status, for all nations were equally his vassals. Thus, the Persian script and language should not be superior to any other. The empire would no longer be called the Persian empire, but, instead, the empire of Achashverosh.

Therefore, he wrote to **each people in its language** and instructed them that every man should **speak the language of his people**, and not the Persian language.[1]

According to Persian law, women had to be subservient to their husbands, obligated to honor them. The directive **that every man should rule his own home** meant that the husband was now given the same power over his wife as that of a master over his slave.

---

1. The usual interpretation of *"speak the language of his people"* is that it excludes speaking the language of his wife's people and was intended to further bolster the husband's standing in the home. The Malbim, though, explains that it comes to exclude speaking the Persian language.

These two enactments dealt with the two matters that Memuchan had raised. Regarding the attainment of unlimited power, Achashverosh instituted that all languages were to be of equal status. Regarding the need for wives to honor their husbands, he legislated that men were to have absolute control over their wives.

Why does our understanding of the Purim miracles require that the Megillah have a long introduction about Achashverosh's acquisition of absolute power?

The most probable explanation seems to be that were it not for Achashverosh's total authority, not limited by the need for ministerial approval, it would have been impossible for him to marry Esther. His ministers would have vetoed the idea of choosing a wife by gathering the most beautiful women for Achashverosh to select from. They would have strongly disapproved of his choice of Esther, a woman of unknown background.[1] The promotion of Haman might never have taken place, and the planned extermination of the entire Jewish nation could not have been contemplated. The whole Purim story required Achashverosh's control to be unlimited.

With this idea, we can understand a teaching of our Sages:

"Were it not for the first letters, the second letters could not have existed"[2] — were it not for the original edict that the king was the sole authority for legislation, it would have been impossible for the king alone to rescind Haman's decree of extermination without ministerial agreement.

Another purpose of this introduction is to highlight the miracle in Achashverosh's acquiescence to Esther's plea to revoke Haman's evil decree. It would be easy to explain it as a husband's heart swayed by the entreaties of his beautiful wife.

---

1. See ch. 2, v. 10.
2. This statement could not be found in available sources. *Megillah* 12b brings a teaching that starts with the same words, *"were it not for the first letters,"* but the continuation is totally different.

However, from the first chapter of the Megillah we see that it is not so simple. Achashverosh was king over a huge empire of one hundred and twenty-seven provinces. He was extremely tenacious, having conquered them all in a very short time. He was fabulously wealthy, as evidenced by the splendor of the tremendous banquet he hosted. He was unusually shrewd, having used all types of strategies in his pursuit of unlimited power. He could not be swayed emotionally; despite his love for Vashti, he put her to death, either for the national benefit that wives should not disrespect their husbands or for the pragmatic aim of attaining absolute power.

We see that this was not a soft man, easily prey to female blandishments. With this background, Esther's success in persuading him to cancel Haman's decree takes on its true, miraculous proportions.

CHAPTER 2

ב א אַחַר הַדְּבָרִים הָאֵלֶּה כְּשֹׁךְ חֲמַת הַמֶּלֶךְ
אֲחַשְׁוֵרוֹשׁ זָכַר אֶת־וַשְׁתִּי וְאֵת אֲשֶׁר־עָשָׂתָה וְאֵת
אֲשֶׁר־נִגְזַר עָלֶיהָ:

1 After these events, when the anger of
King Achashverosh had subsided, he
remembered Vashti, what she had done,
and what was decreed against her.

QUESTIONS

WHY are we told that the king remembered three separate par-
ticulars: *"Vashti," "what she had done,"* and *"what was decreed
against her"*?

COMMENTARY

When the king's anger subsided and he began to consider

finding another woman to be his wife, he had three major concerns.

First, **he remembered Vashti** — her beauty, nobility, and her virtues. He thought that it would be very difficult to find another woman her equal.

Second, he recalled **what she had done** and was afraid that another beautiful, noble woman might act the same way as Vashti. To execute a second wife would give him the undesirable reputation of a habitual wife-killer.

Finally, he remembered **what had been decreed against her** and was concerned that even if he did find a suitable woman, she would not agree to be his wife lest she meet the same fate as Vashti.

ב וַיֹּאמְר֥וּ נַעֲרֵֽי־הַמֶּ֖לֶךְ מְשָׁרְתָ֑יו יְבַקְשׁ֥וּ לַמֶּ֖לֶךְ
נְעָר֥וֹת בְּתוּל֖וֹת טוֹב֥וֹת מַרְאֶֽה: ג וְיַפְקֵ֨ד הַמֶּ֜לֶךְ
פְּקִידִים֮ בְּכָל־מְדִינ֣וֹת מַלְכוּתוֹ֒ וְיִקְבְּצ֣וּ אֶת־כָּל־
נַעֲרָֽה־בְ֠תוּלָה טוֹבַ֨ת מַרְאֶ֜ה אֶל־שׁוּשַׁ֤ן הַבִּירָה֙ אֶל־
בֵּ֣ית הַנָּשִׁ֔ים אֶל־יַ֥ד הֵגֶ֛א סְרִ֥יס הַמֶּ֖לֶךְ שֹׁמֵ֣ר הַנָּשִׁ֑ים
וְנָת֖וֹן תַּמְרֻקֵיהֶֽן:

2 Then the king's servant boys, who ministered to him, said, "Let young, beautiful virgins be sought for the king.

3 Let the king appoint overseers in every province of his kingdom to assemble all the young, beautiful virgins in Shushan the citadel, in the women's quarters, in the charge of Hege the king's chamberlain, custodian of the women, and let their ointments be given them.

Questions

THE advice of the servant boys, to take a woman from the street to be the new wife for the king, seems preposterous. Surely only the most aristocratic of families should come into consideration! How could they suggest something so dishonorable to the king?

FURTHERMORE, they give two apparently contradictory suggestions. They first propose that *"young, beautiful virgins be sought,"* implying with the consent of these women. However, they continue by saying that overseers *"will assemble"* them, implying that they would be coerced. Which were they suggesting?

WHY were the women to be placed *"in the charge of Hege"*?

WHY was it suggested that *"their ointments be given them"*? Why is this important to the subject at hand?

Commentary

When the king revealed his three worries, the servant boys sought to allay each of them:

With regard to finding a woman as beautiful as Vashti, they suggested that there **be sought for the king**, that there be an extensive search for a woman suitable to be his wife. No attention would be paid to lineage;[1] the king was so great that any lineage of his future wife would be irrelevant, and thus finding a wife from a lower class was not dishonorable. The only requirement was that the women from whom the selection be made be **young, beautiful virgins.**

---

1. The assumption in the Malbim's first question on this verse is that aristocratic lineage in a woman would be an asset and that being of common stock would be a disgrace to the king. The Malbim's answer is that the king was so great that the woman's lineage could make no difference.

Concerning the king's third concern, that the woman might not be willing to marry him, the servant boys said that if the search did not provide a suitable woman willing to be his wife, then, and only then, the king should **appoint overseers to assemble all the young, beautiful virgins** — against their will.

The appointment of new overseers would also minimize the danger that wealthy families would attempt to prevent their daughters from being taken by bribing the officials; it is difficult to bribe a new official with whom one is not yet well acquainted.

To reassure the king about his second worry, that Vashti's successor might repeat Vashti's transgression, they advised that the women be placed **in the charge of Hege** and that they should not be allowed to bring their own ointments and cosmetics. Instead, **let their ointments be given them** by the chamberlains. This would ensure that they would feel constantly dependent on Hege and the other chamberlains, and they would be humbled. Once humbled, they would not disobey the king when he ordered them to come with the chamberlains.

ד   וְהַנַּעֲרָה אֲשֶׁר תִּיטַב בְּעֵינֵי הַמֶּלֶךְ תִּמְלֹךְ תַּחַת
וַשְׁתִּי וַיִּיטַב הַדָּבָר בְּעֵינֵי הַמֶּלֶךְ וַיַּעַשׂ כֵּן:

4 **The maiden who pleases the king will reign in place of Vashti." This suggestion pleased the king, and he followed it.**

COMMENTARY

The **maiden**, even if she is not of aristocratic lineage, as long as she **pleases the king** she will be chosen to be his wife.

This suggestion pleased the king — what the ministers

would think was now irrelevant and unnecessary[1] — **and he followed it**.

ה   אִ֣ישׁ יְהוּדִ֔י הָיָ֖ה בְּשׁוּשַׁ֣ן הַבִּירָ֑ה וּשְׁמ֣וֹ מָרְדֳּכַ֗י בֶּ֣ן
יָאִ֧יר בֶּן־שִׁמְעִ֛י בֶּן־קִ֖ישׁ אִ֥ישׁ יְמִינִֽי׃

**5 There was a Jewish man in Shushan the
citadel whose name was Mordechai, the
son of Yair, the son of Shim'i, the son of
Kish, a Benjaminite,**

QUESTIONS

IT would have been sufficient to write, *"There was a Jewish man in
Shushan the citadel whose name was Mordechai."* Why are we told
his lineage?

COMMENTARY

We are now shown the virtuous character of Mordechai and
Esther. On three separate occasions Esther was forcibly abducted;
never did she go willingly to the king. The first time was when
she was taken from her home. The second was when she was de-
tained in Hege's custody for twelve months. The third was when
she was taken to the king's palace after the twelve-month waiting
period.

We are now told about the first abduction. Mordechai had
concealed Esther for a long period of time even though this in-

---

1. See commentary on ch. 1, v. 21, where we learned that the ministers relinquished their legislative powers, leaving the king in sole
control.

volved considerable danger. The king had commanded that anyone with a beautiful daughter must bring her to the overseers.
Disobeying this order would be punished with death, but Mordechai still refused to hand over Esther.

Mordechai's insubordination was especially serious for
eight reasons:

1) **There was a Jewish man** *in Shushan the citadel.* If Mordechai had lived in one of the distant provinces he might have
been able to claim that he was unaware of the king's command.
However, he lived in Shushan, the center to which all the maidens were sent. No one in the city could claim not to know what
was happening.

Furthermore, if Mordechai had arrived in Shushan only re-
cently, he could have asserted that he had not yet heard of the
royal directive. **There was a Jewish man** — the use of the past
tense indicates a state of affairs that had been in existence for a
significant period of time. Mordechai had been living in Shushan
for a long time. To plead ignorance was impossible.

2) If he had been a man of low standing, he could have given
the excuse that he was embarrassed to send his daughter because
of his humble status. However, his **name was Mordechai,** a fa-
mous man of noble descent, scion of the family of King Saul.[1]

ו   אֲשֶׁר הָגְלָה מִירוּשָׁלַיִם עִם־הַגֹּלָה אֲשֶׁר הָגְלְתָה
עִם יְכָנְיָה מֶלֶךְ־יְהוּדָה אֲשֶׁר הֶגְלָה נְבוּכַדְנֶצַּר מֶלֶךְ
בָּבֶל:

6 **who had been exiled with Yechonyah,
the king of Judah, whom Nevuchadnetzar,
the king of Babylon, had exiled.**

---

1. Kish is identified as being the father of Saul. See Shmuel I 9:1-2.

QUESTIONS

WHY is it necessary to mention that Mordechai had been exiled by Nevuchadnetzar?

COMMENTARY

3) His sin was compounded by the fact that he **had been exiled**. An exile living in a foreign land is obligated to show special appreciation to his host country. Disobedience in such circumstances is especially treacherous.

The contention that, since he was a foreigner, he presumed that his daughter could not be a candidate for queen, also would not stand. He had been exiled **with Yechonyah, the king of Judah**, when the elite of Zion had been taken into captivity. Mordechai was clearly of superior rank.

ז וַיְהִי אֹמֵן אֶת־הֲדַסָּה הִיא אֶסְתֵּר בַּת־דֹּדוֹ כִּי אֵין
לָהּ אָב וָאֵם וְהַנַּעֲרָה יְפַת־תֹּאַר וְטוֹבַת מַרְאֶה וּבְמוֹת
אָבִיהָ וְאִמָּהּ לְקָחָהּ מָרְדֳּכַי לוֹ לְבַת:

7 **He had raised Hadassah, that is Esther, his uncle's daughter; she had neither father nor mother and she was of beautiful form and fair appearance. When her father and mother died Mordechai adopted her as his daughter.**

QUESTIONS

WHY does the Megillah state twice that Esther's parents were dead? Once it tells us that *"he had raised Hadassah...she had neither father nor mother,"* why tell us again, *"when her father and mother died Mordechai adopted her"*?

FURTHERMORE, why does a description of Esther's beauty interrupt the account of her adoption?

COMMENTARY

4) Everyone knew that Mordechai raised Esther. Furthermore, she was so renowned herself that she was referred to as **Hadassah**, a reference to her pleasing attributes.[1] She was **his uncle's daughter** and so he was, therefore, responsible for her.

For these reasons he was obligated to ensure that Esther was handed over to the overseers, and any failure to comply was fraught with peril.

5) Since **she had neither father nor mother**, his was the sole responsibility.

6) She was **of beautiful form**. Concealing a girl of such beauty was an unpardonable offense.

7) Mordechai could not pretend that he thought Esther would go of her own accord, because **when her father and mother died Mordechai adopted her as his daughter**; it was inconceivable that she would do anything without her guardian's consent.

ח וַיְהִי בְּהִשָּׁמַע דְּבַר־הַמֶּלֶךְ וְדָתוֹ וּבְהִקָּבֵץ נְעָרוֹת
רַבּוֹת אֶל־ שׁוּשַׁן הַבִּירָה אֶל־יַד הֵגַי וַתִּלָּקַח אֶסְתֵּר
אֶל־בֵּית הַמֶּלֶךְ אֶל־יַד הֵגַי שֹׁמֵר הַנָּשִׁים:

---

1. Although Esther was her real name, she was called "Hadassah" because her good deeds and pleasing character were reminiscent of the "Hadass," the sweet-smelling myrtle. (See *Megillah* 13a.)

8 It happened, when the king's edict and decree became known and many maidens had been assembled in Shushan the citadel, into the charge of Hege, that Esther was taken to the king's house, into the charge of Hege the custodian of the women.

QUESTIONS

SINCE all we need to know is that Esther was abducted, what is the point of the introduction, *"It happened, when the king's edict and decree became known and many maidens had been assembled in Shushan"*?

WHAT difference does it make that *"many maidens had been assembled in Shushan"*?

COMMENTARY

8) In addition to the other incriminating factors against Mordechai, **the king's edict and decree** were known already.

There had been *two* royal commands. The first, referred to as the *"the king's edict,"* requested people to voluntarily hand over their daughters. The second, the *"decree,"* ordered that the women be taken by force.[1] Non-compliance with the second *"decree"* would be punished with the death penalty.

Not only did Mordechai disregard the considerable benefits he would receive by voluntarily handing over Esther at the time of the first *"edict,"* but he even ignored the second, compulsory *"decree."*

---

1. See commentary above on verses 2 and 3 where the king's servant boys propose these two stages.

In addition, **many maidens had been assembled in Shushan.** An inhabitant of Shushan who concealed his own daughter while he witnessed the multitudes of other women being assembled in Shushan could expect to be punished most severely.

Despite Mordechai's attempts to conceal her, **Esther was taken** forcibly, against both her and Mordechai's will.

ט   וַתִּיטַב הַנַּעֲרָה בְעֵינָיו וַתִּשָּׂא חֶסֶד לְפָנָיו וַיְבַהֵל
אֶת־תַּמְרוּקֶיהָ וְאֶת־ מָנוֹתֶהָ לָתֵת לָהּ וְאֵת שֶׁבַע
הַנְּעָרוֹת הָרְאֻיוֹת לָתֶת־לָהּ מִבֵּית הַמֶּלֶךְ וַיְשַׁנֶּהָ
וְאֶת־נַעֲרוֹתֶיהָ לְטוֹב בֵּית הַנָּשִׁים:

9 The maiden pleased him and obtained his kindness. He quickly gave her ointments and portions and the seven maids suitable for her from the king's house. He advanced her and her maids to the best accommodation in the women's quarters.

QUESTIONS

WHY we are told both that *"the maiden pleased him"* and that she *"obtained his kindness"*?

WHY did Hege *"quickly"* give her the ointments?

WHY are we told that Esther received *"portions"*? We are not told that any other women received *"portions."* Nor are we told that they received the *"seven maids"* that Esther was given.

THE phrase *"suitable for her"* implies that they were suitable for Esther alone. Why?

COMMENTARY

Taken against her will and having flagrantly disregarded the king's edict, we would expect Esther to be put to death. However, **the maiden pleased him** — Hege foresaw that this woman was destined to be the queen.

Therefore, to ingratiate himself with the future sovereign, he made sure that Esther **obtained his kindness.** Apart from overlooking her disregard of the royal edict, he **quickly** gave her preferential treatment in four ways.

1) He **quickly gave her ointments.** We see in verse 12 that a woman could not appear in front of the king until she had been treated with ointments for twelve months. Generally, this treatment began either at the start of the summer or at the start of the winter.[1] In Esther's case, the treatment began immediately in order to expedite her appearance before the king.

2) He gave Esther **portions** which were not given to any other woman, because he knew that Achashverosh would choose her.

3) He allocated **seven maids** to wait on her. The queen was attended by seven maids, and even though Esther was not yet queen, they were **suitable for her** when she would become queen. Hege had no doubts about her accession to the throne.

4) Not only do we find that **he advanced her,** but also **her maids,** moving them to **the best accommodation in the women's quarters;** not only were the rooms superior and larger, but the food was of the best quality.

לֹא־הִגִּידָה אֶסְתֵּר אֶת־עַמָּהּ וְאֶת־מוֹלַדְתָּהּ כִּי מָרְדֳּכַי צִוָּה עָלֶיהָ אֲשֶׁר לֹא־תַגִּיד: י

---

1. The commentary on verse 12 explains the need for these twelve months and why they started when they did.

10 **Esther had not revealed her people or her descent because Mordechai had instructed her not to tell.**

QUESTIONS

WHY did Esther not reveal her *"descent"*?

COMMENTARY

The account of the second time when Esther was held against her will — that is, during her stay in the women's quarters under the custody of Hege — is prefaced by a description of the tremendous honor accorded her in the belief that she would become queen. Esther was not swayed by any of the special treatment and refused to reveal **her people or her descent** as Mordechai had enjoined her, in the hope that the king would refuse to take a woman of unknown background to be his queen, and he would expel her.

יא וּבְכָל־יוֹם וָיוֹם מָרְדֳּכַי מִתְהַלֵּךְ לִפְנֵי חֲצַר
בֵּית־הַנָּשִׁים לָדַעַת אֶת־שְׁלוֹם אֶסְתֵּר וּמַה־יֵּעָשֶׂה
בָּהּ:

11 **Every day Mordechai walked in front of the courtyard of the women's quarters to know how Esther was faring and what would become of her.**

QUESTIONS

WHY did Mordechai walk by daily *"to know how Esther was far-ing"*? She would only appear before the king after twelve months, so what was his concern now?

COMMENTARY

Esther placed herself in great danger by continuing to maintain that she was coerced. Mordechai visited daily **to know how Esther was faring and what would become of her** — would she be punished or banished? Mordechai was convinced that her conduct would not be overlooked. Despite the danger, though, Esther remained silent.

יב   וּבְהַגִּיעַ תֹּר נַעֲרָה וְנַעֲרָה לָבוֹא | אֶל־הַמֶּלֶךְ
אֲחַשְׁוֵרוֹשׁ מִקֵּץ הֱיוֹת לָהּ כְּדָת הַנָּשִׁים שְׁנֵים עָשָׂר
חֹדֶשׁ כִּי כֵּן יִמְלְאוּ יְמֵי מְרוּקֵיהֶן שִׁשָּׁה חֳדָשִׁים בְּשֶׁמֶן
הַמֹּר וְשִׁשָּׁה חֳדָשִׁים בַּבְּשָׂמִים וּבְתַמְרוּקֵי הַנָּשִׁים:

12 **When each maiden's turn arrived to come to King Achashverosh, after she had been under the treatment of women for twelve months (for so were the days of their anointing carried out: six months with oil of myrrh and six months with perfumes and women's ointments),**

QUESTIONS

WHY did *"the days of their anointing"* last for twelve months?

COMMENTARY

The third occasion when Esther demonstrated her stubborn opposition to what was being forced upon her was her appearance in front of the king. The women appeared before the king after waiting twelve months. This waiting period was required in order to examine their state of health. A woman, though beautiful, might be unhealthy. She was examined during each of the four seasons, because some illnesses are only apparent at specific times of the year. This period of examination is called **the days of their anointing**. During the six winter months the women were rubbed with **oil of myrrh** which warms the body. In the summer months they used sweet-smelling **perfumes** to counteract undesirable body odors common during this hot time of year.

יג וּבָזֶה הַנַּעֲרָה בָאָה אֶל־הַמֶּלֶךְ אֵת כָּל־אֲשֶׁר
תֹּאמַר יִנָּתֵן לָהּ לָבוֹא עִמָּהּ מִבֵּית הַנָּשִׁים עַד־בֵּית
הַמֶּלֶךְ:

13 **with this the maiden came to the king; anything she requested would be given to her to accompany her from the women's quarters to the king's house.**

QUESTIONS

WHAT is the meaning of *"with this the maiden came to the king"*? Is it a continuation of the previous one which contains only subsidiary clauses? (That is, we are not told what happened *"when each maiden's turn arrived."*)

WHY was each woman given *"anything she requested"*?

COMMENTARY

What was the king looking for in the maidens that came before him? Achashverosh only wanted each maiden to be beautiful and healthy. At the end of the twelve-month examination period, **with this** — her beauty and health — **she came to the king,** and she needed no other attribute.

What could the women expect from the king? When a woman went to the king, she was entitled to ask for anything she desired and it would be granted. By requesting gifts, she demonstrated that she went willingly and was not coerced. She consented to sleep with the king in return for the gifts she received; **with this,** the granting of her request, **she came to the king,** willingly.[1]

בָּעֶרֶב | הִיא בָאָה וּבַבֹּקֶר הִיא שָׁבָה אֶל־בֵּית יד
הַנָּשִׁים שֵׁנִי אֶל־יַד שַׁעֲשְׁגַז סְרִיס הַמֶּלֶךְ שֹׁמֵר
הַפִּילַגְשִׁים לֹא־תָבוֹא עוֹד אֶל־הַמֶּלֶךְ כִּי אִם־חָפֵץ
בָּהּ הַמֶּלֶךְ וְנִקְרְאָה בְשֵׁם:

14 In the evening she went and in the morning she returned to the second quarters of the women, to the charge of Sha'ashgaz, chamberlain of the king,

---

1. According to the Malbim, the word ובזה has two meanings. First, it refers to what she presented to the king —"*with this,*" with her beauty and health, she *"came to the king."* This meaning follows from reading the phrase as a continuation of the previous verse. Second, it refers to what she received from the king — "*with this,*" with the gifts she received, she *"came to the king"*; these gifts were the motivation for her to come to the king. This meaning relates the phrase to the end of this verse.

custodian of the concubines; she would
not return to the king unless he desired
her and she were summoned by name.

COMMENTARY

Each maiden came before the king willingly, despite the fact
that **in the evening she went and in the morning she returned**, permanently confined to the concubines' quarters and
never to **return to the king unless he desired her.**

טו   וּבְהַגִּיעַ תֹּר־ אֶסְתֵּר בַּת־אֲבִיחַיִל | דֹּד
מׇרְדֳּכַי אֲשֶׁר לָקַח־לוֹ לְבַת לָבוֹא אֶל־הַמֶּלֶךְ לֹא
בִקְשָׁה דָּבָר כִּי אִם אֶת־אֲשֶׁר יֹאמַר הֵגַי סְרִיס־הַמֶּלֶךְ
שֹׁמֵר הַנָּשִׁים וַתְּהִי אֶסְתֵּר נֹשֵׂאת חֵן בְּעֵינֵי כָּל־
רֹאֶיהָ:

15 **When it came to the turn of Esther,
daughter of Avichayil the uncle of
Mordechai (who had adopted her as his
daughter), to appear before the king, she
requested nothing, receiving only that
which Hege, the king's chamberlain and
custodian of the women, ordered. Esther
found grace in the eyes of all who saw her.**

QUESTIONS

WHY are we told about Esther's lineage for a second time? We already learned about it in verse 7.

WHY do we need to know that Avichayil was the uncle of Mordechai?

WHY was it that Esther *"requested nothing"*?

WE already know from verse 9 that Esther found favor in people's eyes. Why are we told again that she *"found grace in the eyes of all who saw her"*?

COMMENTARY

Esther was totally different from all the other women. Not only did she possess beauty and excellent health, but she brought with her strength of character and honor as the **daughter of Avichayil**. She had inherited his fine character and high intelligence. Avichayil was the **uncle of Mordechai**, who had developed Esther's potential to the maximum when he **adopted her as his daughter**. This was what she had to offer the king.

Conversely, she wanted nothing from him. When given the opportunity, **she requested nothing**, showing her unwillingness to be there and that she was there only under duress.

When it came to the turn of Esther — only because it was her turn and she was forced to appear did she go. She requested nothing, taking only what **Hege, the king's chamberlain and custodian of the women,**[1] ordered.[2]

---

1. Why are we told that Hege was *"the king's chamberlain and custodian of the women"*? We already know this from verse 3. Perhaps we can suggest that Hege was doubly qualified to decide what Esther should take with her when she appeared before Achashverosh. As *"the king's chamberlain"* he knew the king's tastes and what would please him. As "custodian of the women" he was acquainted with which perfumes and cosmetics would suit each woman. (Ed.)

2. The Malbim does not interpret that Esther requested nothing *except* for what Hege *advised*. He explains that Esther requested *absolutely* nothing, being *ordered* by Hege to take.

Despite her recalcitrance, which was punishable with the death penalty, **she found grace in the eyes of all who saw her.**

טז וַתִּלָּקַ֨ח אֶסְתֵּ֜ר אֶל־הַמֶּ֤לֶךְ אֲחַשְׁוֵרוֹשׁ֙ אֶל־בֵּ֣ית מַלְכוּת֔וֹ בַּחֹ֥דֶשׁ הָעֲשִׂירִ֖י הוּא־חֹ֣דֶשׁ טֵבֵ֑ת בִּשְׁנַת־שֶׁ֖בַע לְמַלְכוּתֽוֹ:

16 **Esther was taken to King Achashverosh, to the house of his sovereignty, in the tenth month, the month of Teves, in the seventh year of his kingdom.**

COMMENTARY

We are informed that Esther's arrival in the king's chambers was entirely under compulsion — **Esther was taken.**

She was not merely taken to his palace, but to **the house of his sovereignty,** his private suite.[1]

יז וַיֶּאֱהַ֨ב הַמֶּ֤לֶךְ אֶת־אֶסְתֵּר֙ מִכָּל־הַנָּשִׁ֔ים וַתִּשָּׂא־חֵ֥ן וָחֶ֛סֶד לְפָנָ֖יו מִכָּל־הַבְּתוּלֹ֑ת וַיָּ֤שֶׂם כֶּֽתֶר־מַלְכוּת֙ בְּרֹאשָׁ֔הּ וַיַּמְלִיכֶ֖הָ תַּ֥חַת וַשְׁתִּֽי:

17 **The king loved Esther more than all the other women; she found grace and favor before him more than all the other**

---

1. The Malbim seems to infer this from the use of the phrase בית מלכותו, literally *"house of his sovereignty,"* rather than בית המלך, *"house of the king."* It may be that the use of the possessive *"his sovereignty"* conveys this idea.

virgins. He placed the royal crown on her head, crowning her as Vashti's successor.

QUESTIONS

WHO are *"the other women"* and who are *"the other virgins"*?

WHAT are the differences between being *"loved"* and finding *"grace and favor"*?

COMMENTARY

Achashverosh already had other wives and concubines. When discussing existing relationships, it is appropriate to use the word *"love." **The king loved Esther more than all the other women,** the wives and concubines he already possessed.

With regard to the virgins from whom Achashverosh would choose his new queen, it is relevant to speak of "finding grace and favor" to be crowned as queen. Esther was superior to these women as well — **she found grace and favor before him more than all the other virgins,** to the extent that he, himself, **placed the royal crown on her head,** immediately **crowning her as Vashti's successor.**

יח וַיַּעַשׂ הַמֶּלֶךְ מִשְׁתֶּה גָדוֹל לְכָל־שָׂרָיו וַעֲבָדָיו אֵת מִשְׁתֵּה אֶסְתֵּר וַהֲנָחָה לַמְּדִינוֹת עָשָׂה וַיִּתֵּן מַשְׂאֵת כְּיַד הַמֶּלֶךְ:

18 The king hosted a great banquet for all his officials and servants — "the banquet of Esther." He granted the provinces a

**reduction in tribute and distributed gifts
as befits a king.**

QUESTIONS

WHY was it called *"the banquet of Esther"*? We already know that
it was in honor of Esther's accession to the throne.

WHY did Achashverosh grant the provinces *"a reduction in tribute"* and distribute *"gifts"*?

COMMENTARY

Having been crowned queen, Esther still did not divulge her
people or descent. Achashverosh attempted three strategies to
persuade her to tell.

First, he **hosted a great banquet for all his officials and
servants** and proclaimed that it was **"the banquet of Esther."** He
hoped that the honor would go to her head, and that to avoid the
embarasssment of the officials querying her unknown background, she would reveal her lineage.

Second, **he granted the provinces a reduction in tribute.**
He hoped that her province of birth would benefit from this reduction and Esther would be encouraged to divulge her province
of origin in order that Achashverosh deal even more generously
with its inhabitants.

Third, he **distributed gifts as befits a king** in the hope that
Esther would want her relatives to receive presents as well, and
thus she would tell him who they were.

יט   וּבְהִקָּבֵץ בְּתוּלוֹת שֵׁנִית וּמָרְדְּכַי יֹשֵׁב בְּשַׁעַר־
הַמֶּלֶךְ:

19 **When the virgins were assembled for the second time, and Mordechai was sitting at the king's gate,**

QUESTIONS

ESTHER had already been crowned queen. Why, then, were the virgins assembled *"for the second time"*?

WHAT is the significance of the fact that *"Mordechai was sitting at the king's gate"*?

COMMENTARY

Achashverosh reasoned that perhaps Esther was afraid to reveal her origins because she was of lowly stock and was worried that the king might divorce her if he knew. He therefore sought to reassure her.

All the remaining virgins who had not yet appeared before the king **were assembled** in order to send them home.[1] Esther could be confident that the king would not choose another woman.

In addition, **Mordechai was sitting at the king's gate**. He had been appointed as one of the judges that sat on the judiciary at the king's gate. This promotion was given to him solely because Esther had been found in his home. How much more honor would be accorded him if the king were to know that Esther was his relative!

---

1. The Malbim does not explain that *"the virgins were assembled for the second time"* in order to select from them, but merely to send them home.

כ אֵין אֶסְתֵּר מַגֶּדֶת מוֹלַדְתָּהּ וְאֶת־עַמָּהּ כַּאֲשֶׁר
צִוָּה עָלֶיהָ מָרְדֳּכָי וְאֶת־ מַאֲמַר מָרְדֳּכַי אֶסְתֵּר עֹשָׂה
כַּאֲשֶׁר הָיְתָה בְאָמְנָה אִתּוֹ:

20 **Esther did not impart her descent or her
people, following Mordechai's command;
she obeyed Mordechai's instruction as
when she had been raised by him.**

QUESTIONS

WE already know from verse 10 that Esther did not reveal *"her
people or her descent."* So why are we told again that she *"did not
impart her descent or her people"*?

IN addition, why in verse 10 is the order *"her people or her descent,"* but here it is *"her descent or her people"*?

THIS verse seems to be a continuation of the previous one. What
is the thematic connection between them?

COMMENTARY

Although Achashverosh had tried to persuade her using the
two approaches mentioned in the previous verse (sending the remaining virgins home and promoting Mordechai), **Esther** still
did not impart her descent or her people.

Originally, in verse 10, we read *"her people or her descent"* because those who met Esther wanted to know who she was, and
their initial question was what was her nation. Here, though,
Achashverosh wanted to show generosity to those close to Esther
— first to her family and only then to her people.

We see Esther's quality of character. Despite her rise to

power, she obeyed Mordechai's instruction as when she had
been raised by him.

כא בַּיָּמִים הָהֵם וּמָרְדֳּכַי יוֹשֵׁב בְּשַׁעַר־הַמֶּלֶךְ קָצַף
בִּגְתָן וָתֶרֶשׁ שְׁנֵי־סָרִיסֵי הַמֶּלֶךְ מִשֹּׁמְרֵי הַסַּף וַיְבַקְשׁוּ
לִשְׁלֹחַ יָד בַּמֶּלֶךְ אֲחַשְׁוֵרֹשׁ:

21 At that time, when Mordechai was
sitting at the king's gate, two of the king's
chamberlains, Bigthan and Seresh, guards
at his door, became enraged and plotted
to assassinate King Achashverosh.

QUESTIONS

WE were told only two verses ago that *"Mordechai was sitting at
the king's gate."* Why are we told this a second time?

COMMENTARY

Before recounting the troubles that befell the Jewish people,
we are told that "the cure had preceded the wound."[1]

We are taught that the Almighty only strikes us in order to
heal us. This is the meaning of the verse: "All the diseases which I
brought on Mitzrayim I will not place upon you, because I am
Hashem Who heals you."[2] Mitzrayim was struck because its people were evil. The Jewish people are told that they will not be
struck in the same manner as Mitzrayim, but because the Almighty is "Hashem Who heals you."

---

1. See *Megillah* 13b.
2. Shemos 15:26.

A surgeon, who makes a cut in order to cure, ensures that the preparations for stemming the blood and healing the wound are ready before the operation starts. Similarly, before bringing decrees upon the Jewish nation, the Omnipotent ensured that the preparations for its salvation were already in place.

The first of these preparations was the appointment of a Jewish woman, Esther, as queen, about which we learned in chapter two.

The second was that Mordechai obtained the king's indebtedness by uncovering the plot to assassinate him. This occurred when **Mordechai was sitting at the king's gate**. This was significant for two reasons:

First, his appointment aroused the jealousy of Bigthan and Seresh. They were furious that Mordechai was *sitting* in ease and honor, while they were *standing* as guards at the king's door.

Second, it was his position at the king's gate that enabled him to uncover the assassination plot.

The Divine hand is apparent in many aspects of this episode:

1) We see that although Mordechai's new position provoked the decree against the Jews — for it was Mordechai's refusal, while sitting at the king's gate, to bow to Haman that initiated Haman's fury — it also contained the seed of redemption. This was miraculous Divine providence.

2) Another miraculous element of this episode was that **Bigthan and Seresh, guards at his door, became enraged.** The position of palace guard, who is directly responsible for the king's security, is only entrusted to the most loyal and trustworthy of men. Yet we see that the Almighty caused them to become enraged against Achashverosh over the most trivial of issues.

3) It was also Divine involvement that led them to plot **to assassinate King Achashverosh.** Usually, only ministers conspire against a king, planning to replace him with one of their own. As chamberlains they could not hope to become king. Thus their conspiracy, which could (and did) lead to their execution, was also extraordinary.

כב וַיִּוָּדַע הַדָּבָר לְמָרְדֳּכַי וַיַּגֵּד לְאֶסְתֵּר הַמַּלְכָּה
וַתֹּאמֶר אֶסְתֵּר לַמֶּלֶךְ בְּשֵׁם מָרְדֳּכָי:

22 The matter became known to Mordechai, who told it to Esther the queen; she informed the king in Mordechai's name.

COMMENTARY

4) The fact that **the matter became known to Mordechai** is also clear evidence of the Divine masterplan.[1]

5) Even though Mordechai had not directed Esther to inform the king in his name, and she always followed his instructions (see verse 20), she did something she was not told to do — **she informed the king in Mordechai's name.**

כג וַיְבֻקַּשׁ הַדָּבָר וַיִּמָּצֵא וַיִּתָּלוּ שְׁנֵיהֶם עַל־עֵץ
וַיִּכָּתֵב בְּסֵפֶר דִּבְרֵי הַיָּמִים לִפְנֵי הַמֶּלֶךְ:

23 When inquiry was made of the matter it was discovered. The two of them were hanged from a gallows, and it was recorded in the book of chronicles before the king.

---

1. In the Hebrew text of the commentary, the miracles are numbered incorrectly, with this miracle and the previous one both being counted as the third miracle. (Ed.)

Questions

WHY are we told that the matter was recorded *"before the king"*?

Commentary

6) When an investigation was made **it was discovered**; that is, the poison with which they planned to kill the king.[1] Although they must have hidden it very carefully it was still found — another component of the Divine design.

7) The fact that Mordechai was not immediately rewarded by the king but **it was recorded** without recompense was also providential. A reminder of Achashverosh's outstanding indebtedness to Mordechai was to prove crucial later on.

8) It was not written in the general book of chronicles, kept in the custody of the king's viceroy. Had it been so, Haman would have had little trouble erasing it. Instead, it was written in the **book of chronicles before the king** — Achashverosh's own personal record, which Haman could not touch.

9) The actual writing took place **before the king**. Were this not the case, the scribe could have easily falsified the account.

---

1. See *Megillah* 13b, where we learn that the method of assassination to be used was poisoning.

CHAPTER 3

גָּ א אַחַר ׀ הַדְּבָרִים הָאֵ֫לֶּה גִּדַּל הַמֶּ֫לֶךְ אֲחַשְׁוֵרוֹשׁ
אֶת־הָמָן בֶּן־הַמְּדָ֫תָא הָאֲגָגִי וַיְנַשְּׂאֵ֫הוּ וַיָּ֫שֶׂם אֶת־
כִּסְא֫וֹ מֵעַ֫ל כָּל־הַשָּׂרִ֫ים אֲשֶׁ֫ר אִתּֽוֹ:

1 After these events, King Achashverosh
promoted Haman, the son of Hamdatha,
the Agagite, and elevated him, placing his
seat above all the officials who were with
him.

QUESTIONS

WHY did Achashverosh elevate Haman to such a high position?

WHY did this occur specifically *"after these events"*?

WHAT is the difference between *"promoted"* and *"elevated"*?

COMMENTARY

Achashverosh recalled that Esther had informed him about the assassination plot. However, he had forgotten that it was Mordechai who had told Esther. He wanted to reward Esther for saving his life and thought she would be delighted if he promoted Memuchan, because it was Memuchan who had suggested that the maidens be assembled, which led to the choice of Esther as queen. Memuchan was one of Haman's other names. Therefore, Achashverosh greatly promoted Haman — just to please Esther.[1]

Having forgotten that it was Mordechai who had uncovered the conspiracy, it was easy for Haman to convince Achashverosh that *he* was the one who had exposed the plot. This caused Achashverosh to further elevate Haman who, thereby, received glory that he did not deserve, but that was really owed to Mordechai. It was Divinely ordained that Haman should temporarily receive this honor until the time came to give it to its rightful recipient.

When a king wishes to advance someone from a low rank to a very high one he does not do so in one act of promotion, but rather, gradually, in stages.[2] Achashverosh initially **promoted** Haman to be one of his officials, and then **elevated** him until Haman reached the pinnacle — **his seat above all the officials**, even those **who were with him** at the peak of power.

ב וְכָל־עַבְדֵי הַמֶּ֫לֶךְ אֲשֶׁר־בְּשַׁעַר הַמֶּ֫לֶךְ כֹּרְעִים וּמִשְׁתַּחֲוִים לְהָמָן כִּי־כֵן צִוָּה־לוֹ הַמֶּ֫לֶךְ וּמָרְדֳּכַי לֹא יִכְרַע וְלֹא יִשְׁתַּחֲוֶה:

---

1. See *Megillah* 12b.
2. See the commentary of the Malbim on Bereishis 45:8 where Yosef says to his brothers, "And He (God) made me a father to Pharaoh" and then "master of all his house" and then "ruler over the whole land of Mitzrayim."

2 **All the king's servants who were at the king's gate were bowing and prostrating themselves before Haman, for this was what the king had commanded him; Mordechai, however, would not bow nor prostrate himself.**

QUESTIONS

WHY was the command to bow issued to those *"at the king's gate"* rather than all the king's servants, wherever they were?

WHY are we told, *"this is what the king had commanded **him**,"* rather than *"this is what the king had commanded **them**"*?

COMMENTARY

Achashverosh gave Haman further glory; **all the king's servants,** even those **who were at the king's gate,** were obligated to bow and prostrate themselves before him. This was remarkable because, usually, where the king is found, it is forbidden to show honor to anyone else, as this would be a slight to the king's honor.[1] The king wanted to forgo this honor and ordered that even those *"at the king's gate"* bow down to Haman.

Achashverosh was determined that Haman receive this honor and would not allow for any possibility that he might forgo it. So **the king had commanded him**[2] to insist on it, pun-

---

1. See *Shabbos* 56a. Uriah HaHiti deserved the death penalty for insubordination against King David because he used the appellation "my master Yoav" (Shmuel II 11:11) in front of the king.
2. There seems to be a significant misprint in the two standard Hebrew editions of the Malbim on Megillas Esther. The text is as follows:

ishing those who transgressed the order of the king.

Despite this, **Mordechai, however, would not bow** and was determined not to do so at all costs. Why? In those days bowing down to someone was considered acknowledgement of the divinity of that person. If a man was unusually wise or strong it was attributed to his being "a son of the gods" or because a "star" or "higher power" rested upon him.[1]

Therefore, Mordechai, as a believing Jew, refused to bow to Haman lest it be interpreted that he ascribed divinity to Haman.

Furthermore, Mordechai was not obligated to bow to Haman because the king's edict applied only to those who were both servants of the king and who sat at the king's gate. Although he sat at the king's gate, Mordechai, as a Jew, was not one of the king's servants; under Persian custom a Jew could not be a servant of the king.

Both of these reasons for Mordechai's refusal to bow — the reluctance to attribute divinity to Haman and his exemption as a Jew — are alluded to in Mordechai's response (verse 4), **he had told them that he was a Jew.**

וגם שלא היה זה רק לכבוד המן שבזה היה בידו למחול רק היה מצות המלך, וגם **לא** להמן צוה זאת שיקפיד ע״ז ויעניש את העובר מצד עברו מצות המלך.

Besides the fact that one edition has the word שיפקיד instead of שיקפיד, the latter seeming more correct, it seems that the word לא should really be לו. If this correction is made, the Malbim's commentary directly answers the question why Achashverosh commanded Haman. (Ed.)

1. See Daniel 2:46. After Daniel interpreted Nevuchadnetzar's dream, "then King Nevuchadnetzar fell on his face and bowed down to Daniel and commanded that they should offer an offering and pleasing odors to him."

ג וַיֹּאמְרוּ עַבְדֵי הַמֶּלֶךְ אֲשֶׁר־ בְּשַׁעַר הַמֶּלֶךְ
לְמָרְדֳּכָי מַדּוּעַ אַתָּה עוֹבֵר אֵת מִצְוַת הַמֶּלֶךְ:
ד וַיְהִי בְּאָמְרָם אֵלָיו יוֹם וָיוֹם וְלֹא שָׁמַע אֲלֵיהֶם
וַיַּגִּידוּ לְהָמָן לִרְאוֹת הֲיַעַמְדוּ דִּבְרֵי מָרְדֳּכַי כִּי־הִגִּיד
לָהֶם אֲשֶׁר־הוּא יְהוּדִי:

3 The king's servants who were at the king's gate said to Mordechai, "Why do you transgress the king's command?"
4 They asked him daily but he did not listen to them. They told Haman to see if Mordechai's claims would stand, for he had told them that he was a Jew.

QUESTIONS

WHAT is the meaning of "if Mordechai's claims would stand, for he had told them that he was a Jew"? They already knew that he was a Jew, so why does it not say "if Mordechai's claims would stand, for he had told them that he would not prostrate himself"?

COMMENTARY

The king's servants were not motivated by hatred when **they told Haman.** They had been instructed to enforce the king's orders and to prevent transgressions. Before they informed Haman they warned Mordechai on many occasions — **they asked him daily** — and yet **he did not listen to them.**

Only then did they tell Haman **to see if Mordechai's claims would stand.** Mordechai had explained that his religion prohibited him from bowing down to Haman. However, this argument was only valid to explain why Mordechai would not bow when Haman was distant from him and was unaware of the bowing — then it would be tantamount to ascribing divinity to Haman.

But if Mordechai was to bow when Haman could see him, this would be merely an act of obeisance with no religious overtones, as it was customary to genuflect before nobles as a sign of servility.

If Mordechai refused to bow in view of Haman, it would not be on religious grounds; it would be an act of defiance. **They told Haman to see,** that he should watch Mordechai,[1] and then they would know **if Mordechai's claim would stand** — that is, the fact that **he had told them** that he did not bow because **he was a Jew.**

ה   וַיַּרְא הָמָן כִּי־אֵין מָרְדֳּכַי כֹּרֵעַ וּמִשְׁתַּחֲוֶה לֹו
וַיִּמָּלֵא הָמָן חֵמָה:

5 **Then Haman saw that Mordechai was not bowing down and prostrating himself before him, and Haman was full of anger.**

QUESTIONS

WHY was Haman furious only when he "*saw that Mordechai was not bowing down*"? Why did he not believe the king's servants when they told him?

---

1. The usual way of interpreting this verse is that "*they told Haman in order to see if Mordechai's claim would stand,*" i.e., they were curious to see. The Malbim, though, understands it to mean "*they told Haman to watch Mordechai, and thereby Haman would know if Mordechai's claim would stand,*" i.e., if it was really genuine.

COMMENTARY

Then Haman saw — that is, he watched Mordechai, and despite this, **Mordechai was not bowing down and prostrating himself.** Now, when Haman was in close proximity to Mordechai and was observing him, respect for his elevated status would demand that Mordechai bow. Haman understood, then, that Mordechai's refusal to bow was clearly out of personal hatred for him; he would not prostrate himself **before *him*.** Therefore, **Haman was full of anger.**

ו   וַיִּבֶז בְּעֵינָיו לִשְׁלֹחַ יָד בְּמָרְדְּכַי לְבַדּוֹ כִּי־הִגִּידוּ
לוֹ אֶת־עַם מָרְדֳּכָי וַיְבַקֵּשׁ הָמָן לְהַשְׁמִיד אֶת־כָּל־
הַיְּהוּדִים אֲשֶׁר בְּכָל־מַלְכוּת אֲחַשְׁוֵרוֹשׁ עַם מָרְדֳּכָי:

6 **Haman considered it disdainful to kill Mordechai alone, because he had been told which was the nation of Mordechai. Haman wanted to exterminate all the Jews, the nation of Mordechai, in the entire kingdom of Achashverosh.**

QUESTIONS

IN what way was the entire *"nation of Mordechai"* culpable? Why should they all be exterminated for the crime of one man?

COMMENTARY

Haman's inhumanity and overweening arrogance were without limit. Even though his anger was essentially directed at

Mordechai, when the king's servants told him **which was the nation of Mordechai**, thereby revealing that his refusal to bow was connected with his Jewish beliefs, he felt hatred towards all Jews and their religion. He **wanted to exterminate all the Jews** because they were **the nation of Mordechai**, sharing the same religion. Haman wanted to extirpate this religion and all who adhered to it.

ז בַּחֹדֶשׁ הָרִאשׁוֹן הוּא־חֹדֶשׁ נִיסָן בִּשְׁנַת שְׁתֵּים
עֶשְׂרֵה לַמֶּלֶךְ אֲחַשְׁוֵרוֹשׁ הִפִּיל פּוּר הוּא הַגּוֹרָל לִפְנֵי
הָמָן מִיּוֹם ׀ לְיוֹם וּמֵחֹדֶשׁ לְחֹדֶשׁ שְׁנֵים־עָשָׂר הוּא־
חֹדֶשׁ אֲדָר:

7 **In the first month, the month of Nissan, of the twelfth year of the reign of Achashverosh, they cast a *pur*, which is a lot, before Haman, from day to day and from month to month, arriving at the twelfth month, the month of Adar.**

QUESTIONS

WHY do we need the phrase *"before Haman"*?

WHAT is the meaning of *"from day to day and from month to month"*?

IN a matter of such critical significance for the Jewish people, it is surely meaningful that the casting of the lot fell on the thirteenth of Adar. Why was this the chosen day?

COMMENTARY

There are various methods of casting lots. The type used by Haman was a *pur*, which he regularly employed in decision-making.

This involved examining each of the upcoming days, on a day by day basis, to see which was most propitious. The casting of the lot to decide when to exterminate the Jewish people took place on the thirteenth day[1] of **the first month, the month of Nissan.**

Haman wanted to rid himself of the Jewish people as soon as possible. He therefore checked whether the very next day, the fourteenth day of Nissan, would be propitious. The lot indicated that it would not. He then tried the fifteenth, then the sixteenth, and so on until the end of Nissan, and each time the lot informed him that the day was inappropriate. Haman then started examining the next month, starting with the first of Iyar and working forward, **from day to day**, until he reached the thirteenth of Iyar. Since, by definition, one day had to be selected, Divine providence ensured that it would be the most distant of the days available for selection, giving the Jewish people the maximum time possible.

Haman, seeing that he had been pushed off from day to day until the last day possible, thought that perhaps the month was an inauspicious one. So he examined each of the months in turn to see which was the most fitting. He started with Nissan, the month the lot-casting was taking place, and the answer was negative. It continued this way **from month to month** until the last available month was reached — **the twelfth month, the month of Adar.**

---

1. See verse 12. The Malbim assumes that the orders to exterminate the Jews were written and sent on the same day that the lot was cast. Given Haman's all-consuming hatred of the Jews, this is very likely to have been the case.

Haman did not cast the lot again to decide which day in Adar should be selected; the original *"day to day"* lot-casting had determined that the thirteenth of a month was the day to be chosen. Thus the day selected was the thirteenth of Adar.

If Haman had selected the month first, and only afterward selected the day, the latest day possible would be the *last* day of Adar. However, since the day was selected first, the last day available was the thirteenth (because he was acting on the thirteenth, and he started the lot-casting from the fourteenth). Since only afterward was the month selected, the latest possible day was the day that the Almighty arranged, the thirteenth of Adar.[1] The Jews

---

1. Slight difficulties still remain. If the earliest that Haman wanted to start killing the Jews was from the next day, the fourteenth of Nissan, and if the *"day to day"* lot-casting determined that the extermination was to take place on the thirteenth of a month, why did Haman examine the month of Nissan first? This would involve waiting a whole year. Why did he not examine the month of Iyar first?

   Furthermore, having determined that the day selected was to be the thirteenth, if the month selected would have been Nissan, the Jews would have gained an extra month, for the extermination would have then taken place after the elapse of a whole year. Why did the Almighty not arrange that the month of Nissan was selected, giving the Jews an extra month?

   Perhaps the resolution is that although Haman wanted to kill the Jews as soon as possible, he would have found it difficult to have started this the very same day. Therefore, he started casting the lot from the next day. When the thirteenth day was the outcome, then Haman was faced with two possible inferences: either that he had been pushed off, inauspiciously, until the last possible day, or that he was to act with alacrity, however technically difficult, and initiate the killing of the Jews the very same day. Haman hoped that the latter was true. Although it would be hard to arrange it the same day, it would be a sign that his plan was blessed with success. Therefore, he examined the month of Nissan first. If Nissan turned out to be the chosen month, he could be confident that he should proceed the very same day. Given his overwhelming

were being given the maximum time possible to ensure their repentance and redemption.

Haman should have seen the Divine intervention in the outcome of the lots. Therefore, they cast the lot **before Haman;** it was prepared in his own presence for his ultimate downfall.

ח וַיֹּ֤אמֶר הָמָן֙ לַמֶּ֣לֶךְ אֲחַשְׁוֵר֔וֹשׁ יֶשְׁנ֣וֹ עַם־אֶחָ֗ד
מְפֻזָּ֤ר וּמְפֹרָד֙ בֵּ֣ין הָֽעַמִּ֔ים בְּכֹ֖ל מְדִינ֣וֹת מַלְכוּתֶ֑ךָ
וְדָתֵיהֶ֞ם שֹׁנ֣וֹת מִכָּל־עָ֗ם וְאֶת־דָּתֵ֤י הַמֶּ֙לֶךְ֙ אֵינָ֣ם
עֹשִׂ֔ים וְלַמֶּ֥לֶךְ אֵין־שֹׁוֶ֖ה לְהַנִּיחָֽם:

8 **Then Haman said to King Achashverosh, "There is a certain people, scattered and dispersed among the peoples in all the provinces of your kingdom. Their religions are different from all people, and they do not adhere to the king's laws. It is not worth it for the king to leave them as they are.**

QUESTIONS (VERSES 8-9)

WHY would a ruler assent to the extermination of an entire people that committed no crime?

IF, in his inhumanity, he had agreed to this genocide, why does he express such surprise when Esther tells him about it, exclaim-

---

hatred of the Jews, Haman did not interpret the selection of the lots of the thirteenth day to mean that he was to wait an entire year.

If so, the latest possible day, with the system of lot-casting used, was the thirteenth of Adar. (Ed.)

ing to her, *"Who is this and what is this, that he dares to do such a thing?"*[1] Is the mass destruction of an entire nation such an insignificant matter that it slipped his memory?

FURTHERMORE, if he did consent to Haman's request, why is Achashverosh so enraged with Haman when Esther tells him of Haman's plan?

WHY does Achashverosh allow Esther to write the whole narrative[2] for posterity, a story in which he will be remembered, for eternity, with disgrace as the ruler who was willing to have the entire Jewish people exterminated?

WHY does Haman not mention the Jewish people by name, saying only that *"there is a certain people"*?

WHY are the words *"scattered"* and *"dispersed"* both used?

WHY say *"their **religions**"* in the plural? Why does it say that *"their religions are different from all people"* ? It should say, *"... are different from the religions of all people."*

WHEN the decree is written by the scribes and distributed by the runners, it commands people *"to destroy, kill, and eradicate all the Jews."* However, Haman, when speaking to Achashverosh, suggests only that they *"should be eradicated."* Why does Haman not speak also of destroying and killing?

COMMENTARY

Haman deceived the king in two respects. First, he never told him that the people he was maligning was the Jewish nation. The Jews were distinguished for their wisdom, and Achashverosh would never have agreed to Haman's request. Haman

---

1. Ch. 7, v. 5.
2. Ch. 9, vs. 29-32.

therefore cunningly said, "**There is a certain people**" — a nation so obscure that they cannot even be referred to by name.

Second, if Achashverosh had been aware that Haman's intention was extermination, he would not have agreed even if the nation concerned was the most lowly and despicable one.

He wanted to vilify this nation as harmful to all the provinces, both in their religion and their behavior. If they were living by themselves, in their own province, they would pose little danger of adversely affecting people living in neighboring provinces. Even if they lived in provinces inhabited by other people but lived separately, in their own towns, the adverse influence would be small and the king would not have condoned their wholesale slaughter.

Therefore, Haman said that they are **scattered** — they do not have their own province. They are also **dispersed** — they do not live in their own separate towns but are found in every area, and they are not confined to a few provinces but they are **among the peoples in all the provinces of your kingdom**. Their harmful influence is to be found everywhere.

Haman then describes how this influence can be dangerous in two areas.

First, in the area of their religion, **their religions are different from all people**. This includes three different aspects:

1) Their religion is **different** from other religions.

2) All religions, by definition, are different from each other. However, they usually differ only in their beliefs and underlying principles. Their religious practices are usually very similar. The Jewish religion, though, has so many laws and practices that it seems to be composed of many **religions**, all of which are radically different from other religions.

3) Not only is their religion different, but the Jews themselves are intrinsically different **from all people**. Their religion separates them from other people through differences in the food they eat and the clothes they wear. This separation leads to

differences in their national character.

Second, in the area of public order they are very dangerous
— **they do not adhere to the king's laws.** Even though these
laws do not conflict with their religious beliefs and only require
compliance with their fiscal duty to the king, they flagrantly disregard them. The possibility that others will learn from their terrible example must be avoided at all costs.

No possible gain from leaving them undisturbed could outweigh the damage they might cause; **it is not worth it for the
king to leave them as they are.**

ט אִם־עַל־הַמֶּלֶךְ טוֹב יִכָּתֵב לְאַבְּדָם וַעֲשֶׂרֶת
אֲלָפִים כִּכַּר־כֶּסֶף אֶשְׁקוֹל עַל־יְדֵי עֹשֵׂי הַמְּלָאכָה
לְהָבִיא אֶל־גִּנְזֵי הַמֶּלֶךְ:

9 **If it pleases the king, let it be written
that they should be eradicated, and I will
weigh ten thousand talents of silver from
those who will do the work to be brought
into the king's treasuries."**

QUESTIONS

THE usual translation of this verse is, *"I will pay ten thousand talents of silver **into the hands of those who will do the work** to bring
it into the king's treasuries."* Why is the money paid into the hands
of *"those who will do the work"* and not directly into the hands of
"stewards" or "treasurers"?

IT is unheard of in history for a king to sell one of his subject peoples. Why would Achashverosh agree to such a sale?

IF the Jews were going to be slaves, it might have been appropriate for Haman to pay the king. However, since the Jews were going to be killed, why should money be paid?

COMMENTARY

The second way in which Haman deceived the king was that he did not say he wanted to destroy this people but that **they should be eradicated.**[1] That is, their old form should be wiped away and, compelled to be like the other nations, they would become a "new product" that could be allowed to remain in the kingdom without any danger of adverse influence. Achashverosh never realized that Haman's real intention was total annihilation.

To achieve this transformation and to "convert" the members of this nation into normal members of society would require much intensive work. This could be expected to be a very expensive process. Haman reassured Achashverosh that he would not need to pay for experienced officials to carry out this task. There would be **those who will do the work** voluntarily and would be so happy to have this chance to act for the public welfare that they would pay for the opportunity. Haman assured the king, "From those who will do the work **I will** be able to **weigh ten thousand talents of silver**" which would be brought **into the king's treasuries.**[2]

---

1. The Malbim's explanation is based on the fact that the Hebrew word לאבד has two meanings. The first is "to destroy." The second is "to change the form of something" causing it to lose its old form. Haman, when speaking to the king, used it with its second meaning, "to change the form." In the text of the decree (verse 13), the word is used to mean "destroy." In Haman's speech to the king the phrase *"should be eradicated"* was used, attempting to convey this double meaning of either removing the old form, or, as in verse 13, the idea of destruction.
2. Unlike the usual understanding of this verse according to which

Achashverosh was convinced that everyone would be pleased to have the chance to return these miscreants to the correct path.

וַיָּסַר הַמֶּלֶךְ אֶת־טַבַּעְתּוֹ מֵעַל יָדוֹ וַיִּתְּנָהּ לְהָמָן
בֶּן־הַמְּדָתָא הָאֲגָגִי צֹרֵר הַיְּהוּדִים:

י

10 **The king removed his ring from his hand and gave it to Haman, the son of Hamdatha, the Agagite, the Jews' oppressor.**

QUESTIONS

WHY is it significant that Achashverosh gave his ring to Haman?

WHY is Haman's lineage mentioned here when we already know it from verse 1?

WHY, specifically here, is Haman referred to as *"the Jews' oppressor"*?

---

the money is paid *to* those who do the work, the Malbim interprets it to mean that those who do the work will *pay* the money, enabling Haman to weigh it and have it brought into the king's treasuries.

The Hebrew construction seems to support the Malbim's interpretation. First, Haman did not say he would *"pay"* but that he would *"weigh."* If he were paying the money himself, the verb *"pay"* would be far more appropriate. Second, if Haman is to pay the money from his own pocket, why is it significant that it will be weighed by *"those who will do the work"*? According to the Malbim, however, they are very important, being the ones who will donate the money.

COMMENTARY

We are now shown that the king was not at all culpable. Haman tricked Achashverosh by not telling him that the Jews were the nation involved and that his aim was extermination. If the king himself would have read and signed the edict, he would have immediately seen that he had been doubly duped. Achashverosh, with full trust in Haman, gave him the royal signet ring with which to sign on his behalf. Haman was then able to change the wording and write *"to destroy, kill, and eradicate."*

Achashverosh was not to blame. It was only Haman who was **the Jews' oppressor.** He was the sole mastermind of the plot to kill the Jews, spurred by the hatred passed down from his ancestors and destined to remain for eternity since he was an **Agagite.**

יא וַיֹּאמֶר הַמֶּלֶךְ לְהָמָן הַכֶּסֶף נָתוּן לָךְ וְהָעָם
לַעֲשׂוֹת בּוֹ כַּטּוֹב בְּעֵינֶיךָ:

11 **The king said to Haman, "The silver is given to you, and you can do with the people as you see fit."**

QUESTIONS

SINCE the king was not giving Haman anything, but merely forgoing the money that Haman had offered, instead of saying, *"The silver is given to you,"* why does he not say simply, *"The silver is yours"*?

COMMENTARY

We are shown again the innocence of Achashverosh. No one should think that he was motivated by greed and a lust for money. On the contrary, he told Haman, **"The silver is given to you"** — he was willing to spend his own money[1] to correct this deviant people, to destroy their evil religion and improve their character. The money was to be given to Haman together **with the people.** Haman could do with them as he would **see fit** in order to rectify them.

יב וַיִּקָּרְאוּ סֹפְרֵי הַמֶּלֶךְ בַּחֹדֶשׁ הָרִאשׁוֹן בִּשְׁלוֹשָׁה
עָשָׂר יוֹם בּוֹ וַיִּכָּתֵב כְּכָל־אֲשֶׁר־צִוָּה הָמָן אֶל
אֲחַשְׁדַּרְפְּנֵי־הַמֶּלֶךְ וְאֶל־הַפַּחוֹת אֲשֶׁר | עַל־מְדִינָה
וּמְדִינָה וְאֶל־שָׂרֵי עַם וָעָם מְדִינָה וּמְדִינָה כִּכְתָבָהּ
וְעַם וָעָם כִּלְשׁוֹנוֹ בְּשֵׁם הַמֶּלֶךְ אֲחַשְׁוֵרֹשׁ נִכְתָּב
וְנֶחְתָּם בְּטַבַּעַת הַמֶּלֶךְ:

12 The king's scribes were summoned in the first month, on the thirteenth day thereof, and all that Haman dictated was written to the king's satraps, to the governors that were over every province and the officials of every people; to each province in its script and to each people in its language. It was written in the name

1. The usual explanation of the phrase *"The silver is given to you"* is that it refers to the silver that Haman was offering to pay the king. To answer the question as to why the word *"given"* is used, the Malbim explains that it refers to money that the king was willing to pay from his own funds for the project that Haman was proposing.

of King Achashverosh and sealed with the
king's ring.

Questions

HAVING determined that the date for the Jews' annihilation was
to be the thirteenth of Adar, eleven months away, why did Haman rush to summon the king's scribes the very same day?

Commentary

Haman now attempted to secure the success of his plan. He
had tricked the king and obtained the royal signet ring. However,
there was always the possibility that Achashverosh might discover that the people in question were the Jews and that Haman
intended to annihilate them. If this happened his plan would be
thwarted. To avoid this, **the king's scribes were summoned** that
same day. We are told that **all that *Haman* dictated was written**
and not "all that the King dictated," because Achashverosh was
totally unaware what was afoot.

Each province contained several peoples. Therefore, two letters were written to each province as a whole, one to the **satraps**
and one to the **governors**. In addition, letters were sent to each
of the peoples within each province to be delivered to the **officials of every people**.

In general, every people had its own language. Each province, even though made up of several peoples, usually was united
in its own style of writing. Therefore, letters were sent **to each
province in its script and to each people in its language.**

יג וְנִשְׁלוֹחַ סְפָרִים בְּיַד הָרָצִים֩ אֶל־כָּל־מְדִינוֹת
הַמֶּלֶךְ֙ לְהַשְׁמִיד֩ לַהֲרֹג וּלְאַבֵּד אֶת־כָּל־הַיְּהוּדִים
מִנַּעַר וְעַד־ זָקֵן טַף וְנָשִׁים֙ בְּיוֹם אֶחָד בִּשְׁלוֹשָׁה
עָשָׂר לְחֹדֶשׁ שְׁנֵים־עָשָׂר הוּא־חֹדֶשׁ אֲדָר וּשְׁלָלָם
לָבוֹז:

13 Letters were sent by runners to all the
king's provinces to destroy, kill, and
eradicate all the Jews, from young to old,
infants and women, on one day — the
thirteenth of the twelfth month, the
month of Adar, and their wealth for
plundering.

COMMENTARY

The **letters were sent by runners** on the same day. This was
to ensure that even if the king wanted to rescind the decree he
would not be able to, *"for a document written in the king's name and
signed with the king's ring may not be revoked."*[1]

The mass annihilation was to take place **on one day** in all
the provinces, leaving the Jews with no possibility of escaping.
The letters did not specify that the decree applied to all the provinces;[2] this was done purposely, in order that each official and
governor would think that his was the sole province involved.
This would ensure that they would be afraid to disobey an order
that they believed was directed specifically to them, rather than a
general order to the empire as a whole.

---

1. Ch. 8, v. 8.
2. This is in contrast to Mordechai's letter, which clearly stated that it
   applied to all the provinces (see ch. 8, v. 11). The commentary on
   chapter 8 analyzes other differences in the wording of the letters of
   Mordechai and Haman.

יד פַּתְשֶׁגֶן הַכְּתָב לְהִנָּתֵן דָּת בְּכָל־מְדִינָה וּמְדִינָה
גָּלוּי לְכָל־ הָעַמִּים לִהְיוֹת עֲתִדִים לַיּוֹם הַזֶּה:

14 A synopsis of the writing was to be given out for an decree in every province, revealed to all the peoples, that they should be ready for that day.

QUESTIONS

WHAT was the *"synopsis of the writing"*? Letters had been sent to every province; what was the need for a synopsis? It cannot be that the synopsis was to clarify the original letter because the synopsis itself was extremely vague.

THE fact that the synopsis was *"revealed to all the peoples"* seems to imply that the original letters were sealed and concealed. Why should this have been so?

WHAT is the meaning of *"they should be ready"* — ready for what, and why?

COMMENTARY

Haman's plan was ingenious in its cunning. The letters sent to the officials of the provinces were sealed with the king's ring. On the outside were clear instructions that they were not to be opened until the thirteenth of Adar. The meaning of **sealed with the king's ring**[1] is not that it was used merely in place of the king's signature at the bottom of the documents, but that the documents were sealed closed with a seal bearing the imprint of the king's signet ring. No one was to know, yet, the contents of

---

1. Verse 12.

the letters — that the Jews were to be killed.

Together with these sealed letters Haman sent open letters, a **synopsis** of the sealed letters. These were **revealed to all the peoples**, merely telling them **that they should be ready** for the thirteenth of Adar to do battle. On that day they were to open the sealed letters, and they would then discover whom they were to fight.

This would ensure that no one would know what was to happen until the appointed time, and the Jews would be unable to seek help or petition the king for clemency. Nor would the Jews try to flee outside Achashverosh's empire or hide themselves. They, too, would think that they should be ready with everyone else, unaware that they were the ones to be killed — until it was too late.

טו הָרָצִים יָצְאוּ דְחוּפִים בִּדְבַר הַמֶּלֶךְ וְהַדָּת נִתְּנָה
בְּשׁוּשַׁן הַבִּירָה וְהַמֶּלֶךְ וְהָמָן יָשְׁבוּ לִשְׁתּוֹת וְהָעִיר
שׁוּשָׁן נָבוֹכָה:

15 **The runners went out hastened by the king's order, and the decree was given out in Shushan the citadel. The king and Haman sat down to drink, but the city of Shushan was confused.**

QUESTIONS

WHY was the decree promulgated in Shushan only after the runners departed? Why was it not first issued in the capital city as we might expect?

HOW could the king be so inhuman as to sit down to drink immediately after selling an entire nation to be annihilated?

WHY was the city of Shushan *"confused"*?

COMMENTARY

Haman ensured that **the runners went out hastened,** giving the king no time to change his mind. Only after their departure was **the decree given out in Shushan the citadel.** Haman was worried that the king might change his mind and decide not to send the letters. He ensured that Achashverosh would not know anything until the runners were already on their way.

As further proof that the king was oblivious to what was happening, we are told that he **sat down to drink** with Haman. If he had been aware that an entire nation had been condemned to death, it is not feasible that he would have acted this way; after sentencing someone to capital punishment, judges customarily refrain from drinking wine for the entire day. How much more so when an entire nation had been condemned!

The reason that **the city of Shushan was confused** was that no one knew what was written in the sealed letters. The synopsis only specified that they should be ready, and they did not know for what.

Haman's plan was working just as he had hoped. The king had no idea what was happening, nor did anyone else in the city. However, the Almighty was yet to thwart Haman's evil designs through the agency of Mordechai.

Chapter 4

ד א וּמָרְדֳּכַ֗י יָדַע֙ אֶת־כָּל־אֲשֶׁ֣ר נַעֲשָׂ֔ה וַיִּקְרַ֤ע
מָרְדֳּכַי֙ אֶת־בְּגָדָ֔יו וַיִּלְבַּ֥שׁ שַׂ֖ק וָאֵ֑פֶר וַיֵּצֵא֙ בְּת֣וֹךְ
הָעִ֔יר וַיִּזְעַ֛ק זְעָקָ֥ה גְדֹלָ֖ה וּמָרָֽה׃

1 Mordechai knew all that had transpired.
Mordechai rent his clothes and put on
sackcloth with ashes and went out into
the middle of the city, crying loudly and
bitterly.

Questions

WHAT is the significance in the fact that *"Mordechai knew all that
had transpired"*? Surely everyone knew what had transpired from
the letters that had been sent to every province.

IF what Mordechai knew was the sum of money that Haman had
promised Achashverosh, why should this have any relevance
now to the situation of the Jews?

WHY did Mordechai merely go out *"into the middle of the city, crying loudly and bitterly"* rather than taking practical steps to try and have the decree rescinded?

COMMENTARY

In spite of all of Haman's efforts at secrecy, Divine providence intervened and ensured that Mordechai became aware and **knew all that had transpired** between Haman and the king and how Achashverosh had been deceived.

Mordechai responded in two ways. First, he **rent his clothes and put on sackcloth with ashes** in repentance and prayer to the Almighty, who controls the hearts of kings.

Only after this did he make practical efforts to avert the decree. His first course of action was to ensure that the true nature of the decree be exposed to both the nations of the empire and to the king himself. Then, representatives could be sent to Achashverosh to beseech mercy.

Therefore, he **went out into the middle of the city crying loudly and bitterly** to attract attention and publicize what he knew.

ב וַיָּבוֹא עַד לִפְנֵי שַׁעַר־הַמֶּלֶךְ כִּי אֵין לָבוֹא
אֶל־שַׁעַר הַמֶּלֶךְ בִּלְבוּשׁ שָׂק:

2 **He came until the king's gate but no further, because no one was allowed to enter the king's gate wearing sackcloth.**

QUESTIONS

WHY did Mordechai come *"until the king's gate"*?

COMMENTARY

Following this, Mordechai **came until the king's gate** in order that the truth of the matter be known in the court of the king, be it to Esther or to the king himself.

We are told that **no one was allowed to enter the king's gate wearing sackcloth** for two reasons: first, to understand why Mordechai did not enter, and second, so we realize that it would have been an unusual sight to have someone standing outside the king's gate wearing sackcloth. This would quickly become public knowledge in the court of the king.

ג וּבְכָל־מְדִינָה וּמְדִינָה מְקוֹם אֲשֶׁר דְּבַר־הַמֶּלֶךְ
וְדָתוֹ מַגִּיעַ אֵבֶל גָּדוֹל לַיְּהוּדִים וְצוֹם וּבְכִי וּמִסְפֵּד
שַׂק וָאֵפֶר יֻצַּע לָרַבִּים:

3 In every province, wherever the king's edict and decree reached, the Jews were in great mourning with fasting, weeping, and lamenting; sackcloth with ashes was worn by the masses.

QUESTIONS

THIS verse is out of place and should have been written at the end of chapter 3. After telling us that *"the runners went out hastily,"* it would be appropriate to tell us that wherever they reached *"the Jews were in great mourning."*

WHY in chapter 8, verse 17 was the king's decree saving the Jews *"in every province and in every city,"* whereas here only *"in every province"* is mentioned and not *"in every city"*?

WHAT is the difference between *"the king's edict"* and his *"decree"*?

COMMENTARY

Before Mordechai revealed the true nature of the decree, no one knew of the matter besides Haman. Once Mordechai had publicized it in Shushan, the news quickly spread by word of mouth to different corners of the empire.

Wherever *both* **the king's edict** — the public copy telling people to be ready for the thirteenth of Adar — *and* the **decree** — the revelation of the contents of the sealed letters (that is, the impending annihilation of the Jewish people) — had **reached**, the consequence was that **the Jews were in great mourning.**[1]

Since the letters were not sent to every city but only to the capital city of each province, it would be incorrect to say here *"in every city."*

ד ‏וַתָּבוֹאֶינָה נַעֲרוֹת אֶסְתֵּר וְסָרִיסֶיהָ וַיַּגִּידוּ לָהּ וַתִּתְחַלְחַל הַמַּלְכָּה מְאֹד וַתִּשְׁלַח בְּגָדִים לְהַלְבִּישׁ אֶת־ מָרְדֳּכַי וּלְהָסִיר שַׂקּוֹ מֵעָלָיו וְלֹא קִבֵּל:

4 **Esther's maids and chamberlains came and told her. The queen was greatly distressed and sent clothing to dress**

---

1. Further thought is required to explain how the identical phrase, *"the king's edict and decree,"* is to be explained above in ch. 2, v. 8.(Ed.)

Mordechai and to remove his sackcloth
from over him, but he did not accept.

QUESTIONS

IF Esther *"sent clothing to dress Mordechai"* it is obvious that his
sackcloth was to be removed first. Why then is there a need to
write, *"and to remove his sackcloth from over him"*?

COMMENTARY

Esther wanted to know what was troubling Mordechai and
she **sent clothing to dress Mordechai** *over* his sackcloth and
thereby **remove his sackcloth from over him** — that is, it would
not be the outermost layer of his clothing. That way he would
not need to remove the sackcloth, but at least it would not be
visible.

ה וַתִּקְרָא אֶסְתֵּר לַהֲתָךְ מִסָּרִיסֵי הַמֶּלֶךְ אֲשֶׁר
הֶעֱמִיד לְפָנֶיהָ וַתְּצַוֵּהוּ עַל־מָרְדֳּכָי לָדַעַת מַה־זֶּה
וְעַל־מַה־זֶּה:

5 **Esther called for Hasach, one of the
king's chamberlains whom he had
appointed to attend her, and she
instructed him about Mordechai to know
what this was about and why it was.**

QUESTIONS

WHY did Esther choose Hasach to go to Mordechai?

WHY are we told that Hasach was a chamberlain whom *"he had appointed to attend her"*?

WHY did Esther instruct him *"about Mordechai"* instead of the more correct phrase, *"and sent him to Mordechai"*?

COMMENTARY

When Esther realized that an important, secret matter was at stake she **called for Hasach** who was loyal and trustworthy. He was **one of the king's chamberlains whom he had appointed** specifically **to attend her** and had become her trusted confidant.

She did not know whether Mordechai would divulge any secrets to Hasach and therefore did not *send him to Mordechai* but **instructed him** to find out **about Mordechai** and what was troubling him.

More specifically, he was to investigate **what this was about** — what was his distress — **and why it was** — what was the cause of the distress. Just as an illness has both a cause and symptoms, and the cure must deal with the cause and not just the symptoms, so, too, Esther wanted to know Mordechai's distress and its underlying cause.

וַיֵּצֵא הֲתָךְ אֶל־מָרְדֳּכָי אֶל־רְחוֹב הָעִיר אֲשֶׁר
לִפְנֵי שַׁעַר־הַמֶּלֶךְ:

6 Hasach went out to Mordechai, to the city square which was in front of the king's gate.

COMMENTARY

Hasach went out to Mordechai to investigate the matter at its source.

ז וַיַּגֶּד־לוֹ מָרְדְּכַי אֵת כָּל־אֲשֶׁר קָרָהוּ וְאֵת ׀ פָּרָשַׁת
הַכֶּסֶף אֲשֶׁר אָמַר הָמָן לִשְׁקוֹל עַל־גִּנְזֵי הַמֶּלֶךְ
בַּיְּהוּדִיִּים לְאַבְּדָם:

7 Mordechai told him everything that had happened to him and the explanation of the money which Haman had promised to pay to the king's treasuries in order to eradicate the Jews.

QUESTIONS

WHY did Mordechai tell Hasach *"everything that had happened to him"*? The decree applied to all Jews, not just to Mordechai.

WHY write *"the **explanation** of the money which Haman had promised,"* rather than simply *"about the money which Haman had promised"*?

COMMENTARY

First, Mordechai revealed to Hasach the original cause of the misfortune — **everything that had happened to him** — his refusal to bow to Haman and his subsequent denouncement by the king's servants.

Then, he told him **the explanation of the money**. When Haman spoke with Achashverosh, he told him that ten thousand talents of silver would be paid by those who would do the work of "converting" the Jews. Achashverosh had understood that they would be paying the money happily from their own funds for the privilege of contributing to the national welfare. The true **explanation**, though, was that Haman intended to raise this sum from the assets of the Jews who were to be slaughtered.

ח וְאֶת־פַּתְשֶׁגֶן כְּתָב־הַדָּת אֲשֶׁר־נִתַּן בְּשׁוּשָׁן לְהַשְׁמִידָם נָתַן לוֹ לְהַרְאוֹת אֶת־אֶסְתֵּר וּלְהַגִּיד לָהּ וּלְצַוּוֹת עָלֶיהָ לָבוֹא אֶל־הַמֶּלֶךְ לְהִתְחַנֶּן־לוֹ וּלְבַקֵּשׁ מִלְּפָנָיו עַל־עַמָּהּ: ט וַיָּבוֹא הֲתָךְ וַיַּגֵּד לְאֶסְתֵּר אֵת דִּבְרֵי מָרְדֳּכָי:

8 He gave him a synopsis of the writing of the decree to destroy them, which had been given out in Shushan, to show Esther, to tell her, and to order her to come to the king and to beseech him and to plead before him for her people.
9 Hasach came and told Mordechai's words to Esther.

QUESTIONS

IF the *"synopsis of the writing"* was the one *"revealed to all the peoples,"*[1] it contained no mention of "destruction," but only instructed people to be ready for the thirteenth of Adar. If so, how could Mordechai give *"the synopsis of the writing of the decree* **to destroy them**"?

---

1. Ch. 3, v. 14.

IF Mordechai gave Hasach one of the sealed letters, sent only to the officials, how did he obtain it?

HAVING instructed Hasach *"to show Esther,"* why was there any need *"to tell her"*?

COMMENTARY

The sealed letter which ordered the annihilation of the Jews was held by the governor of Shushan and was not accessible to Mordechai. He could only obtain **a synopsis of the writing** that was available to everyone, telling them to be ready for the thirteenth of Adar.

Mordechai knew that this synopsis concealed the secret **decree to destroy them.**[1] He gave Hasach a copy of the **synopsis of the writing** which he was **to show Esther** and thereby clearly indicate that something was astir. He ordered Hasach then **to tell her,** verbally, what stood behind the synopsis — the impending mass murder of the Jews.

Therefore, Hasach was to **order her to come to the king** to save the Jewish nation.

וַתֹּאמֶר אֶסְתֵּר לַהֲתָךְ וַתְּצַוֵּהוּ אֶל־מָרְדֳּכָי: י

10 **Esther spoke with Hasach and instructed him to return the following message to Mordechai:**

---

1. The Malbim's interpretation is based on the extra words *"of the decree to destroy them,"* which do not appear in ch. 3, v. 14, where the phrase *"the synopsis of the writing"* is used without any mention of *"the decree to destroy them."*

Questions

THE use of both *"spoke with"* and *"instructed him"* seems repetitive. Why write both?

Commentary

Esther was afraid to send Hasach to Mordechai a second time. She did not want Haman's agents to see Hasach conveying messages back and forth between herself and Mordechai. So she **spoke with Hasach,** explaining this problem, **and instructed him** to find someone **to return the following message to Mordechai.**[1]

יא כָּל־עַבְדֵי הַמֶּלֶךְ וְעַם מְדִינוֹת הַמֶּלֶךְ יֹדְעִים
אֲשֶׁר כָּל־אִישׁ וְאִשָּׁה אֲשֶׁר יָבוֹא־אֶל־הַמֶּלֶךְ אֶל־
הֶחָצֵר הַפְּנִימִית אֲשֶׁר לֹא־יִקָּרֵא אַחַת דָּתוֹ לְהָמִית
לְבַד מֵאֲשֶׁר יוֹשִׁיט־לוֹ הַמֶּלֶךְ אֶת־שַׁרְבִיט הַזָּהָב
וְחָיָה וַאֲנִי לֹא נִקְרֵאתִי לָבוֹא אֶל־הַמֶּלֶךְ זֶה שְׁלוֹשִׁים
יוֹם:

11 **"All the king's servants and people of the king's provinces know that any man or woman who comes before the king, into the inner court, without being summoned, there is only one law for him:**

---

1 This explanation is confirmed by an examination of verse 12, which says, *"They told Esther's words to Mordechai."* If Hasach himself had relayed the message, the verse would say, *"He told Esther's words to Mordechai."* The use of the plural indicates messengers sent by Hasach. (Ed.)

to be killed. Unless the king extends the golden scepter to him, then he shall live. I have not been summoned to come to the king for thirty days."

QUESTIONS

WHY did Esther mention both the *"king's servants"* and the *"people of the king's provinces"*?

WHAT is the meaning of *"there is only one law for him"*?

WHY say *"to be killed"* rather than *"he will die"*?

ESTHER'S reluctance to put her life at risk when she hears of the impending destruction of the Jewish nation seems astounding. Why did she not display greater courage upon hearing these tidings?

"I have not been summoned... for thirty days" seems irrelevant. Why did Esther want Mordechai to know this?

COMMENTARY

Esther's response to Mordechai was twofold:

First, she argued that if she went to the king immediately, she would be placing herself in great danger and would be unlikely to succeed in her mission of pleading for the Jewish people.

All the king's servants know the law, Esther argued, so she would be unable to plead ignorance; **and people of the king's provinces know,** so Achashverosh would be unable to overlook this offense even if he wanted to, for it would be a blatant and public transgression, just like Vashti's.

It was not possible to contend that the law did not apply to everyone. It was known **that any man or woman** faced the same punishment.

One might think that the law applied only to those who came without a genuine justification and that one who came to save an entire nation whose lives were in danger would not be punished. This was not so. Anyone **who comes...without being summoned,** for whatever reason, **there is only one law for him,** even if he is someone worthy of special treatment or someone who performs work critical to the interests of the empire; his punishment is **to be killed** — he is considered dead as soon as he enters.

His death is inevitable **unless the king extends the golden scepter to him,** pardoning him of his crime — **then he shall live.** In other words, his death has already been determined[1] and it is only the king's mercy that has given him a reprieve.

Esther argued that if she entered without being summoned, even if the king forgave her, she would be unable to beseech clemency on behalf of the Jewish people because she would already have received great mercy from Achashverosh when he revoked the automatic death penalty to which she was subject.

Esther's second point was that although even the most improbable and unlikely efforts must be made to save those whose lives are in danger, this is only true after more feasible methods have been tried first.

---

1. The Malbim infers this from the use of the phrase *"to be killed,"* להמית, rather than *"he will die,"* יומת. The latter indicates that his death will take place in the future; the former has the connotation that he is *"to be killed"* immediately, and it is as if he is a dead man now.

   To make the translation readable we used the phrase *"to be killed."* In fact, the verb is not a passive one, but is active, literally meaning *"to cause to die"* or *"to kill."* The Malbim does not discuss why, instead of a passive form of the verb, the active *"to kill"* is used. Rabbi Joseph Pearlman suggested that the use of the active implies that it was incumbent on anyone present to immediately kill the offender, a further indication that someone entering without permission was considered as already dead. (Ed.)

She was telling Mordechai that since she had **not been summoned to come to the king for thirty days**, it was certain that she would be called within the next few days, and then she could plead on behalf of her people far more effectively. It was much better to wait a few days.

יב   וַיַּגִּידוּ לְמָרְדֳּכָי אֵת דִּבְרֵי אֶסְתֵּר:

12 They told Esther's words to Mordechai.

QUESTIONS

WHO are *"they"*?

COMMENTARY

They — the messengers sent by Hasach — **told Esther's words to Mordechai.**

יג   וַיֹּאמֶר מָרְדֳּכַי לְהָשִׁיב אֶל־אֶסְתֵּר אַל־תְּדַמִּי בְנַפְשֵׁךְ לְהִמָּלֵט בֵּית־הַמֶּלֶךְ מִכָּל־הַיְּהוּדִים:

13 Mordechai told them to reply to Esther, "Do not think to yourself that you can escape in the king's house more than all the Jews.

QUESTIONS

WHY did Mordechai say, *"Do not think **to yourself**"* when *"Do not think"* would have sufficed?

COMMENTARY

Mordechai informed Esther of several fundamental principles:

1) Any time something unusual and extraordinary occurs, we must realize that the Almighty has brought this about as a means to achieving some important providential end. Esther's remarkable elevation to the position of queen was clearly Divinely determined for some significant purpose. With the revelation of the decree to annihilate the Jewish people, it was now obvious that Esther was intended to help save the Jews.

2) For any tragedy that befalls the Jews, there is a specific time and day ready for their deliverance by certain prepared means. If these means are not actualized, then the Omnipotent will prepare other means to save them.

3) Anything that does not exist for itself, but to help something else, has its entire existence dependent on what it was destined to help. For example, if a gardener wants to plant certain flowers in the winter, he will construct a special greenhouse with a heating system to help these flowers grow. If he changes his mind and wants the flowers to flourish in the summer, when there is an abundance of natural light and heat from the sun, he will dismantle the greenhouse, for it is no longer required.

Mordechai was telling Esther that her position in the royal house was not for her own benefit, but for the sake of the Jews. If Esther decided not to help rescue them, the Almighty undoubtedly had other means and methods of bringing about their redemption, regardless of how improbable they might seem.

Since Esther was granted her position as queen only in order to help the Jews, and since the date for their salvation had already been determined, if she did not act immediately she might miss the appointed time and the Almighty would use other agents to effect their deliverance.

This was Mordechai's warning to Esther. **Do not think** that your elevation to royalty is **to yourself,** for your own benefit, so **that you can escape in the king's house,** rather than for saving the Jewish nation. The opposite is true: it is only to enable you to rescue the Jews.

כִּי אִם־הַחֲרֵשׁ תַּחֲרִישִׁי בָּעֵת הַזֹּאת רֶוַח וְהַצָּלָה יד
יַעֲמוֹד לַיְּהוּדִים מִמָּקוֹם אַחֵר וְאַתְּ וּבֵית־אָבִיךְ
תֹּאבֵדוּ וּמִי יוֹדֵעַ אִם־לְעֵת כָּזֹאת הִגַּעַתְּ לַמַּלְכוּת:

14 **For if you will remain quiet at this time, relief and deliverance will arise for the Jews from elsewhere and you and your father's house will perish. Who knows whether it was for such a time that you came to royal position?"**

QUESTIONS

WHY did Mordechai say *"at this time"*?

WHAT was the rush? The decree was not to be carried out for another eleven months.

WHAT is the meaning of *"for such a time"*?

COMMENTARY

Since a time had been determined for the Jews to be saved,[1] **if you will remain quiet at this time, relief and deliverance will arise for the Jews from elsewhere.** What will follow from

---

1. As Mordechai explained in the second point in the commentary on verse 13.

this is that **you and your father's house will perish,** since your royal status will become pointless.[1]

Do not think that you can help in a few days time when you will be summoned to the king, because perhaps the designated time will already have passed and, with it, your opportunity of being instrumental in saving the Jews. **Who knows whether it was for such a time** — that is, now — **that you came to royal position?**

טו וַתֹּאמֶר אֶסְתֵּר לְהָשִׁיב אֶל־מָרְדֳּכָי: טז לֵךְ
כְּנוֹס אֶת־כָּל־ הַיְּהוּדִים הַנִּמְצְאִים בְּשׁוּשָׁן וְצוּמוּ
עָלַי וְאַל־תֹּאכְלוּ וְאַל־תִּשְׁתּוּ שְׁלֹשֶׁת יָמִים לַיְלָה
וָיוֹם גַּם־אֲנִי וְנַעֲרֹתַי אָצוּם כֵּן וּבְכֵן אָבוֹא אֶל־
הַמֶּלֶךְ אֲשֶׁר לֹא־כַדָּת וְכַאֲשֶׁר אָבַדְתִּי אָבָדְתִּי:

15 Esther told them to reply to Mordechai, 16 "Go, gather all the Jews found in Shushan and fast for me. Do not eat or drink for three days, night and day. I and my maidens will similarly fast, and so I will come to the king, against the law, and if I perish, so I perish."

QUESTIONS

WHY did Esther say *"fast for me,"* rather than ordering them to fast and pray that the decree be rescinded?

WHAT is the meaning of *"and if I perish, so I perish"*? Why the repetition?[2]

---

1. Following the third point of Mordechai in the commentary on verse 13.

2. The actual question asked by the Malbim is slightly different. The

COMMENTARY

Once Mordechai had assured Esther that the Jewish people would certainly be saved from extermination and that this was not dependent on her, she agreed to go before the king. Even if she was killed, the Jews would be saved anyway.

Therefore, she asked that at least they should **fast for me** and pray for Divine mercy on her behalf. Then Esther would **come to the king, against the law.**

Esther, with utter selflessness, told Mordechai, **if I perish** for transgressing the king's command, **so I perish** — only me, but the Jewish people will survive no matter what.

יז וַיַּעֲבֹר מָרְדֳּכָי וַיַּעַשׂ כְּכֹל אֲשֶׁר־צִוְּתָה עָלָיו אֶסְתֵּר:

17 **Mordechai passed and did all that Esther had commanded him.**

COMMENTARY

Mordechai passed through all the Jewish streets announcing the fast as **Esther had commanded him.**

Hebrew words are כאשר אבדתי אבדתי, which literally mean, "As I have perished, so I have perished," and is widely understood to mean, "As I have perished so I will perish." The Malbim asks how had Esther already perished? See *Megillah* 15a for an answer how Esther could be considered to have already perished.

The Malbim's answer is that the repetition of the verb is not to indicate both the past and future tenses, but to highlight that if Esther dies, it is only Esther that dies and not the entire Jewish nation. Our formulation of the question is easier to understand and is answered just the same by the Malbim's answer. (Ed.)

CHAPTER 5

ה א וַיְהִי ׀ בַּיּוֹם הַשְּׁלִישִׁי וַתִּלְבַּשׁ אֶסְתֵּר מַלְכוּת
וַתַּעֲמֹד בַּחֲצַר בֵּית־הַמֶּלֶךְ הַפְּנִימִית נֹכַח בֵּית הַמֶּלֶךְ
וְהַמֶּלֶךְ יוֹשֵׁב עַל־כִּסֵּא מַלְכוּתוֹ בְּבֵית הַמַּלְכוּת נֹכַח
פֶּתַח הַבָּיִת׃

1 On the third day Esther was robed in
majesty and stood in the inner court of
the king's house, opposite the king's
house. The king was sitting on his royal
throne in the royal house opposite the
door of the house.

QUESTIONS

WOULD it not be more correct to write that *"Esther was robed in
majestic clothes"* rather than *"robed in majesty"*?

WHAT is the difference between *"the king's house"* and *"the royal
house"*?

COMMENTARY

Esther was robed in majesty — she had an aura of majesty such that all who saw her recognized that she was ideally suited to be queen.

The royal house adjoined the court. Here the king sat on his throne when he judged the people. Behind the royal house was the king's house, his private quarters, where he retired when he was not dealing with state affairs.

Esther stood **opposite the king's house** — where he was expected to be at that time. Divine providence, however, had arranged that **the king was sitting**, not in the king's house, but **in the royal house** next to the court in which Esther stood. Furthermore, the **royal throne** had been placed **opposite the door of the house** so that Achashverosh would see Esther immediately when she entered.

ב וַיְהִי כִרְאוֹת הַמֶּלֶךְ אֶת־אֶסְתֵּר הַמַּלְכָּה עֹמֶדֶת
בֶּחָצֵר נָשְׂאָה חֵן בְּעֵינָיו וַיּוֹשֶׁט הַמֶּלֶךְ לְאֶסְתֵּר
אֶת־שַׁרְבִיט הַזָּהָב אֲשֶׁר בְּיָדוֹ וַתִּקְרַב אֶסְתֵּר וַתִּגַּע
בְּרֹאשׁ הַשַּׁרְבִיט:

2 When the king saw Esther the queen standing in the court, she obtained favor in his eyes and the king extended to Esther the golden scepter in his hand; Esther drew near and touched the top of the scepter.

Commentary

Such was the king's love for Esther that it never occurred
to him that the decree prohibiting entrance to the king's inner court without prior permission applied to Esther. He en-
joyed her presence so much, even in the royal house, that he
did not think that she needed to wait until he extended the
scepter.

Therefore, **when the king saw Esther** was humbly **standing in the court** waiting for permission to enter, even though
she was **the queen** and Achashverosh's beloved wife to whom
the decree did not apply, **she obtained favor in his eyes** for
her genuine humility. Achashverosh responded as she had
hoped and **extended to Esther the golden scepter.** Even
though the king was not sitting in judgment at that moment,
and only when the king sits in judgment does he hold the scepter, the Almighty had providentially arranged that it was **in his
hand.**

ג וַיֹּאמֶר לָהּ הַמֶּלֶךְ מַה־לָּךְ אֶסְתֵּר הַמַּלְכָּה וּמַה־
בַּקָּשָׁתֵךְ עַד־חֲצִי הַמַּלְכוּת וְיִנָּתֵן לָךְ:

3 The king said to her, "What disturbs you,
Esther the queen, and what is your
petition? Up to half of the kingdom and it
shall be given to you."

Questions

WHY did Achashverosh ask *"what disturbs you"* and also *"what is
your petition"*?

HERE Achashverosh said about Esther's petition *"and it shall be given to you."* However, on other occasions he said *"and it shall be done."*[1] Why the difference?

COMMENTARY

Achashverosh understood that Esther must have some urgent reason for appearing before him. He assumed that her urgent appearance must be either to prevent some harm occurring or to obtain some benefit from him.

At first, he asked, "**What disturbs you** — is there any potential injury affecting you?" Then, he asked, "Or **what is your petition** — what benefit do you want me to give you?"

This is the first time Esther came to make a petition from the king. Achashverosh did not respond *"and it shall be done"* because this would imply that it would be done even if the petition was on behalf of somebody else. Achashverosh was only interested in helping Esther herself, and he expressed this by emphasizing **and it shall be given to *you.***

ד וַתֹּאמֶר אֶסְתֵּר אִם־עַל־הַמֶּלֶךְ טוֹב יָבוֹא הַמֶּלֶךְ
וְהָמָן הַיּוֹם אֶל־הַמִּשְׁתֶּה אֲשֶׁר־עָשִׂיתִי לוֹ:

4 **Esther replied, "If it seems good to the king, let the king and Haman come today, to the banquet that I have prepared for him."**

QUESTIONS

HERE Esther only said *"if it seems good to the king,"* whereas on

---

1. Ch. 5, v. 6; ch. 7, v. 2; ch. 9, v. 12.

other occasions she introduces this with the phrase *"if I have found favor."*[1] Why did she omit this introduction here?

WHAT was Esther's motivation in inviting Haman to the banquet?

COMMENTARY

Many reasons are suggested for Esther's inviting Haman to the banquet. The most likely seem to be:

1) Esther did not want Achashverosh to think that she wanted Haman killed because of personal animosity. By inviting him she demonstrated that she had no hatred for Haman, but was merely trying to save her life and the lives of her people.

2) She wanted to confront Haman with her accusations suddenly so that he would have no time to present a reasoned response. At the opportune moment, when the king's anger could be easily inflamed under the influence of the wine at the banquet, Esther hoped that Achashverosh would speedily sentence a bewildered Haman.

3) Once a person's good fortune has reached its zenith, it starts to wane. Esther saw that Haman had risen to the pinnacle of success: he was second only to the king. By inviting only the king and Haman, she was equating Haman's importance with the king's, as Haman himself acknowledged.[2] Now Haman's fortunes could start their downward turn.

Esther did not say *"if I have found favor"* because she was not making a substantial request but only asking Achashverosh to come to a banquet.[3] This only requires **if it seems good to the**

---

1. Ch. 5, v. 8; ch. 7, v. 3; ch. 8, v. 5.
2. Verse 12.
3. According to this explanation we need to consider why, in ch. 9, v. 13, Esther says *"if it seems good to the king"* without *"if I have found favor."* There, the queen is asking for the Jews of Shushan to have

king to come to eat and drink at *the banquet that I have prepared,* everything is *already* prepared. Esther wanted them to
come right away and not to postpone the banquet to a later date.

ה וַיֹּאמֶר הַמֶּלֶךְ מַהֲרוּ אֶת־הָמָן לַעֲשׂוֹת אֶת־דְּבַר
אֶסְתֵּר וַיָּבֹא הַמֶּלֶךְ וְהָמָן אֶל־הַמִּשְׁתֶּה אֲשֶׁר־עָשְׂתָה
אֶסְתֵּר:

5 Then the king ordered, "Rush Haman to
do Esther's command." The king and
Haman came to the banquet that Esther
had prepared.

QUESTIONS

WHY did Achashverosh say *"to do Esther's command"*?

---

another day to kill their enemies and to publicly hang Haman's ten
sons. These are substantial requests.

Perhaps we can suggest that there, Esther is asking for the
death of the enemies of her people. A king should not decide to
have people killed based on the feelings he has for his wife. However, in ch. 7, v. 3 and ch. 8, v. 5, Esther is pleading for clemency on
behalf of the Jews; in this situation it is relevant to speak about
"finding favor."

Ch. 5, v. 8 is merely a precursor of the request she is going to
make at the second banquet in ch. 7, v. 3, and so Esther says *"if I
have found favor."* Some commentators explain that Esther intended making her request at this point, but changed her mind,
deciding that the time was not yet ripe. Others understand that Esther pretended as though she was going to make the request now.
These interpretations would both explain the use of *"if I have found
favor."* (Ed.)

COMMENTARY

By saying **to do Esther's command** Achashverosh was indicating Haman would not be honoring Esther by his presence at
the banquet. Haman's attendance was due only to Esther's order,
and he was obligated to do the will of his masters.

ו   וַיֹּאמֶר הַמֶּלֶךְ לְאֶסְתֵּר בְּמִשְׁתֵּה הַיַּיִן מַה־שְּׁאֵלָתֵךְ
וְיִנָּתֵן לָךְ וּמַה־בַּקָּשָׁתֵךְ עַד־חֲצִי הַמַּלְכוּת וְתֵעָשׂ:

6 The king said to Esther at the banquet of
wine, "What is your request? It shall be
given to you. What is your petition? Up to
half of the kingdom and it shall be done."

QUESTIONS

WHAT is the difference between *"request"* and *"petition"*?

WHY, when referring to the *"request,"* did Achashverosh say *"it
shall be given to you,"* while concerning the *"petition"* he said *"it
shall be done"*?[1]

COMMENTARY

The Malbim writes that commentators have distinguished
between שאלה, *"request"*, and בקשה, *"petition."* In any appeal
there is the *"request,"* or that which is being asked, and there is

---

1. See verse 8 where Esther uses similar terminology: *"to grant* (literally, *to give*) *my petition and to perform* (literally, *to do*) *my request."*
See also ch. 7, v. 2 and ch. 9, v. 12, where Achashverosh uses the
same terms as here.

the *"petition,"* the purpose for which it is being asked. For example, if someone asks for a large sum of money to enable him to buy a plot of land, the money will be the *"request"* and the land will be the *"petition."*[1] According to this, Esther's response was that her *"petition"* and *"request"* were not distinct and different, but they were identical; she was asking the king and Haman to come to a second banquet with no ulterior motives.

The Malbim, himself, makes a different distinction between the two terms. Asking for something small is a *"request,"* whereas a *"petition"* is far more substantial. Anything the queen would ask for herself would be a *"request,"* something that the king would easily grant. An appeal on behalf of someone else would be a *"petition,"* which requires imploring and entreating.

When Esther came to Achashverosh to invite him to the first banquet, he asked her *"what is your petition? Up to half of the kingdom and it shall be given to you."*[2] He referred to something that Esther might want for herself as a *"petition"* since it might be very considerable — *"up to half the kingdom."* This, he said in verse 3, *"shall be given to you"* — it concerns *you.*

Now, though, having already assured Esther in verse 3 that anything that was for herself *"shall be given to you,"* appeals for herself are regarded only as **your request** which **shall be given to you.** Something, though, that she asks for on behalf of others is still **your petition** — this still requires entreaties and persuasion before **it shall be done** for others.

---

1. This distinction is borne out by the words themselves. שאלה, *"request,"* comes from the verb לשאול, *"to ask,"* as in "When your son will ask you" (Devarim 6:20). This is what he is asking.

    בקשה, *"petition,"* comes from the verb לבקש which connotes intention or desire. A clear example is "He (Joseph) wanted (ויבקש) to cry." Here the meaning cannot be *"to ask."* Therefore, בקשה implies the ultimate intention. See, also, the Malbim's commentary on Tehillim 27:4.

2. Verse 3.

ז וַתַּעַן אֶסְתֵּר וַתֹּאמַר שְׁאֵלָתִי וּבַקָּשָׁתִי: ח אִם־
מָצָאתִי חֵן בְּעֵינֵי הַמֶּלֶךְ וְאִם־עַל־הַמֶּלֶךְ טוֹב לָתֵת
אֶת־ שְׁאֵלָתִי וְלַעֲשׂוֹת אֶת־בַּקָּשָׁתִי יָבוֹא הַמֶּלֶךְ וְהָמָן
אֶל־ הַמִּשְׁתֶּה אֲשֶׁר אֶעֱשֶׂה לָהֶם וּמָחָר אֶעֱשֶׂה כִּדְבַר
הַמֶּלֶךְ:

7 Esther answered and said, "My request and my petition... 8 if I have found favor in the eyes of the king and if it seems good to the king to grant my request and to perform my petition, let the king and Haman come to the banquet that I shall prepare for them and tomorrow I will do as the king has said."

QUESTIONS

WHY did Esther say both *"if I have found favor in the eyes of the king"* and also *"if it seems good to the king"*?

WHY does Esther repeat the words *"request"* and *"petition"* in verse 8 having already used them in her introductory phrase in verse 7?

WHAT did Esther mean when she told Achashverosh that *"tomorrow I will do as the king has said"*?

COMMENTARY

Esther's response was very intelligent. She said that all she asked of the king was to find favor in his eyes so that he would want to fulfill her request. The main thing she wanted was to obtain his favor; the fulfillment of her request was incidental.

This is what Esther meant when she said, "**My request and my petition** is essentially to **have found favor in the eyes of the king,** and an incidental consequence will be that **if it seems good to the king** then he will **grant my request.**"

Esther demanded that two conditions be satisfied before the king grant her request. First, **if I have found favor in the eyes of the king** — Esther herself should be desirable to the king so that he would want to do as she asked. Second, **if it seems good to the king** — the petition itself should be something the king would want to do irrespective of the one making the request. Esther did not want to ask for anything that went against the king's will.

If these conditions were satisfied, then **let the king and Haman come to the banquet** which would take place the next day.

Then, **tomorrow I will do as the king has said,** that is, to tell him my request. Esther subtly implied that the only reason she would tell the king her request was because he had commanded her to do so.

ט וַיֵּצֵא הָמָן בַּיּוֹם הַהוּא שָׂמֵחַ וְטוֹב לֵב וְכִרְאוֹת הָמָן אֶת־מָרְדֳּכַי בְּשַׁעַר הַמֶּלֶךְ וְלֹא־קָם וְלֹא־זָע מִמֶּנּוּ וַיִּמָּלֵא הָמָן עַל־מָרְדֳּכַי חֵמָה:

9 Haman went out on that day happy and with a glad heart, but when Haman saw Mordechai at the king's gate and he did not rise or move in his presence, Haman was full of anger against Mordechai.

QUESTIONS

THE phrase *"on that day"* seems to be unnecessary. Why was it written?

WHY are we told that Mordechai *"did not rise"* and also that he did not *"move"*?

HERE we are told that *"Haman was full of anger against Mordechai"* whereas, in chapter 3, verse 5, when Haman saw for the first time that Mordechai did not bow, we are told that *"Haman was full of anger"* without the words "against Mordechai." Why the difference?

COMMENTARY

We now learn the true evil of Haman's character. Despite his tremendous success, he had never had a happy day in his life. Nothing he acquired gave him satisfaction; he always wanted more. Now, though, he had reached the absolute pinnacle — he was equated with the king. For the first time, **on that day**, he was **happy and with a glad heart.**

His happiness did not last long. As soon as he saw Mordechai, his emotions became sad and bitter ones.

Haman saw that apart from the fact that Mordechai **did not rise**, he did not even **move in his presence** — Mordechai was not at all intimidated by Haman even though he could have Mordechai killed. Even if Mordechai refrained from bowing to Haman for reasons of religion,[1] Haman reasoned that Mordechai should at least exhibit fear in front of someone who could severely punish him.

When, in chapter 3, verse 5, he saw that Mordechai did not bow, and this could at least be partially attributed to Mordechai's religion, *"he was full of anger"* — not against Mordechai himself, but against his religion and those who adhered to it. But now, when he saw that Mordechai was not even slightly in awe of him, **Haman was full of anger against Mordechai** himself.

---

1. See commentary to ch. 3, v. 4.

י   וַיִּתְאַפַּק הָמָן וַיָּבוֹא אֶל־בֵּיתוֹ וַיִּשְׁלַח וַיָּבֵא אֶת־
אֹהֲבָיו וְאֶת־ זֶרֶשׁ אִשְׁתּוֹ:

10 Nevertheless, Haman restrained himself and went home. He sent for and fetched his friends and Zeresh his wife.

QUESTIONS

"HAMAN restrained himself and went home" implies that if he had not restrained himself, he would have gone somewhere else. Where?

COMMENTARY

Haman initially thought of of returning to the king, denouncing Mordechai, and having him killed. However, **Haman restrained himself and went home** to consult with **his friends and Zeresh his wife.**

יא   וַיְסַפֵּר לָהֶם הָמָן אֶת־כְּבוֹד עָשְׁרוֹ וְרֹב בָּנָיו
וְאֵת כָּל־אֲשֶׁר גִּדְּלוֹ הַמֶּלֶךְ וְאֵת אֲשֶׁר נִשְּׂאוֹ עַל־
הַשָּׂרִים וְעַבְדֵי הַמֶּלֶךְ:

11 He recounted to them the glory of his wealth, the large number of his sons, and all the details of how the king had promoted him, elevating him above the officials and servants of the king.

QUESTIONS

WHY did Haman now recount the *"glory of his wealth"*?

COMMENTARY

Haman had not ordered Mordechai's execution. Rather, he decreed the extermination of the entire Jewish nation, because he deemed it beneath his dignity to to quarrel with a lowly, solitary Jew for not bowing down to him. Haman's importance was a reason for ignoring the insult of such a lowly individual

On the one hand, Haman's greatness multiplied the severity of Mordechai's offence. On the other hand, it was an obstacle to punishing Mordechai.

Therefore, Haman started by recounting his exalted stature. This was the root cause of his need for advice as to how to handle Mordechai.

Wordly success takes three forms: wealth, children, and power. Haman gloried in his accomplishments in all three areas — **the glory of his wealth, the large number of his sons, and how the king had promoted him.**

יב וַיֹּאמֶר הָמָן אַף לֹא־הֵבִיאָה אֶסְתֵּר הַמַּלְכָּה
עִם־הַמֶּלֶךְ אֶל־הַמִּשְׁתֶּה אֲשֶׁר־עָשָׂתָה כִּי אִם־אוֹתִי
וְגַם־לְמָחָר אֲנִי קָרוּא־לָהּ עִם־הַמֶּלֶךְ:

12 **Haman said, "Furthermore, Esther the queen brought no one to the banquet which she made for the king except for me; also tomorrow I am invited to her, together with the king.**

QUESTIONS

HAMAN'S statement that *"Esther the queen brought no one... except for me"* implies that she should have brought others to the banquet. Why did Haman emphasize that others were not invited, and not simply emphasize that he *had* been invited?

COMMENTARY

Haman continued by saying that he had reached the absolute pinnacle of success. It would have been appropriate for the queen to invite all the king's ministers to the banquet, for it was unheard of to make a banquet for one or two people.[1] Haman reasoned that he was so important in the queen's eyes that he was considered the equal of all the other ministers together. Therefore, **the queen brought no one to the banquet** — none of the other ministers — **except for me**; by inviting me it was as if all the ministers were present.

Haman added that **also tomorrow I am invited to her**. "See how great I am! The queen has a request to make of the king, and she is afraid that he might not agree. Therefore, she also invited me, in order to entreat on her behalf. This shows that I am greater than the queen and she needs my help."

יג   וְכָל־זֶה אֵינֶנּוּ שֹׁוֶה לִי בְּכָל־עֵת אֲשֶׁר אֲנִי רֹאֶה
אֶת־מָרְדֳּכַי הַיְּהוּדִי יוֹשֵׁב בְּשַׁעַר הַמֶּלֶךְ:

13 **All this is worth nothing to me every time I see Mordechai the Jew sitting at the king's gate."**

---

1. See, for example, ch. 2, v. 18, *"The king hosted a great banquet for all his officials and servants."*

COMMENTARY

All this is worth nothing to me — it does not help me when **I see Mordechai the Jew.** Although my stature compounds Mordechai's guilt by increasing the severity of his insolence, it is an obstacle to my punishing him; it is beneath my dignity to stoop to deal with such an insignificant individual.

Haman, therefore, was asking advice how to kill Mordechai without compromising his prestige.

יד וַתֹּאמֶר לוֹ זֶרֶשׁ אִשְׁתּוֹ וְכָל־אֹהֲבָיו יַעֲשׂוּ־עֵץ
גָּבֹהַּ חֲמִשִּׁים אַמָּה וּבַבֹּקֶר | אֱמֹר לַמֶּלֶךְ וְיִתְלוּ
אֶת־מָרְדֳּכַי עָלָיו וּבֹא־עִם־הַמֶּלֶךְ אֶל־הַמִּשְׁתֶּה שָׂמֵחַ
וַיִּיטַב הַדָּבָר לִפְנֵי הָמָן וַיַּעַשׂ הָעֵץ:

14 Zeresh his wife and all his friends said to him, "Let a gallows be built, fifty cubits tall, and in the morning speak to the king that Mordechai should be hanged on it. Then go happily to the banquet with the king." This suggestion pleased Haman, and he had the gallows built.

QUESTIONS

WHAT was so shrewd about the suggestion to build the gallows?

WHY should the gallows be *"fifty cubits tall"*?

WHY should Haman speak to the king *"in the morning"*?

COMMENTARY

Haman's friends and wife gave him shrewd advice how to kill Mordechai without lowering himself. If he were to hang Mordechai for the offense of not bowing down to him, it would be humiliating to have had a quarrel with a despicable Jew who had slighted him. However, occasionally, the king ordered the execution of a dissident to create an atmosphere of fear and to instill discipline into his subjects. For this purpose one of the lowliest individuals was chosen and hanged publicly on a tall gallows, so that everyone could see and learn the appropriate lesson.

If Mordechai was hanged for this purpose, it would not embarass Haman to have killed such an abject individual. It would not be because of the offense of not bowing to Haman, but to set an example to the king's subjects.

Haman was advised how to demonstrate that this was the motivation behind Mordechai's execution. First, he should be hanged on a gallows **fifty cubits tall**, in full view of the king's subjects, to show clearly that his death was intended to be a public example.

Second, the hanging should take place early **in the morning**. This was the time that those who were killed to inspire public discipline were executed. That way people would see the corpse hanging from the gallows as soon as they left their homes in the morning, and they would be suitably affected by the sight.

If Mordechai were to be killed for his offence against Haman, the trial would continue until the afternoon and he would not be hanged from such tall gallows.

Having solved his dilemma, Haman could **go happily to the banquet.**

CHAPTER 6

ו א   בַּלַּ֣יְלָה הַה֔וּא נָדְדָ֖ה שְׁנַ֣ת הַמֶּ֑לֶךְ וַיֹּ֗אמֶר לְהָבִ֞יא
אֶת־סֵ֤פֶר הַזִּכְרֹנוֹת֙ דִּבְרֵ֣י הַיָּמִ֔ים וַיִּהְי֥וּ נִקְרָאִ֖ים לִפְנֵ֥י
הַמֶּֽלֶךְ:

1 That night the king's sleep was
disturbed. He ordered that the book of
records of the chronicles be brought, and
they were read before the king.

QUESTIONS

WHAT was the reason for the king's inability to sleep?

WHY is there a need to write both *"the book of records"* and *"the
chronicles"*?

COMMENTARY

When the king saw the lengths that Esther had gone to in order to speak with him, he knew that she had a substantial petition to make and, therefore, he had told her he would grant it even *"up to half of the kingdom."*[1] Esther had used two expressions, *"if I have found favor in the eyes of the king"* and *"if it seems good to the king."*[2] From the former expression, he inferred that it was something that he would personally want to do. From the latter expression, he inferred that her request was also something fitting for him as benevolent ruler of the empire.

It occurred to him that perhaps he had omitted to reward someone who had been of service to him and that Esther wanted him to rectify this neglect. This preyed on his mind, depriving him of sleep. So he ordered that the book of chronicles be brought before him.

The Malbim brings the explanation of other commentators who have explained that the book of chronicles was the annal in which events were recorded in full. In addition, there was an index listing brief summaries of the entries in the book of chronicles. Accordingly, the episode of Bigthan and Seresh's assassination plot was recorded fully in *"the book of chronicles"*[3] and a summary was recorded in the index — *"the book of records of the chronicles."*

The Malbim, himself, has a different interpretation. According to the Malbim, there were two books of chronicles. The first was written for posterity and recorded all the king's deeds and exploits, good and bad. This record was not in the custody of the king but was in the care of his chief minister, Haman. The second book of chronicles was written in the king's presence and was to remind the king of events that had happened. This was called **the**

1. Ch. 5, v. 6.
2. Ibid., v. 8.
3. Ch. 2, v. 23.

book of records of the chronicles.

We have already seen that Achashverosh had forgotten who had uncovered the plot to assassinate him and had informed Esther of it.[1] He did not know whom to reward. He, therefore, rewarded Esther (since Esther had been the one who had directly informed him of the plot) by promoting Haman, also known as Memuchan, whose advice had led to Esther being chosen as queen.

Haman slyly deceived Achashverosh into thinking that he had been the one who had informed Esther, leading to his further elevation above all other ministers. It was easy for Haman to erase all mention of Mordechai in the book of chronicles recorded for posterity, which was in his custody as chief minister, and write in his own name instead. However, the true version of the story remained written in the *"the book of records of the chronicles,"* the king's own private record.

ב וַיִּמָּצֵא כָתוּב אֲשֶׁר הִגִּיד מָרְדֳּכַי עַל־בִּגְתָנָא
וָתֶרֶשׁ שְׁנֵי סָרִיסֵי הַמֶּלֶךְ מִשֹּׁמְרֵי הַסַּף אֲשֶׁר בִּקְשׁוּ
לִשְׁלֹחַ יָד בַּמֶּלֶךְ אֲחַשְׁוֵרוֹשׁ:

2 It was found written that Mordechai had informed about Bigthan and Seresh, two of the king's chamberlains, guards at his door, who had plotted to take King Achashverosh's life.

QUESTIONS

"IT was found written" seems to imply that it would not be expected to be written there, as if one might think it would have been erased. Why should this be so?

---

1. See commentary to ch. 3, v. 1.

COMMENTARY

It was found written because Haman had been unable to erase the name Mordechai from the king's private record. So there it was discovered that it was not Haman who had told Esther but that **Mordechai had informed** her.

Now Achashverosh was aware that his promotion of Haman, in the belief that he had been instrumental in saving his life, had been mistaken. All the honor and authority that had been given to Haman really belonged to Mordechai.

We see Divine providence in the fact that at the very moment that Haman comes to ask the king to hang Mordechai, Achashverosh discovers that Haman's prominence really belonged to Mordechai.

ג וַיֹּאמֶר הַמֶּלֶךְ מַה־נַּעֲשָׂה יְקָר וּגְדוּלָּה לְמָרְדֳּכַי
עַל־זֶה וַיֹּאמְרוּ נַעֲרֵי הַמֶּלֶךְ מְשָׁרְתָיו לֹא־נַעֲשָׂה עִמּוֹ
דָּבָר:

3 The king asked, "What honor or eminence was conferred on Mordechai for this?" The king's servant boys who attended him replied, "Nothing was done for him."

QUESTIONS

WHY did Achashverosh ask about both *"honor"* and *"eminence"*? Furthermore, in verse 6, Achashverosh said, *"whose honor the king desires,"* without mentioning *"eminence."*

WHY did Achashverosh need to say *"for this"*? It is obvious that he is talking about a reward for the episode that has just been read to him.

COMMENTARY

Achashverosh reasoned that Mordechai deserved two types of reward. First, he deserved **honor**, immediately, to show that he had saved the king's life. Second, he merited **eminence**, in the future, with promotion above other ministers. Achashverosh knew that Mordechai had been appointed a judge who sat at the king's gate. That position had been given because Esther had been found in Mordechai's home.[1] He was asking what reward had he received **for this** — for saving his life.

וַיֹּאמֶר הַמֶּלֶךְ מִי בֶחָצֵר וְהָמָן בָּא לַחֲצַר בֵּית־ ד
הַמֶּלֶךְ הַחִיצוֹנָה לֵאמֹר לַמֶּלֶךְ לִתְלוֹת אֶת־מָרְדֳּכַי
עַל־הָעֵץ אֲשֶׁר־הֵכִין לוֹ: ה וַיֹּאמְרוּ נַעֲרֵי הַמֶּלֶךְ
אֵלָיו הִנֵּה הָמָן עֹמֵד בֶּחָצֵר וַיֹּאמֶר הַמֶּלֶךְ יָבוֹא:

4 **The king asked, "Who is in the court?" (Haman had just come to the outer court of the king's house to speak to the king about hanging Mordechai on the gallows that he had prepared for him.) 5 The king's servant boys answered him, "Behold, Haman is standing in the court." The king ordered, "Let him enter."**

---

1. See commentary on ch. 2, v. 19.

COMMENTARY

We see the miraculous juxtaposition of events — at the same moment that Achashverosh was planning to honor Mordechai, Haman came to have Mordechai hanged on the gallows (which would be used later to execute Haman himself).

וְ וַיָּבוֹא הָמָן וַיֹּאמֶר לוֹ הַמֶּלֶךְ מַה־לַעֲשׂוֹת בָּאִישׁ
אֲשֶׁר הַמֶּלֶךְ חָפֵץ בִּיקָרוֹ וַיֹּאמֶר הָמָן בְּלִבּוֹ לְמִי יַחְפֹּץ
הַמֶּלֶךְ לַעֲשׂוֹת יְקָר יוֹתֵר מִמֶּנִּי:

6 Haman entered, and the king asked him, "What should be done with the man whose honor the king desires?" Haman thought to himself, "Whom would the king desire to honor more than me?"

QUESTIONS

WHY was Achashverosh so eager to reward Mordechai immediately, early in the morning?[1]

---

1. The Malbim does not appear to answer this question directly. It could be that the answer implied by the commentary is that since the king wanted Haman to suggest Mordechai's reward, and since Haman "happened" to be there, it was an opportune time to arrange that Mordechai receive his just reward.

   Alternatively, perhaps the intended answer is that the wrong done to Mordechai by giving his promotion to Haman demanded immediate rectification. Although reward can wait, righting wrongs cannot.

   In his commentary to verse 10, the Malbim writes that Achashverosh inferred from Haman's reply that Haman's ambition extended to the trappings of royalty. This had to be quickly thwarted.

COMMENTARY

Achashverosh knew that Haman would mistakenly infer that the king intended this reward for him. He wanted Mordechai to receive the reward that Haman desired for himself. This

---

Thus, perhaps the commentary to verse 10 provides the answer to this question. The rush was not to reward Mordechai, but to foil Haman. If this is true, though, the question would have been better placed on verse 10, in connection with the word *"quickly,"* rather than on verse 6.

Maybe we can suggest that this question really related to verse 3. In verse 3, Achashverosh openly talks about Mordechai's reward, which he does not do in verse 6. If so it was a continuation of the last question asked there: "Why did Achashverosh need to say *'for this'* — surely it is obvious that he is talking about a reward for the episode that has just been read to him. And why was Achashverosh so eager to reward Mordechai immediately?"

In some printed editions of the Malbim's commentary, the questions in each verse are prefaced by the verse number to which they relate. In other editions, no such numbers are included.

If the Malbim himself included these verse numbers, the error could have arisen because the Malbim wrote ומדוע, "And why...," which the printer mistakenly read as ו מדוע — that is, a question on verse 6 (represented by the Hebrew letter ו) which starts "Why...." Alternatively, perhaps the Malbim never wrote verse numbers to his questions, and the printer assumed that the question belonged with verse 6. The error was facilitated by the fact that there are no other questions between verses 3 and 7.

If this conjecture is correct, then the answer to this question should be found in the commentary to verse 3. There, the Malbim distinguishes between "honor" given immediately to acknowledge that Mordechai had saved the king's life, and "eminence," future elevation above other ministers. The reason to reward Mordechai as soon as possible was to publicly link the reward with the action that it was acknowledging. The sooner this could be done, the better. The bestowal of "eminence" was not quite so pressing. (Ed.)

was only appropriate since really all Haman's glory belonged to Mordechai.

Therefore, Achashverosh did not ask, "What shall be done for the man whose honor and eminence the king desires," using both terms mentioned in verse 3, because then Haman would realize that he was not the intended recipient since he had already reached the pinnacle of eminence, above all other ministers. By asking only about *"honor,"* Haman would assume that the king had him in mind and would suggest an incredible display of honor, which could then be given to Mordechai.

Furthermore, there was no need to ask about *"eminence,"* since Achashverosh intended to transfer all of Haman's eminence to Mordechai, who was really entitled to it.

זְ וַיֹּאמֶר הָמָן אֶל־הַמֶּלֶךְ אִישׁ אֲשֶׁר הַמֶּלֶךְ חָפֵץ
בִּיקָרוֹ:

7 So Haman replied to the king, "A man whose honor the king desires,

QUESTIONS

WHY did Haman echo the phrase *"man whose honor the king desires,"* which the king had used?

COMMENTARY

Haman responded obsequiously that the answer to the question *"What should be done with the man whose honor the king desires?"* was that he should be *"A man whose honor the king desires"* — this was the greatest possible honor.[1]

---

1. This explanation is supported by a subtle difference in the phrase

Therefore, in response to the question what should be done with him, the answer was that it should be publicized that he was **a man whose honor the king desires** — this was the highest prestige that could be bestowed. The royal robe and horse were only to convey this to the king's subjects.

ח   יָבִ֙יאוּ֙ לְב֣וּשׁ מַלְכ֔וּת אֲשֶׁ֥ר לָבַשׁ־בּ֖וֹ הַמֶּ֑לֶךְ וְס֗וּס אֲשֶׁ֙ר רָכַ֤ב עָלָיו֙ הַמֶּ֔לֶךְ וַאֲשֶׁ֙ר נִתַּ֛ן כֶּ֥תֶר מַלְכ֖וּת בְּרֹאשֽׁוֹ:

8 let a royal robe be brought, which the king has worn, and a horse that the king rode, with a royal crown being placed on his head,

COMMENTARY

The phrase **a royal crown being placed on his head** is understood in two different ways. Some explain it to mean that the crown was placed on the horse's head, in accordance with the custom of the time. Others interpret it to mean that the horse used should be the one that Achashverosh rode when the crown was placed on his head — that is, at his coronation.

According to the first interpretation, the head in question is that of the horse; according to the second, it is Achashverosh's head.

---

used in the king's question and the phrase used in Haman's response. Achashverosh asked, *"What should be done **with the man** (באיש) whose honor the king desires?"* Haman, in his response, did not say *"**With the man...**"* but merely *"A man (איש) whose honor the king desires..."* — nothing else need be done with him. (Ed.)

ט וְנָתוֹן הַלְּבוּשׁ וְהַסּוּס עַל־יַד־אִישׁ מִשָּׂרֵי הַמֶּלֶךְ הַפַּרְתְּמִים וְהִלְבִּישׁוּ אֶת־הָאִישׁ אֲשֶׁר הַמֶּלֶךְ חָפֵץ בִּיקָרוֹ וְהִרְכִּיבֻהוּ עַל־הַסּוּס בִּרְחוֹב הָעִיר וְקָרְאוּ לְפָנָיו כָּכָה יֵעָשֶׂה לָאִישׁ אֲשֶׁר הַמֶּלֶךְ חָפֵץ בִּיקָרוֹ:

9 and let the robe and the horse be given to one of the king's most noble officers, and let them attire the man whose honor the king desires, and let them ride him on horseback through the city square, proclaiming before him, 'So will be done for the man whose honor the king desires.' "

COMMENTARY

When Haman said *"and let **them** attire...and let **them** ride him... proclaiming before him,"* his intention was to magnify the honor by having many ministers involved in the process of attiring, leading, and proclaiming. That is why the plural form was used.

י וַיֹּאמֶר הַמֶּלֶךְ לְהָמָן מַהֵר קַח אֶת־הַלְּבוּשׁ וְאֶת־הַסּוּס כַּאֲשֶׁר דִּבַּרְתָּ וַעֲשֵׂה־כֵן לְמָרְדֳּכַי הַיְּהוּדִי הַיּוֹשֵׁב בְּשַׁעַר הַמֶּלֶךְ אַל־תַּפֵּל דָּבָר מִכֹּל אֲשֶׁר דִּבַּרְתָּ:

10 The king ordered Haman, "Quickly, take the robe and the horse as you described and do this to Mordechai the Jew, who sits at the king's gate. Do not

omit anything from all that you have described."

QUESTIONS

HAMAN had said *"let **them** attire... and let **them** ride him,"* implying many were to be involved. Why did Achashverosh order Haman to do it all by himself?

COMMENTARY

Achashverosh realized that Haman's power and prestige really belonged to Mordechai. He now saw the full extent of Haman's arrogance, wanting to use the trappings of royalty.[1] In his fury, he ordered that the honor that Haman proposed should quickly be bestowed upon Mordechai, its true recipient, and that Haman should be the one to carry this out; as the one who had "stolen" Mordechai's position he should be the one to serve him and run before him as his slave.

He therefore commanded Haman, **"Do not omit anything"** — because Mordechai genuinely deserves all of it. He ordered Haman that he alone should be the one to attire and lead Mordechai's horse; **from all that you have described** indicates that every detail of the attiring, leading, and proclaiming should be carried out by Haman himself.

---

1. See Melachim I 1:5 where Adoniyahu adopted the trappings of royalty during the lifetime of King David, his father, and was killed by David's son and successor, King Solomon (ibid. 2:25), for this rebellious act against King David.

יא וַיִּקַּח הָמָן אֶת־הַלְּבוּשׁ וְאֶת־הַסּוּס וַיַּלְבֵּשׁ אֶת־
מָרְדֳּכָי וַיַּרְכִּיבֵהוּ בִּרְחוֹב הָעִיר וַיִּקְרָא לְפָנָיו כָּכָה
יֵעָשֶׂה לָאִישׁ אֲשֶׁר הַמֶּלֶךְ חָפֵץ בִּיקָרוֹ: יב וַיָּשָׁב
מָרְדֳּכַי אֶל־שַׁעַר הַמֶּלֶךְ וְהָמָן נִדְחַף אֶל־בֵּיתוֹ אָבֵל
וַחֲפוּי רֹאשׁ:

**11 Haman took the robe and the horse,
attired Mordechai, and rode him through
the city square, proclaiming before him,
"So will be done for the man whose honor
the king desires." 12 Mordechai then
returned to the king's gate, while Haman
hurried home, grieving, and with his
head covered.**

COMMENTARY

Mordechai then returned to his prestigious position at **the
king's gate**, while Haman started his decline to ignominy. In
spite of all of man's machinations, it is the Divine will that pre-
vails.

יג וַיְסַפֵּר הָמָן לְזֶרֶשׁ אִשְׁתּוֹ וּלְכָל־אֹהֲבָיו אֵת
כָּל־אֲשֶׁר קָרָהוּ וַיֹּאמְרוּ לוֹ חֲכָמָיו וְזֶרֶשׁ אִשְׁתּוֹ אִם
מִזֶּרַע הַיְּהוּדִים מָרְדֳּכַי אֲשֶׁר הַחִלּוֹתָ לִנְפֹּל לְפָנָיו
לֹא־תוּכַל לוֹ כִּי־נָפוֹל תִּפּוֹל לְפָנָיו:

13 **Haman recounted to Zeresh his wife and all his friends everything that had happened to him. His wise men and Zeresh his wife said to him, "If Mordechai is of Jewish offspring, since you have started to fall before him, you will not prevail against him, but you will be sure to fall before him."**

QUESTIONS

WHY did Haman recount such bad tidings to his friends and family? Surely he should have kept quiet about such a shameful experience.

THE phrase *"that had happened to him"* implies that it had "just happened" by chance. Why is this connotation used?

HOW can they be *"wise men"* if they tell Haman that he *"will be sure to fall,"* a statement that is bound to cause discouragement?

COMMENTARY

Haman feared that his family and friends had heard of his misfortune and might have assumed that his degradation was a result of his having asked Achashverosh to hang Mordechai. As a result of the ensuing investigation, perhaps the king now realized that he had been duped, and that was the reason that he had publicly shamed Haman. If this was the case, the situation could not be saved.

Haman sought to reassure them with good tidings: it had merely **happened to him**, a chance occurence, and he had not yet asked the king to have Mordechai killed. There was still hope that at a later date the king would agree to his request, Mordechai having already received his reward.[1]

However, his wise men and advisors counseled him not to try to engage in further confrontation with Mordechai. Any attempt to have him killed was doomed to failure.

Haman's presumption that what had occurred was only by chance was erroneous. **If Mordechai is of Jewish offspring**, a people under the special care of the Almighty, what had happened could not be mere chance, but was definitely part of a Divine plan. Since **you have started to fall before him**, it shows that the Almighty does not want the Jews to come to harm and you cannot prevail.

The proof that his advisors adduced, **since you have started to fall before him**, contains two ideas. First, **since you have started to fall** — the fall was initiated by your own actions.[2] No one else was trying to cause your downfall; it was the result of *your* rushing to the king's palace, and you yourself proposed the reward that Mordechai received.

Second, you have started to fall **before him** — i.e., before he has started to fall.[3] This was a clear omen that Mordechai was under Divine protection due to the merit of his prayer and fasting.

If so, **you will not prevail against him** *unless* **you will be sure to fall before him**. His wise men were not being prophets of doom, but were giving him sound advice: Your only chance is to humble yourself in front of him. Thereby, Mordechai might be-

---

1. This explanation is attributed to Rav Eliezer Ashkenazy. See footnote, p. 11.
2. The Malbim infers this from the use of the word החלות — *"you have started."* The form of the verb is *hiphil*, causitive, and the literal meaning of the word is that *"you have caused to start,"* i.e., you have initiated your own fall. (Ed.)
3. The Malbim does understand the word *"before"* to mean "in front of," but as "prior to." See commentary on ch. 1, v. 3 for a similar interpretation.

come overconfident, lowering his guard and ceasing his prayer and fasting. Then he can be overcome. But as long as you openly oppose him, he will continually place his trust in the Almighty, giving you no chance of victory.

יד עוֹדָם מְדַבְּרִים עִמּוֹ וְסָרִיסֵי הַמֶּלֶךְ הִגִּיעוּ
וַיַּבְהִלוּ לְהָבִיא אֶת־הָמָן אֶל־הַמִּשְׁתֶּה אֲשֶׁר־עָשְׂתָה
אֶסְתֵּר:

14 **While they were still speaking with him, the king's chamberlains arrived and hurried to bring Haman to the banquet which Esther had prepared.**

QUESTIONS

WHY are we told that the king's chamberlains arrived while *"they were still speaking"*?

COMMENTARY

It was also a mark of Divine providence that the chamberlains arrived in the middle of the discussion. They overheard Haman say that he still wished to try to persuade the king to allow him to hang Mordechai, while his close friends advised against opposing Mordechai. It was at this point that Charvonah, one of these chamberlains, learned that Haman had constructed a gallows to hang Mordechai. This enabled him to report this fact to the king at the opportune moment.[1]

---

1. Ch. 7, v. 9. This explanation is attributed to Rav Eliezer Ashkenazy. See footnote, p. 11.

CHAPTER 7

ז א וַיָּבֹא הַמֶּ֫לֶךְ וְהָמָן֙ לִשְׁתּ֣וֹת עִם־אֶסְתֵּ֣ר הַמַּלְכָּֽה:
ב וַיֹּ֩אמֶר֩ הַמֶּ֨לֶךְ לְאֶסְתֵּ֜ר גַּ֣ם בַּיּ֤וֹם הַשֵּׁנִי֙ בְּמִשְׁתֵּ֣ה
הַיַּ֔יִן מַה־שְּׁאֵלָתֵ֛ךְ אֶסְתֵּ֥ר הַמַּלְכָּ֖ה וְתִנָּ֣תֵֽן לָ֑ךְ וּמַה־
בַּקָּשָׁתֵ֛ךְ עַד־חֲצִ֥י הַמַּלְכ֖וּת וְתֵעָֽשׂ:

1 The king and Haman came to drink with
Esther the queen. 2 The king asked Esther
again on the second day at the wine feast,
"What is your request, Esther the queen?
It shall be given to you. What is your
petition? Up to half of the kingdom and it
shall be done."

QUESTIONS

WHY does Achashverosh refer to Esther as *"Esther the queen"*?[1]

COMMENTARY

Out of his love for her, Achashverosh, by adding the phrase *"Esther the queen,"* was telling her that even if she requested

---

1. The intent of this question is not straightforward. If it is asking why he addresses her as *"Esther the queen"* rather than *"Esther,"* this does not seem to be a strong question. Prior to this verse, the Megillah records two other instances where Achashverosh spoke with Esther. In the first, ch. 5, v. 3, Achashverosh also addressed Esther as *"Esther the queen."* In the second, ch. 5, v. 6, he does not address her with any name or title.

   However, in ch. 5, v. 5, he refers to her as *"Esther,"* without title. Also, further ahead in the Megillah, in ch. 8, v. 7, in speaking to Esther and Mordechai, Achashverosh uses her name without any title. Perhaps these references are the basis for the question according to this understanding.

   More likely, however, the Malbim is asking why the king used any name when talking to Esther directly. This is confirmed by the answer, which speaks of the king adding the phrase *"Esther the queen,"* rather than adding just the title *"the queen."* This question would be based on the last occasion Achashverosh addressed Esther, in ch. 5, v. 6, where no name or title was used. What remains unanswered, though, is why Achashverosh did say *"Esther the queen"* in ch. 5, v. 3? Why was the question not asked there? Perhaps the basis for the question, therefore, is that the king's questions to Esther in this verse and in ch. 5, v. 6 are identical, apart from the inclusion, this time, of the phrase *"Esther the queen."*

   This question is answered by saying that Achashverosh's growing love prompted him, in an identical formulation of his statement, to add the phrase *"Esther the queen,"* expressing that he would grant a request even on a scale that befits a queen. (Ed.)

something very substantial, befitting her status as **Esther the queen**, it would still be granted her.

ג וַתַּעַן אֶסְתֵּר הַמַּלְכָּה וַתֹּאמַר אִם־ מָצָאתִי חֵן
בְּעֵינֶיךָ הַמֶּלֶךְ וְאִם־עַל־הַמֶּלֶךְ טוֹב תִּנָּתֶן־ לִי נַפְשִׁי
בִּשְׁאֵלָתִי וְעַמִּי בְּבַקָּשָׁתִי:

3 **Esther the queen replied and said, "If I have found favor in your eyes, your majesty, and if it seems good to the king, then let my life be given to me as my request and my people as my petition.**

QUESTIONS

WHY did Esther connect her *"request"* to her life and her *"petition"* to her people?

COMMENTARY

We have already explained[1] that a *"request"* is something which a person asks for himself, whereas a *"petition"* is made on behalf of others.

Esther was saying that all she was asking for herself was her life, and what she was petitioning on behalf of her people was not wealth or honor, but that their lives be spared.

We quoted another interpretation[2] of the commentators: *"request"* is that which is asked for, and *"petition"* is the purpose that the request is intended to achieve. According to this ap-

1. See commentary on ch. 5, v. 6.
2. Quoted in commentary on ch. 5, v. 6.

proach, in the case of one who asks for his friend's life to be spared, the *"request"* will be that his friend is not killed. The *"petition,"* though, the reason for which the *"request"* is made, is that one cannot bear to see harm befall one's friend. The *"petition,"* then, is really for oneself.

One might think, therefore, that in asking for her people to be spared Esther's main concern was that she should not experience the pain of seeing harm befall them, the pain that she herself describes in chapter 8, verse 6.

Therefore, Esther explained that this was not so. Her people were so dear to her that she, herself, would be prepared to die as long as their lives would be spared. Although her *"request"* was for own life, her *"petition"* — her ultimate desire — was for her people.

ד   כִּי נִמְכַּרְנוּ אֲנִי וְעַמִּי לְהַשְׁמִיד לַהֲרוֹג וּלְאַבֵּד וְאִלּוּ לַעֲבָדִים וְלִשְׁפָחוֹת נִמְכַּרְנוּ הֶחֱרַשְׁתִּי כִּי אֵין הַצָּר שֹׁוֶה בְּנֵזֶק הַמֶּלֶךְ:

4 **For I and my people have been sold to be destroyed, killed, and eradicated. If we had been sold as slaves and slave-girls, I would have remained silent, for the adversary is not worth the king's damage."**

QUESTIONS

WHY would Esther have remained quiet if she and her people were sold as slaves?

WHAT is the meaning of *"for the adversary is not worth the king's damage"*? This is a phrase that has challenged the commentators.

COMMENTARY

Esther made two points. First, she told the king that the sale was essentially intended against her, that Haman's main intention was to kill her. She accused him of vilifying her people and intending to denounce her and have her executed with them.

This is the meaning of **"For I and my people have been sold"** — Esther mentioned herself before her people because she wanted the king to believe that she was the intended target, and her people were only sold as a means of killing her.

Second, she highlighted that the sale was not into slavery, but **to be destroyed** and **killed**.[1] She thus revealed to the king how he had been deceived by Haman in two respects.[2]

First, Haman had said, *"There is a certain people"* — a little-known nation. He gave no indication that he was talking about the Jews. Esther exposed this deception by saying that Haman's real intention had been **I and my people** — the nation in question is the nation to which I belong.

Second, Haman had proposed to the king that this nation *"should be eradicated,"* that is, that their national identity and religion should be done away with, enabling them to be members of the empire without being a harmful influence. Achashverosh never realized that Haman intended to *"destroy, kill, and eradicate"*[3] this people.

---

1. The Malbim comments that, following this interpretation, we can understand why Esther introduces her requests to the king by saying both *"if I have found favor"* and *"if it seems good to the king."* Finding favor relates to her own life being spared. This required that she, personally, found favor before the king. The phrase *"if it seems good to the king"* relates to her people. This does not necessitate finding favor, since sparing their lives is the "good" thing to do: it would be dishonorable for the king to kill an entire nation, innocent of any crime.

2. See ch. 3, vs. 8-9, with commentary.

3. Ch. 3, v. 13.

Esther revealed that Achashverosh had been duped. **If we had been sold as slaves** and the king would have only been deceived as to the identity of the nation, **I would have remained silent.** I would not have reported Haman's duplicity, since the king made an innocent mistake. However, since the king has been totally deceived and the affair will cause the king's reputation to be disgraced, it is only right that the rogue who perpetrated this nefarious plot should be punished.

Haman had said that *"it is not worth it for the king to leave them as they are"*[1] because they are harming the king. Esther responded in kind by saying, **the adversary is not worth the king's damage** — it is not worth leaving Haman alive because of the tremendous destruction he intends to cause to the empire.

ה וַיֹּאמֶר הַמֶּלֶךְ אֲחַשְׁוֵרוֹשׁ וַיֹּאמֶר לְאֶסְתֵּר הַמַּלְכָּה מִי הוּא זֶה וְאֵי־זֶה הוּא אֲשֶׁר־מְלָאוֹ לִבּוֹ לַעֲשׂוֹת כֵּן:

5 **King Achashverosh spoke, and he said to Esther the queen, "Who is this and what is this, that he dares to do such a thing?"**

QUESTIONS

WHY write both *"spoke"* and *"said"*?[2]

WHY did Achashverosh say both *"who is this"* and *"what is this"*?

---

1. Ch. 3, v. 8.
2. The question is even stronger than might appear from a reading of the English translation. In fact, the literal translation is *"King Achashverosh said, and he said to Esther."* The exact same word, וַיֹּאמֶר, is used twice. To make the translation more readable, the first *"said"* was changed to *"spoke."* (Ed.)

WHY did Achashverosh express such surprise on hearing of Haman's plan to annihilate the Jews — the king himself had granted Haman express permission to carry it out![1]

COMMENTARY

The astounded king initially **spoke** to his retinue, which included Haman, asking if they knew the identity of the culprit. No one answered him.

So then **he said to Esther the queen, "Who is this?"** — who is the man who has perpetrated such a terrible deed? **"And what is this?"** — what is the reason that motivated him to do it, such that he **dares to do such a thing?**

וַתֹּאמֶר אֶסְתֵּר אִישׁ צַר וְאוֹיֵב הָמָן הָרָע הַזֶּה   ו
וְהָמָן נִבְעַת מִלִּפְנֵי הַמֶּלֶךְ וְהַמַּלְכָּה:

6 Esther replied, "An adversary and an enemy! This evil Haman!" Haman was bewildered before the king and queen.

QUESTIONS

WHY did Esther say both *"adversary"* and *"enemy"*?

COMMENTARY

In response to the king's second question, what was the mo-

---

1. See ch. 3, vs. 8-9, where this question is asked in the list of questions and answered in the commentary.

tivation that spurred him to such evil, Esther responded that is
was because he was **an adversary and an enemy.**

Each of these terms has a different meaning. *"Adversary,"* צַר,
connotes one who has actively harmed his antagonist.[1] *"Enemy,"*
אוֹיֵב, means one who seeks to harm, but has not actually done so
yet.[2]

Unless someone is unusually cruel, he will only be an *"enemy"* until he becomes an *"adversary"*; once he has become an
"adversary," and has succeeded in harming his foe, the desire to
plan further harm will pass.

Haman's cruelty was so overpowering that even after he actively harmed the Jews, he still remained an *"enemy,"* harboring
feelings of hatred in his heart which spurred him to further harm
the Jewish people.

Esther replied to Achashverosh's first question, who was the
man responsible, by revealing that it was **this evil Haman!**

Haman was bewildered. If only the king had been present,
Haman could have stuck by his story. He could have insisted that
what he told the king about the harmful influnce of the Jews[3] was
absolutely true. However, since the queen was present as well,
she would be infuriated by his maligning her people.

If only Esther had been present, then he could have tried to
persuade her that he had acted without realizing that the Jews
were her people, and assure her that he would now speak on their
behalf and have the letters of decree recalled. However, since the
king was present, to appease the queen in such a way would enrage the king. Haman would be demonstrating that his attempt

---

1. See, for example, Bemidbar 10:9, "And when you go to war against
    the adversary (הַצֹּרֵר) who oppresses you," i.e., the adversary has al-
    ready harmed you.
2. See, for example, Devarim 21:10, "When you go out to war against
    your enemies" — you are going out to those who have not yet
    harmed you.
3. See ch. 3, v. 8.

to exterminate the Jews had not been motivated by a genuine concern for the welfare of the empire. If his concern had been sincere and he really believed that they should be destroyed for the good of the empire, why was he now trying to spare them merely out of fear of the queen?

Therefore, Haman was bewildered *because* he was **before the king and queen**, that is, before both of them together.

ז   וְהַמֶּ֜לֶךְ קָם֩ בַּחֲמָת֨וֹ מִמִּשְׁתֵּ֤ה הַיַּ֨יִן֙ אֶל־גִּנַּ֣ת הַבִּיתָ֔ן
וְהָמָ֣ן עָמַ֗ד לְבַקֵּ֤שׁ עַל־נַפְשׁוֹ֙ מֵֽאֶסְתֵּ֣ר הַמַּלְכָּ֔ה כִּ֣י
רָאָ֔ה כִּֽי־כָלְתָ֥ה אֵלָ֛יו הָרָעָ֖ה מֵאֵ֥ת הַמֶּֽלֶךְ:

7 The king rose in anger from the wine banquet and went out to the palace garden. Haman stayed to plead for his life from Esther the queen because he saw that he was destined to a bad end from the king.

QUESTIONS

WHY did Haman *"plead for his life from Esther the queen"* rather than from the king and queen together?

COMMENTARY

We saw in the previous verse that any arguments in his defense that Haman could offer the king would infuriate Esther, and any points he might make to placate the queen would enrage Achashverosh.

When the king **went out to the palace garden**, Haman had a chance to plead in front of the queen alone.

ח   וְהַמֶּ֡לֶךְ שָׁב֩ מִגִּנַּ֨ת הַבִּיתָ֜ן אֶל־בֵּ֣ית ׀ מִשְׁתֵּ֣ה הַיַּ֗יִן
וְהָמָן֙ נֹפֵ֔ל עַל־הַמִּטָּה֙ אֲשֶׁ֣ר אֶסְתֵּ֣ר עָלֶ֔יהָ וַיֹּ֣אמֶר
הַמֶּ֗לֶךְ הֲגַ֛ם לִכְבּ֥וֹשׁ אֶת־הַמַּלְכָּ֖ה עִמִּ֣י בַּבָּ֑יִת הַדָּבָ֗ר
יָצָא֙ מִפִּ֣י הַמֶּ֔לֶךְ וּפְנֵ֥י הָמָ֖ן חָפֽוּ׃

8 The king returned from the palace
garden to the wine banquet. Haman had
fallen on the couch with Esther. The king
exclaimed, "Does he intend to vanquish
the queen while she is with me in the
house?" The statement left the king's
mouth and they covered Haman's face.

COMMENTARY

The king had been told by Esther that Haman intended to
kill her as part of the elimination of the entire Jewish nation. Returning to the banquet, and seeing that **Haman had fallen on
the couch with Esther**, Achashverosh was convinced that Haman was trying to kill her then and there.

Does he intend to vanquish the queen — even if he intends killing the Jewish people, does he really dare to include the
queen herself in this annihilation?

Furthermore, does he dare to do so **while she is with me in
the house?** Someone sentenced to death who fled to the royal
palace could not be killed there. So how does Haman dare to kill
someone right here in the palace?

Then **they covered Haman's face.** It was the Persian custom to cover the face of someone with whom the king was angry,
so that the king should not see his face and, thereby, his wrath
would be assuaged.[1]

---

1. This explanation is attributed to Rav Avraham Ibn Ezra
   (1089–1164).

ט וַיֹּאמֶר חַרְבוֹנָה אֶחָד מִן־הַסָּרִיסִים לִפְנֵי הַמֶּלֶךְ
גַּם הִנֵּה־הָעֵץ אֲשֶׁר־עָשָׂה הָמָן לְמָרְדֳּכַי אֲשֶׁר דִּבֶּר־
טוֹב עַל־הַמֶּלֶךְ עֹמֵד בְּבֵית הָמָן גָּבֹהַּ חֲמִשִּׁים אַמָּה
וַיֹּאמֶר הַמֶּלֶךְ תְּלֻהוּ עָלָיו:

9 Then Charvonah, one of the chamberlains who attended the king, said, "Also see
the gallows which Haman prepared for
Mordechai, who spoke good for the
king. It is standing in Haman's house,
fifty cubits tall." The king said, "Hang
him on it!"

QUESTIONS

HOW did the chamberlain know about the gallows and its intended victim?

WHY did he mention *"who spoke good for the king"*?

WHAT difference did it make if the gallows was *"standing in Haman's house"* at that moment or not?

WHY was it important that the gallows was *"fifty cubits tall"*?

COMMENTARY

Charvonah was **one of the chamberlains** who had brought
Haman to the banquet. When he had arrived at Haman's home,
he heard Haman discussing with his wife and friends his hope and
intention to hang Mordechai in spite of all that had transpired, including the honor that the king had accorded to Mordechai.[1]

---

1. See ch. 6, v. 14 with commentary.

Also see the gallows — Charvonah brought proof that Haman only had the king's worst interests at heart. He had constructed a gallows to kill Mordechai, whose only "crime" was that he **spoke good for the king.** The fact that Mordechai had saved the king's life had evidently infuriated Haman, a clear sign that Haman wanted to see the king killed.

Furthermore, the gallows is **standing in Haman's house** and it is **fifty cubits tall,** ensuring that it could be seen by all. This was a disgrace to the king. While Mordechai was wearing a royal robe and being led with public proclamation that this was the man whom the king wanted to honor, at that very moment a gallows was standing, visible to all, prepared to kill the same man! Haman was publicly demonstrating that the man whom the king wished to honor was about to be hanged. There could be no greater sign of disloyalty and rebellion against the king. Upon hearing this, Achashverosh immediately sentenced Haman to the fate that he deserved — to be hanged on the same gallows he had prepared for Mordechai.

"So let all Your enemies perish, O Lord."[1]

י וַיִּתְלוּ אֶת־הָמָן עַל־הָעֵץ אֲשֶׁר־הֵכִין לְמָרְדֳּכָי
וַחֲמַת הַמֶּלֶךְ שָׁכָכָה׃

10 They hanged Haman on the gallows which he had prepared for Mordechai. Then the king's anger subsided.

---

1. Shoftim 5:31.

CHAPTER 8

ח א   בַּיּוֹם הַהוּא נָתַן הַמֶּלֶךְ אֲחַשְׁוֵרוֹשׁ לְאֶסְתֵּר
הַמַּלְכָּה אֶת־בֵּית הָמָן צֹרֵר הַיְּהוּדִיִּים וּמָרְדֳּכַי בָּא
לִפְנֵי הַמֶּלֶךְ כִּי־הִגִּידָה אֶסְתֵּר מַה הוּא־לָהּ:

1 That same day King Achashverosh gave
Esther the queen the house of Haman,
oppressor of the Jews. Then Mordechai
came before the king, for Esther had
divulged whom he was to her.

QUESTIONS

WHY did Achashverosh give Haman's house to Esther?

WHAT was so noteworthy about Mordechai coming before the
king? Surely anyone could have an audience with the king if necessary.

WHY is Haman referred to here as *"oppressor of the Jews"*?

COMMENTARY

The law in those days was that when someone was sentenced to death by the king, his estate passed to the king himself. If Haman had been killed for rebellion against the king, his property would belong to Achashverosh. Achashverosh, though, wanted to demonstrate that Haman was not executed for rebelling against the king, but for opposing the queen and her people. It was only appropriate, therefore, that Haman's estate should go to Esther.

Haman is referred to as the **oppressor of the Jews** to highlight the reason that his property was given to Esther — he had been killed as punishment for his conspiracy against Esther and the Jews.

Then Mordechai came — Achashverosh imediately promoted him, permitting him to appear before the king whenever he wanted, without having to wait until he was summoned and with no need for the royal scepter to be extended to him.

בוַיָּסַר הַמֶּלֶךְ אֶת־טַבַּעְתּוֹ אֲשֶׁר הֶעֱבִיר מֵהָמָן וַיִּתְּנָהּ לְמָרְדֳּכָי וַתָּשֶׂם אֶסְתֵּר אֶת־מָרְדֳּכַי עַל־בֵּית הָמָן:

2 **The king took off his ring which he had removed from Haman and gave it to Mordechai. Esther placed Mordechai in charge of Haman's house.**

QUESTIONS

THE phrase *"which he had removed from Haman"* is apparently redundant. What does it teach us?

WHY are we told that *"Esther placed Mordechai in charge of Haman's house"*?

COMMENTARY

From the moment that Achashverosh had given his ring to Haman[1] the king's chief minister had been in charge of the ring. Upon Haman's death, Achashverosh immediately gave the ring to Mordechai, without even placing it on his own finger first.[2]

Haman had boasted about *"the glory of his wealth"* and *"how the king had promoted him."*[3] Now, it was Mordechai who was granted both. The promotion to Haman's position was indicated by the fact that **the king took off his ring which he had removed from Haman and gave it to Mordechai.** The transfer of Haman's wealth to Mordechai took place when **Esther placed Mordechai in charge of Haman's house.**

ג   וַתּוֹסֶף אֶסְתֵּר וַתְּדַבֵּר לִפְנֵי הַמֶּלֶךְ וַתִּפֹּל לִפְנֵי
רַגְלָיו וַתֵּבְךְּ וַתִּתְחַנֶּן־לוֹ לְהַעֲבִיר אֶת־רָעַת הָמָן
הָאֲגָגִי וְאֵת מַחֲשַׁבְתּוֹ אֲשֶׁר חָשַׁב עַל־הַיְּהוּדִים:

---

1. Ch. 3, v. 10.
2. Many understand that the king removed the ring from his own finger, and the phrase *"which he had removed from Haman"* describes the ring we are discussing. The Malbim, though, explains the phrase *"which he had removed from Haman"* as indicating that he gave it to Mordechai immediately after removing it from Haman. The inference seems to be from the apparently unnecessary inclusion of the words *"which he had removed"* — the verse could have been written, *"The king took off his ring from Haman."* The extra words imply *"which he had only now removed from Haman."*
3. Ch. 5, v. 11.

3 **Esther once again spoke before the king. She fell before his feet, crying, and beseeched him to revoke the evil of Haman the Agagite and his scheme which he had plotted against the Jews.**

QUESTIONS

ESTHER had already appealed on behalf of her people.[1] Why did Esther *"once again"* speak before the king, pleading even more fervently than previously?

WHAT is the need for all the different phrases describing Esther's plea to Achashverosh — *"spoke," "fell before his feet," "crying,"* and *"beseeched"*?

WHAT is the difference between *"the evil of Haman"* and *"his scheme"*?

COMMENTARY

Esther saw that Achashverosh had promoted Mordechai and had given her Haman's house, but he had ignored the essence of her request. She was afraid that the king had abandoned any idea of granting her request and was trying to placate her with other presents. If he genuinely intended to do as she had asked, he would have reassured her on this point before giving her other, less important favors. The granting of these favors was a reason for even greater alarm and prompted Esther to implore the king with all her might.

Esther tried all possible approaches to persuade Achashverosh. Some people are convinced by a rhetorical speech ex-

---

1. Ch. 7, vs. 3-4.

plaining the correctness of the request. So first, Esther **spoke before the king**, setting out logical reasons to grant her request.

Others are won over by tearful supplication that arouses their feelings of mercy. Esther also used this emotional approach. **She fell before his feet, crying, and beseeched him.**

Esther asked the king to send runners to recall the letters that Haman had dispatched and to nullify the decree. She did not want him to send other letters, also to be opened on the thirteenth of Adar, countermanding the first ones (which is what would actually happen).[1] This was because she was afraid of two possible scenarios.

First, before the time came to open the letters, when it would be known that the decree had been overturned, enemies might already start persecuting the Jews. It was no secret[2] that the Jews had been condemned to annihilation, and pogroms might already begin before the appointed time. With this concern, she entreated Achashverosh **to revoke the evil of Haman**, that is, the evil that posed an immediate threat.

The second scenario was that when the time came to open both sets of letters, the provinces would read the letters that Haman had dictated in which he besmirched and denigrated the Jews in the most forceful manner. The consequence might be that they would not believe that the second set of letters, rescinding the first, was genuine. With this in mind, Esther begged Achashverosh to thwart **his scheme which he had plotted against the Jews.**[3]

---

1. Verses 8-14.
2. Although Haman had not indicated in the "open" letters what was to take place (see commentary on ch. 3, v. 14), Mordechai had publicized the content of the sealed letters (see commentary on ch. 4, vs. 1-3).
3. The phrase *"his scheme"* in Hebrew is מחשבתו, which literally means *"his thought."* Hence it indicates something that has not yet been realized in the realm of action.

Esther was aware that, in Persian law, any decree written in the name of the king could not be revoked.[1] By using the phrase *"his scheme"* she put forward two reasons why the king did not have to be concerned about this law, neither from his own point of view nor from that of the ministers.

The king himself did not need to be apprehensive about contravening the law against rescinding his decrees. Achashverosh, himself, had never personally issued the decree. It had been the work of Haman — *"his scheme"* alone. The king had never known that the Jews were the nation concerned, nor that Haman intended to annihilate them.[2]

Nor did Achashverosh need to worry about an adverse reaction from his ministers. Esther pointed out that the details of the decree were in letters that were still sealed. The "open" letters only told everyone to be ready for the thireenth of Adar without specifying for what.[3] Esther advised Achashverosh to recall only the letters which stated explicitly Haman's decree — the sealed letters. The king need not be anxious about recalling Haman's letters since they were only *"his scheme"* — they remained in the realm of thought, not having been publicized yet. If they were brought back and others sent in their place, no one would know that Achashverosh had retracted any decree.[4]

---

1. See verse 8.
2. See commentary on ch. 3, vs. 8-13.
3. See commentary on ch. 3, v. 14.
4. There is a slight problem with this explanation. Earlier in the commentary on this verse, when describing the first possible scenario that worried Esther, the Malbim wrote that it was already known that the Jews had been condemned to extermination. Here, though, the Malbim writes that if Achashverosh recalled the sealed letters, no one would know that the decree had been revoked.

   Perhaps a reconciliation could be that the Malbim means that no one would know with certainty and with the ability to prove that Achashverosh had revoked a royal decree. (Ed.)

ד　וַיּ֤וֹשֶׁט הַמֶּ֙לֶךְ֙ לְאֶסְתֵּ֔ר אֵ֖ת שַׁרְבִ֣יט הַזָּהָ֑ב וַתָּ֣קָם
אֶסְתֵּ֔ר וַתַּֽעֲמֹ֖ד לִפְנֵ֥י הַמֶּֽלֶךְ׃

4 The king extended the golden scepter to
Esther, and Esther rose and stood before
the king.

COMMENTARY

The king extended the golden scepter to Esther, giving
her permission to stand and state her case in detail.

ה　וַתֹּ֗אמֶר אִם־עַל־הַמֶּ֤לֶךְ טוֹב֙ וְאִם־מָצָ֨אתִי חֵ֜ן
לְפָנָ֗יו וְכָשֵׁ֤ר הַדָּבָר֙ לִפְנֵ֣י הַמֶּ֔לֶךְ וְטוֹבָ֥ה אֲנִ֖י בְּעֵינָ֑יו
יִכָּתֵ֞ב לְהָשִׁ֣יב אֶת־הַסְּפָרִ֗ים מַחֲשֶׁ֜בֶת הָמָ֤ן בֶּֽן־הַמְּדָ֙תָא֙
הָאֲגָגִ֔י אֲשֶׁ֣ר כָּתַ֔ב לְאַבֵּד֙ אֶת־הַיְּהוּדִ֔ים אֲשֶׁ֖ר בְּכָל־
מְדִינ֥וֹת הַמֶּֽלֶךְ׃

5 She said, "If it seems good to the king
and if I have found favor before him, and
if the matter seems correct to the king and
I am good in his eyes, let it be written to
recall the letters, the scheme of Haman
the son of Hamdatha, the Agagite, which
he wrote to eradicate the Jews in all the
provinces of the king.

QUESTIONS

WHY did Esther use so many different phrases of introduction
before stating her request?

WHY did Esther need to say *"the scheme of Haman"*? We know that the letters were the work of Haman.

COMMENTARY

Someone who grants a request does so either because he desires to do the will of the one making the request, or because of the request itself. Each of these factors can have an influence in one of two ways. Either the petitioner or the request itself finds favor before the person granting the request, or he anticipates obtaining some benefit or advantage from either the petitioner or from the fulfillment of the request itself.

Esther addressed each of these four possibilities. **If it seems good to the king** — if the request itself is pleasing to the king; **and if I have found favor before him** — if I, the petitioner, am pleasing to the king. Esther then addressed the two aspects of benefit that could accrue to the king. First, **if the matter seems correct to the king** — it will be advantageous to the king to be seen doing that which is just and correct. Second, if **I am good in his eyes** — if the king benefits at all from having me as his wife, then he should grant my request so that I do not die from seeing the calamity that will befall my people. Esther demonstrated to Achashverosh that there were all four types of reasons for fulfilling her entreaty.

If so, Esther continued, **let it be written to recall the letters.** Runners should be sent to bring back the sealed letters which contained **the scheme of Haman.** Esther once again emphasized that they were, as yet, only the *"scheme of Haman,"* unknown to the officials. There would be no problem in recalling the letters.

ו כִּי אֵיכָכָה אוּכַל וְרָאִיתִי בָּרָעָה אֲשֶׁר־יִמְצָא
אֶת־עַמִּי וְאֵיכָכָה אוּכַל וְרָאִיתִי בְּאָבְדַן מוֹלַדְתִּי:

6 For how can I bear to see the evil which
will happen to my people, and how can I
bear to see the eradication of my
kindred?"

QUESTIONS

WHY did Esther say both halves of this verse; they seem to be repetitive?

COMMENTARY

Esther proceeded to give two reasons why it would not be
possible to remedy the situation by sending a second set of letters
that would also be opened on the thirteenth of Adar, to countermand the first set.

**For how can I bear to see the evil which will happen to
my people** — even before the thirteenth of Adar, with pogroms
and pillaging of the Jews.

Second, **how can I bear to see the eradication of my kindred** — even when the thirteenth of Adar would arrive, people
might not accept the authenticity of the second set of letters and
they would follow the directive of the first — to annihilate the
Jews.

These two reasons correspond to the two possible scenarios
that frightened Esther and to which she alluded in verse 3 with
the phrases *"the evil of Haman"* and *"his scheme."*[1]

---

1. See commentary on verse 3.

ז וַיֹּאמֶר הַמֶּלֶךְ אֲחַשְׁוֵרֹשׁ לְאֶסְתֵּר הַמַּלְכָּה
וּלְמָרְדֳּכַי הַיְּהוּדִי הִנֵּה בֵית־הָמָן נָתַתִּי לְאֶסְתֵּר וְאֹתוֹ
תָּלוּ עַל־הָעֵץ עַל אֲשֶׁר־שָׁלַח יָדוֹ בַּיְּהוּדִיים:

7 King Achashverosh said to Esther the queen and to Mordechai the Jew, "See, I have given Haman's house to Esther, and I have hanged him on the gallows for attacking the Jews.

QUESTIONS

ACHASHVEROSH'S response to Esther, telling her about Haman's house and the hanging of Haman himself, seems irrelevant to the point she raised — the potential destruction of the Jewish people. Why did the king not allay Esther's fears immediately?

ח וְאַתֶּם כִּתְבוּ עַל־הַיְּהוּדִים כַּטּוֹב בְּעֵינֵיכֶם בְּשֵׁם
הַמֶּלֶךְ וְחִתְמוּ בְּטַבַּעַת הַמֶּלֶךְ כִּי־כְתָב אֲשֶׁר־נִכְתָּב
בְּשֵׁם־הַמֶּלֶךְ וְנַחְתּוֹם בְּטַבַּעַת הַמֶּלֶךְ אֵין לְהָשִׁיב:

8 You may write concerning the Jews whatever seems right to you, and sign it with the king's ring, for a document written in the king's name and signed with the king's ring may not be revoked."

QUESTIONS

ACHASHVEROSH'S suggestion has puzzled the commentators. Since *"a document written in the king's name... may not be revoked,"* how could the king tell Mordechai and Esther to *"write... whatever seems right to you"*? On the one hand, it was not permissible to rescind the first letters; on the other hand, if they were not rescinded, the Jews were doomed to death!

COMMENTARY (VERSES 7-8)

The king would not agree to Esther's proposal that the sealed letters should be recalled. This was because of the law that *"a document written in the king's name and signed with the king's ring may not be revoked."* However, he suggested two ideas how the sealed letters could remain where they were without any harm befalling the Jews.

His first suggestion was as follows. The decree written in the sealed letters gave the command *"to destroy, kill, and eradicate all the Jews"*;[1] that is, *"the Jews"* were the object of the verbs. It was possible, though, to interpret this command with *"the Jews"* being the subject of the verbs. According to this reading, the people who were *"to destroy, kill, and eradicate all"* were *"the Jews."* However, according to this interpretation, no indication was given as to whom would be killed. This uncertainty would be clarified by a second set of letters which would state explicitly that those carrying out the destruction were to be the Jews — **the king had given authority to the Jews**, and that those to be killed were **all the forces of any people or province that trouble them.**[2]

The consequence would be that the second set of letters did not countermand the first set, but merely clarified and added to the first letters.

---

1. Ch. 3, v. 13.
2. Verse 11.

However, this course of action alone would not be fool-proof. The new interpretation of the original letters was some-what farfetched. Furthermore, the first letters had been sent out in many languages; in some of those languages this new interpre-tation would be impossible.

Achashverosh's second idea would remove any problems. If someone orders "Reuven should hit Shimon" and then says "Reuven should not hit Shimon" it is clear that these orders con-tradict each other. If, however, he orders "Reuven should hit Shi-mon" and then "Shimon should hit Reuven" there is no contra-diction — both orders can be obeyed.

Similarly, if Achashverosh was to issue a second set of letters ordering the king's subjects *not* to kill the Jews, this would clearly contradict the first orders. Instead, Achashverosh wrote that the Jews had authority to kill all those who attacked them. Now the letters would not be at variance with each other — each group had permission to fight the other.

However, the Jews would still be in danger. Their enemies had authority to kill them, and although they were allowed to fight back there was no certainty who would prevail. For this rea-son Achashverosh prefaced his remarks by saying, *"See, I have given Haman's house to Esther and I have hanged him on the gallows for attacking the Jews."* We shall now explain the significance of this response.

Achashverosh addressed all of Esther's concerns.[1] Just as Ha-man had done, Achashverosh sent out sealed letters, to be opened on the thirteenth of Adar — the same date as Haman's letters were to be opened. These are described in verses 10 to 12. Also like Haman, Achashverosh issued an "open" synopsis. This is described in verse 13.

Esther had been afraid that since the provinces had received "open" letters telling them to be prepared for the thirteenth of

---

1. See commentary on verses 3 and 6.

Adar, and since they had heard rumors that the Jews were to be killed, if Achashverosh sent letters to be opened on the thirteenth of Adar together with Haman's sealed letters, they might start a rampage before the appointed date.

Achashverosh argued that his first idea removed this danger. The "open" letters only ordered readiness, without specifying who should be ready or for what. Achashverosh's "open" synopsis stated categorically that it was the Jews who were to be ready and that they were to be ready to avenge themselves on their enemies. No one would dare attack the Jews against this explicit directive which clarified the first "open" letters.

An additional peril that worried Esther was that when Haman's sealed letters would be opened, on the thirteenth of Adar, there would be languages in which the Haman's sealed letters were unambiguous. Even though Achashverosh's sealed letters clearly authorized the Jews to kill all who attacked them, they might be overpowered by their enemies. These enemies might be aided by the governors and officials who felt they could choose which of the contradictory orders to follow.

Therefore, Achashverosh's first words were **"See, I have given Haman's house to Esther, and I have hanged him on the gallows for attacking the Jews."** Everyone knew that Achashverosh's chief minister had been hanged and his estate given to Esther for trying to exterminate the queen and her people.[1] The governors and officials would clearly understand that the first letters had been written without the king's approval and against his will. When they would open both sets of "sealed" letters they would dispose of the first ones, afraid of meeting the same fate as Haman. They would do their utmost to help the Jews. The masses would never know the contents of Haman's sealed letters.

The Jews would be saved.

---

1. See commentary on verse 1.

ט וַיִּקָּרְאוּ סֹפְרֵי־ הַמֶּלֶךְ בָּעֵת־הַהִיא בַּחֹדֶשׁ
הַשְּׁלִישִׁי הוּא־חֹדֶשׁ סִיוָן בִּשְׁלוֹשָׁה וְעֶשְׂרִים בּוֹ
וַיִּכָּתֵב כְּכָל־אֲשֶׁר־צִוָּה מָרְדֳּכַי אֶל־הַיְּהוּדִים וְאֶל
הָאֲחַשְׁדַּרְפְּנִים־וְהַפַּחוֹת וְשָׂרֵי הַמְּדִינוֹת אֲשֶׁר ׀ מֵהֹדּוּ
וְעַד־כּוּשׁ שֶׁבַע וְעֶשְׂרִים וּמֵאָה מְדִינָה מְדִינָה
וּמְדִינָה כִּכְתָבָהּ וְעַם וָעָם כִּלְשֹׁנוֹ וְאֶל־הַיְּהוּדִים
כִּכְתָבָם וְכִלְשׁוֹנָם:

9 The king's scribes were summoned at that time, the twenty-third day of the third month, that is the month of Sivan. All that Mordechai dictated was written to the Jews, as well as to the satraps, governors, and officials of the provinces, from India to Ethiopia, a hundred and twenty-seven provinces, to each province in its script and to each people in its language, and to the Jews in their script and language.

QUESTIONS

WHY did Achashverosh wait until the twenty-third of Sivan before sending his letters?

COMMENTARY

Achashverosh waited until the twenty-third of Sivan because he wanted the same messengers who had delivered Haman's letters to be the couriers of the second letters as well. This would confirm the authenticity of these second letters. The last messengers to return arrived back in Shushan on the twenty-third of Sivan.[1]

In addition to writing to **the satraps, governors, and officials of the provinces,** Mordechai ensured that letters were **written to the Jews.** This gave greater authority to the second letters. The governors and officials who received two contradictory sets of letters might decide that they could follow whichever they wanted. However, since the second set of letters had been sent also to people who had not received the first letters, this option no longer remained. It was clear that the second letters were authoritative, countermanding the first set.

יְ וַיִּכְתֹּב בְּשֵׁם הַמֶּלֶךְ אֲחַשְׁוֵרֹשׁ וַיַּחְתֹּם בְּטַבַּעַת הַמֶּלֶךְ וַיִּשְׁלַח סְפָרִים בְּיַד הָרָצִים בַּסּוּסִים רֹכְבֵי הָרֶכֶשׁ הָאֲחַשְׁתְּרָנִים בְּנֵי הָרַמָּכִים:

10 He wrote in the name of King Achashverosh and signed them with the king's ring and sent the letters by fast couriers, on horseback, riding on the swift steeds used in the royal service, bred of stud mares,

QUESTIONS

WHY did Mordechai send his couriers on horseback, whereas Haman had sent them by foot?[2]

---

1. This commentary is attributed to Rav Eliezer Ashkenazy. See footnote, p. 11.
2. See ch. 3, v. 15 where no mention of horses is made. Unless such mention is made, the word רצים, literally "runners," indicates "by foot."

COMMENTARY

Mordechai sent his couriers on horseback for one of two possible reasons: either because they were exhausted, having just returned from delivering Haman's letters;[1] or, because the Jews were in danger, Mordechai wanted to act in the quickest possible manner.

יא אֲשֶׁר֩ נָתַ֨ן הַמֶּ֜לֶךְ לַיְּהוּדִ֣ים ׀ אֲשֶׁ֣ר בְּכָל־עִיר־
וָעִ֗יר לְהִקָּהֵל֮ וְלַעֲמֹ֣ד עַל־נַפְשָׁם֒ לְהַשְׁמִיד֩ וְלַהֲרֹ֨ג
וּלְאַבֵּ֜ד אֶת־כָּל־חֵ֧יל עַ֣ם וּמְדִינָ֗ה הַצָּרִ֤ים אֹתָם֙ טַ֣ף
וְנָשִׁ֑ים וּשְׁלָלָ֖ם לָבֽוֹז׃

11 **stating that the king had given authority to the Jews in every city to assemble and defend themselves, to destroy, kill, and eradicate all the forces of any people or province that trouble them, their children or women, and their wealth for plundering,**

QUESTIONS

WHEN Haman issued his decree he wrote *"to destroy, kill, and eradicate all the Jews...on one day...and their wealth for plundering."*[2] This implies that the plundering was to take place only after the

---

1. See commentary on the previous verse. As soon as they returned from delivering Haman's letters, they were sent out again with Mordechai's letters.
2. Ch. 3, v. 13.

day on which the Jews were killed.[1] Mordechai, however, authorized the Jews *"to destroy, kill, and eradicate...and their wealth for
plundering, on one day,"* implying that the plundering was to take
place on the same day. Why the difference?

COMMENTARY

Mordechai did not want the Jews to take spoils from the
property of their enemies. This would bring them into disrepute.
People would say that their main motivation in attacking their
enemies was greed and a desire for material possessions.

However, as we saw, the first letters could not be revoked,
and the second letters were written to be a "clarification" of the
first. It was, therefore, impossible to omit explicit parts of the first
letters. The first had spoken expressly about *"and their wealth for
plundering."* This could not be removed. Mordechai, ingeniously,
made a slight modification. He permitted plunder only on the
thirteenth of Adar, the day when the Jews were authorized to
avenge themselves on their enemies. The Jews would not neglect
the main task of eliminating their foes in order to take spoils. It
would be understood that they were not meant to touch the possessions of their enemies.

Haman, though, knew that the consequence of authorizing
plunder before the Jews had been killed would be that everyone
would rush to seize spoils before others took them. No one would
be interested in killing Jews. Therefore, he ordered that no spoils
were to be plundered on the thirteenth of Adar. The day was to be
devoted to annihilating the Jews. After this had been achieved,
their property could be plundered.

---

1. The inference is from the observation that the phrase *"on one day"*
    comes after *"to destroy, kill, and eradicate all the Jews"* and before
    "and their wealth for plundering." It cannot, therefore, describe both
    phrases.

יב בְּיוֹם אֶחָד בְּכָל־מְדִינוֹת הַמֶּלֶךְ אֲחַשְׁוֵרוֹשׁ
בִּשְׁלוֹשָׁה עָשָׂר לְחֹדֶשׁ שְׁנֵים־עָשָׂר הוּא־חֹדֶשׁ אֲדָר:

12 **on one day, in all the provinces of King
Achashverosh, the thirteenth day of the
twelfth month, the month of Adar.**

QUESTIONS

MORDECHAI wrote that his decree would apply to *"all the provinces of King Achashverosh."* Haman never wrote this, so why did
Mordechai?

COMMENTARY

Haman never mentioned that his decree was to apply to *"all
the provinces of King Achashverosh."* He was concerned that if the
officials knew that all the Jews had been condemned to death,
they might be reluntant to be involved with the annihilation of
an entire nation. Haman wanted each province to think that the
decree applied to it alone.[1]

Mordechai, on the other hand, wanted everyone to know
that the Jews' fortunes had turned to *"happiness and joy"*[2] in **all
the provinces of King Achashverosh.**

יג פַּתְשֶׁגֶן הַכְּתָב לְהִנָּתֵן דָּת בְּכָל־מְדִינָה וּמְדִינָה
גָּלוּי לְכָל־הָעַמִּים וְלִהְיוֹת הַיְּהוּדִיים עֲתִידִים לַיּוֹם
הַזֶּה לְהִנָּקֵם מֵאֹיְבֵיהֶם:

---

1. See commentary on ch. 3, v. 13, according to which it would follow
   that another reason for Haman not mentioning that the decree applied to *"all the provinces of King Achashverosh"* would be to ensure
   fear of the consequences of disobedience.
2. Verse 16.

13 A synopsis of the writing was to be given out for an edict in every province, revealed to all the peoples, that on this day the Jews should be ready to avenge themselves on their enemies.

COMMENTARY

A synopsis of the writing — see commentary on verses 7 and 8.

יד הָרָצִים רֹכְבֵי הָרֶכֶשׁ הָאֲחַשְׁתְּרָנִים יָצְאוּ
מְבֹהָלִים וּדְחוּפִים בִּדְבַר הַמֶּלֶךְ וְהַדָּת נִתְּנָה בְּשׁוּשַׁן
הַבִּירָה:

14 The fast couriers, riding on the swift steeds used in the royal service, went out rushed and hastened by the king's order, and the decree was given out in Shushan the citadel.

QUESTIONS

WHY are we told that the couriers *"went out rushed and hastened by the king's order,"* whereas when Haman sent them they only *"went out hastened by the king's order"*[1] and were not *"rushed"*?

---

1. Ch. 3, v. 15.

COMMENTARY

The fast couriers...went out rushed — they had no idea[1] why they were being sent out again immediately.

Wisely, Mordechai arranged that **the decree was given out in Shushan** only after the couriers had left. Like Haman before him with the first letters, he wanted to ensure that no one in Shushan would try to dissuade Achashverosh from sending out the second set of letters.

טו וּמָרְדֳּכַי יָצָא ׀ מִלִּפְנֵי הַמֶּלֶךְ בִּלְבוּשׁ מַלְכוּת
תְּכֵלֶת וָחוּר וַעֲטֶרֶת זָהָב גְּדוֹלָה וְתַכְרִיךְ בּוּץ
וְאַרְגָּמָן וְהָעִיר שׁוּשָׁן צָהֲלָה וְשָׂמֵחָה:

15 **Mordechai went out from the presence of the king wearing a royal robe of blue and white, with a large golden crown and cloak of fine linen and purple. The city of Shushan was jubilant and happy.**

QUESTIONS

SINCE we are told in the next verse that *"For the Jews there was light and happiness, joy and honor,"* we can infer that *"the city of Shushan was jubilant and happy"* refers to non-Jews. Why were they happy?

---

1. The word מבוהלים connotes both "rushed" and "confused." The Malbim explains that, in this verse, it has the connotation of being "confused."

COMMENTARY

We see Mordechai's quality of character from the fact that he accepted no honor for himself until he was certain that there was light and salvation for his troubled people. Only then did he go out **wearing a royal robe.**

The city of Shushan was jubilant and happy — a fulfillment of the words of King Solomon, "When the righteous become great, the people rejoice."[1] Everyone was happy with Mordechai's rise to power.

טז   לַיְּהוּדִים הָיְתָה אוֹרָה וְשִׂמְחָה וְשָׂשֹׂן וִיקָר:

16 **For the Jews there was light and happiness and joy and honor.**

COMMENTARY

For **the Jews** especially there was extra happiness and open joy, with great honor being accorded them.

יז   וּבְכָל־מְדִינָה וּמְדִינָה וּבְכָל־עִיר וָעִיר מְקוֹם
אֲשֶׁר דְּבַר־הַמֶּלֶךְ וְדָתוֹ מַגִּיעַ שִׂמְחָה וְשָׂשׂוֹן
לַיְּהוּדִים מִשְׁתֶּה וְיוֹם טוֹב וְרַבִּים מֵעַמֵּי הָאָרֶץ
מִתְיַהֲדִים כִּי־נָפַל פַּחַד־הַיְּהוּדִים עֲלֵיהֶם:

17 **In every province and in every city, wherever the king's edict and decree reached, there was happiness and joy for**

---

1.   Mishlei (Proverbs) 29:2.

the Jews, a feast and a holiday. Many of
the people of the land became Jews
because the fear of the Jews had fallen
upon them.

QUESTIONS

WHEN Haman sent out his letters, we are told that *"in every province, wherever the king's edict and decree reached, the Jews were in great mourning."*[1] No mention was made of *"and in every city."* Why is this phrase added here?

COMMENTARY

Haman's "open" synopsis had merely told people to be prepared for the thirteenth of Adar. Only those communities which also knew, through word of mouth, that Haman's real intention was the annihilation of the Jewish people, were in mourning. Not every city knew this.

Mordechai's "open" synopsis was explicit — the Jews were to avenge themselves on their enemies. Therefore every city knew the good news as soon as it received the "open" letter.

---

1. Ch. 4, v. 3.

CHAPTER 9

ט א וּבִשְׁנֵים֩ עָשָׂ֨ר חֹ֜דֶשׁ הוּא־חֹ֣דֶשׁ אֲדָ֗ר בִּשְׁלוֹשָׁ֨ה
עָשָׂ֥ר יוֹם֘ בּ֣וֹ אֲשֶׁ֣ר הִגִּ֧יעַ דְּבַר־הַמֶּ֛לֶךְ וְדָת֖וֹ לְהֵעָשׂ֑וֹת
בַּיּ֗וֹם אֲשֶׁ֨ר שִׂבְּר֜וּ אֹיְבֵ֤י הַיְּהוּדִים֙ לִשְׁל֣וֹט בָּהֶ֔ם
וְנַהֲפ֣וֹךְ ה֔וּא אֲשֶׁ֨ר יִשְׁלְט֧וּ הַיְּהוּדִ֛ים הֵ֖מָּה בְּשֹׂנְאֵיהֶֽם:

1 In the twelfth month, the month of
Adar, on the thirteenth day, the time
arrived for the king's edict and his decree
to come into force. On the day when the
Jews' enemies had anticipated dominating them, it was turned about; the Jews
themselves dominated those who hated
them.

QUESTIONS

THE word *"themselves"* seems to be superfluous. What does it
teach us?

COMMENTARY

We have seen how the Jews were saved from all persecution in the period before the thirteenth of Adar. Were it not for the second set of letters, the Jews would have been assaulted. Only Mordechai's "open" letter saved them by stating that it was the Jews who were to be ready to attack their enemies.

Now we discover what happened when both sets of sealed letters were opened at the appointed time. When **the time arrived for the king's edict and his *decree* to come into force,** the decree that had been written in Achashverosh's sealed letters was revealed.[1] Since it was the time for the decree *"to come into force,"* it was impossible to be passive. A peaceful resolution was impossible because the king had commanded war.

On that day the fortunes and constellation of the Jews were at their nadir, whereas those of Amalek were at their zenith. This motivated Haman to choose this day.[2] It was **the day when the Jews' enemies had anticipated dominating them** — the day itself had encouraged this anticipation.

The Almighty demonstrated His unceasing concern for His people. Not only did the Jews' enemies not vanquish them, but

---

1. See commentary on ch. 4, v. 3, in which the Malbim explained that the *"edict"* refers to the "open" synopsis, while *"decree"* refers to the contents of the sealed letters.
2. How is this to be reconciled with the fact that Haman cast lots to decide on which day to annihilate the Jews? Furthermore, the commentary on ch. 3, v. 7 explains how the thirteenth of Adar was Divinely ordained, being the most distant day given the system of lot-casting used, to provide the Jews with the maximum time in which to repent.

   It could be that if the day decided by the lots would have been a day which the constellations deemed to be inauspicious, Haman would have disregarded the lots. Since the outcome of the lots coincided with a day that the constellations showed to be very propitious, Haman accepted it. (Ed.)

the complete reverse occurred. These enemies fell from the pinnacle of good fortune to the deepest of pits, while the Jews rose from the depths to the greatest heights of success.

There were two aspects of the miraculous here. First, that the situation **was turned about**, from one extreme to the other. Second, that it happened in a highly extraordinary manner. Someone whose fortunes are at their lowest point can hope to succeed if he joins forces with another whose fortunes are succeeding. A partner's success can outweigh one's own bad fortune. Here, though, it was the Jews *themselves*, without any assistance from others, who **dominated those who hated them.**

ב נִקְהֲלוּ הַיְּהוּדִים בְּעָרֵיהֶם בְּכָל־מְדִינוֹת הַמֶּלֶךְ אֲחַשְׁוֵרוֹשׁ לִשְׁלֹחַ יָד בִּמְבַקְשֵׁי רָעָתָם וְאִישׁ לֹא־עָמַד לִפְנֵיהֶם כִּי־נָפַל פַּחְדָּם עַל־כָּל־הָעַמִּים:

2 The Jews assembled in their cities in all the provinces of King Achashverosh, to attack those who sought their harm. No man stood up to them, because their fear had fallen upon all the people.

QUESTIONS

THIS verse seems to say the same as verse 16. Why do we need both?[1]

WHY did the fear of the Jews fall upon *"the people,"* whereas, in verse 3, it is *"the fear of Mordechai"* that fell on the *"officials, satraps, and governors"*?

---

1. This question is answered by the combination of the commentary on this verse and that on verse 16.

COMMENTARY

We now learn what happened in the large fortified cities. These were the bases of the governors, officials, and army battalions who now protected the Jews from their enemies. This ensured that those who hated the Jews were afraid to approach or stand against them.

This explains why, when **the Jews assembled in their cities**, the large fortified cities which were **in all the provinces of King Achashverosh**, they discovered that **no man stood up to them**.

There was a fundamental difference between *"the people"* and *"the officials."* The former did not know what had been written in the sealed letters, and were unaware that the first letters gave them the authority to fight and kill the Jews. Therefore they were afraid of the Jews themselves, who had been empowered by the king's "open" letter to annihilate their enemies.

ג וְכָל־שָׂרֵי הַמְּדִינוֹת וְהָאֲחַשְׁדַּרְפְּנִים וְהַפַּחוֹת
וְעֹשֵׂי הַמְּלָאכָה אֲשֶׁר לַמֶּלֶךְ מְנַשְּׂאִים אֶת־הַיְּהוּדִים
כִּי־נָפַל פַּחַד־מָרְדֳּכַי עֲלֵיהֶם:

3 The officials, satraps, and governors, and those who worked for the king, all supported the Jews, because the fear of Mordechai had fallen upon them.

COMMENTARY

The officials, however, knew the contents of the sealed letters. They were not afraid of the Jews because they were aware that according to the first sealed letters it was permissible to attack and kill the Jews. They could choose to follow the first letters and assist the Jews' enemies or, at least, stand aside and watch each group fight the other. They did neither, but instead **supported the Jews** against their foes, concealing the first letters. This was not done out of fear of the Jews, but **because the fear of Mordechai had fallen upon them,** and they were terrified that he would avenge any wrongs perpetrated against his people.

ד   כִּי־גָדוֹל מָרְדֳּכַי בְּבֵית הַמֶּלֶךְ וְשָׁמְעוֹ הוֹלֵךְ
בְּכָל־הַמְּדִינוֹת כִּי־הָאִישׁ מָרְדֳּכַי הוֹלֵךְ וְגָדוֹל:

4 For Mordechai was powerful in the king's palace and his reputation had spread throughout all the provinces, for the man Mordechai grew increasingly greater.

QUESTIONS

WHAT is the meaning of *"for the man Mordechai grew increasingly greater"?*

COMMENTARY

Different government officials have different responsibilities. Certain ministers are responsible for the administration of the king's palace. Others control the government of the provinces. A third type is in charge of wars against hostile countries and foreign conquest. The success of this third type depends on continued conquest and victory in battle.

Mordechai was preeminent in all three areas. He **was pow-**

erful in the king's palace, responsible for its administration.
Also **his reputation had spread throughout all the provinces,**
being the king's second-in-charge of government of the provinces. Furthermore, **the man Mordechai grew increasingly
greater,** subduing other countries under Achashverosh's dominion, as we will see in the final chapter.[1]

ה   וַיַּכּוּ הַיְּהוּדִים בְּכָל־אֹיְבֵיהֶם מַכַּת־חֶרֶב וְהֶרֶג
וְאַבְדָן וַיַּעֲשׂוּ בְשֹׂנְאֵיהֶם כִּרְצוֹנָם:

**5 The Jews smote all their enemies with
the sword, killing and eradicating, and
they did as they wanted with those who
hated them.**

QUESTIONS

WHAT is the difference between the *"enemies"* of the Jews and
"those who hated them"?[2]

COMMENTARY

The Jews certainly did not have permission to kill whoever
they wanted. The king's decree only authorized the deaths of
those *"that trouble them."*[3] In the large cities *"no man stood up to
them."*[4] Thus they could only kill those whose enmity toward the
Jews was clear and who still displayed an intention to harm

---

1. See ch. 10, v. 1, with commentary.
2. This question also applies to verse 16.
3. Ch. 8, v. 11.
4. Verse 2.

them.[1] **The Jews smote all their enemies with the sword** —
those whose enmity was still revealed. There were others who
now kept their hatred hidden. These could not be killed, but they
could be humiliated. The Jews **did as they wanted with those
who hated them**, shaming and disgracing them.

וּ וּבְשׁוּשַׁן הַבִּירָה הָרְגוּ הַיְּהוּדִים וְאַבֵּד חֲמֵשׁ מֵאוֹת
אִישׁ: ז וְאֵת׀ פַּרְשַׁנְדָּתָא וְאֵת ׀ דַּלְפוֹן וְאֵת׀
אַסְפָּתָא: ח וְאֵת ׀ פּוֹרָתָא וְאֵת ׀ אֲדַלְיָא וְאֵת ׀
אֲרִידָתָא: ט וְאֵת ׀ פַּרְמַשְׁתָּא וְאֵת ׀ אֲרִיסַי וְאֵת ׀
אֲרִידַי וְאֵת ׀ וַיְזָתָא: י עֲשֶׂרֶת בְּנֵי הָמָן בֶּן־הַמְּדָתָא
צֹרֵר הַיְּהוּדִים הָרָגוּ וּבַבִּזָּה לֹא שָׁלְחוּ אֶת־יָדָם:

**6 In Shushan the citadel, the Jews killed
and eradicated five hundred men. 7 and
Parshandatha and Dalphon and Aspatha 8
and Poratha and Adalya and Aridatha 9
and Parmashta and Arisai and Aridai and
Vaizatha 10 the ten sons of Haman, son of
Hamdatha, the Jews' oppressor, they killed,
but they did not touch the spoils.**

יא בַּיּוֹם הַהוּא בָּא מִסְפַּר הַהֲרוּגִים בְּשׁוּשַׁן הַבִּירָה
לִפְנֵי הַמֶּלֶךְ:

---

1. See commentary on ch. 7, v. 6, where the Malbim distinguishes between an "*adversary*" (צר) who has succeeded in harming his foe,
and an "*enemy*" (אויב) who seeks to harm but has not yet done so.
Here a third type is introduced — one who hates his opponent.
With this third type the hatred is hidden, unlike the first two.

11 **On that day the number of those killed in Shushan the citadel was reported to the king.**

COMMENTARY

Achashverosh had only permitted the Jews to kill those whose enmity was open and who still intended to harm them. From the number of those killed, one could estimate how many enemies the Jews really had. For this reason they arranged that **on that day,** immediately, **the number of those killed in Shushan the citadel was reported to the king.** If, even after the king's decree, there were still five hundred men who publicly displayed anti-Jewish sentiments and who had been killed, one could begin to imagine the total number of those that wanted to persecute the Jews.

יב וַיֹּאמֶר הַמֶּלֶךְ לְאֶסְתֵּר הַמַּלְכָּה בְּשׁוּשַׁן הַבִּירָה הָרְגוּ הַיְּהוּדִים וְאַבֵּד חֲמֵשׁ מֵאוֹת אִישׁ וְאֵת עֲשֶׂרֶת בְּנֵי־הָמָן בִּשְׁאָר מְדִינוֹת הַמֶּלֶךְ מֶה עָשׂוּ וּמַה־שְּׁאֵלָתֵךְ וְיִנָּתֵן לָךְ וּמַה־בַּקָּשָׁתֵךְ עוֹד וְתֵעָשׂ:

12 **The king said to Esther the queen, "In Shushan the citadel the Jews have killed and eradicated five hundred men and the ten sons of Haman. What then have they done in the rest of the king's provinces? What is your request? It shall be given to you. What is your petition yet? It shall be done."**

QUESTIONS

ACHASHVEROSH seems to have been annoyed with the large number of men killed, saying *"What then have they done in the rest of the king's provinces?"* Why, then, did he ask Esther what else she wanted? Was the bloodshed to continue unabated?

IN light of Achashverosh's displeasure, his agreement to permit a second day of slaughter of citizens of his empire (verse 14) is startling!

COMMENTARY

Once Achashverosh realized how many enemies the Jews had, he understood that the efforts to save the Jewish people had to be redoubled. If **in Shushan the citadel**, where the king resided and fear of the monarch would be the greatest, there were still so many who openly professed their hatred of the Jews, such that **the Jews have killed and eradicated five hundred men**, who knows **what then have they done in the rest of the king's provinces?** Who knows whether they have succeeded in vanquishing the multitude of foes in distant provinces, where the fear of the king and his decrees was not as strong?[1]

What is your request?...What is your petition yet? What else can be done to remove the danger that threatens the Jews? **It shall be done.**

---

1. In his questions, the Malbim assumed, as many commentaries explain, that the phrase *"What then have they done in the rest of the king's provinces?"* expresses amazement and consternation. In his commentary the Malbim explains that it expresses concern how the Jews fared in distant provinces, where fear of the king would not be so great.

יג   וַתֹּאמֶר אֶסְתֵּר אִם־עַל־הַמֶּלֶךְ טוֹב יִנָּתֵן גַּם־
מָחָר לַיְּהוּדִים אֲשֶׁר בְּשׁוּשָׁן לַעֲשׂוֹת כְּדָת הַיּוֹם וְאֵת
עֲשֶׂרֶת בְּנֵי־הָמָן יִתְלוּ עַל־הָעֵץ:

13 Esther replied, "If it seems good to the
king, let the Jews of Shushan be granted
permission to do tomorrow like the decree
that applied today, and let Haman's ten
sons be hanged on the gallows."

QUESTIONS

HAVING heard Achashverosh express amazement at the large
number of those killed, how did Esther dare ask for yet another
day of carnage?

USUALLY the king's capital city is referred to as *"Shushan the citadel."* Why, with reference to the killing on the fourteenth of Adar,
is it referred to only as *"Shushan"* without *"the citadel"*?[1]

COMMENTARY

The time was opportune for Esther to make her request. She
proposed that the Jews of Shushan be given one more day to kill

---

1. According to the straightforward reading of the Malbim's question,
he seems to ask why, throughout the entire Megillah, only the
phrase *"Shushan the citadel"* is used, whereas, with reference to the
second day of killing, the words *"the citadel"* are omitted.

However, there are various instances of *"Shushan"* without *"the
citadel"* previously in the Megillah. Therefore, it seems that the
thrust of the question is why, from this point on, the words *"the
citadel"* are not used. See commentary and the next footnote for an
analysis of when *"the citadel"* is included and when it is omitted.

their enemies. Seeing that the king's decree was still in force against them would strike fear into the hearts of those that wished the Jews harm.

Esther did not mention *"Shushan the citadel,"* but **Shushan** — the city. This is because Shushan was divided into two parts — *"the citadel,"* where the king and his ministers resided, and the city, which was referred to as *"Shushan."*[1] On the thirteenth, the Jews had already killed their enemies in *"Shushan the citadel."* Esther wanted permission, on the fourteenth, to kill enemies in

---

1. With this distinction we can understand when the phrase *"the citadel"* is included.

Ch. 1, vs. 2 and 5 discuss the king's residence and the banquet in the palace. Therefore this phrase is used there.

Ch. 2, v. 3 recounts the assembling of the maidens in the royal quarters. The phrase is used.

Ch. 2, v. 5 tells us where Mordechai lived. As one of the Jewish nobility (see commentary on ch. 2, v. 6), he lived in proximity to the aristocracy of Shushan. The phrase is used.

Haman's edict was given out first in the locality of the citadel (ch. 3, v. 15), but the news spread quickly to the city of Shushan so that residents of the city were confused (also ch. 3, v. 15).

By the time Mordechai spoke with Hasach (ch. 4, v. 8), the edict was known throughout all of Shushan. Therefore, *"it was given out in Shushan"* — the entire city.

The majority of Jews lived in the city, not the citadel. Therefore, Esther told Mordechai to *"gather all the Jews found in Shushan and fast for me"* (ch. 4, v. 16).

Like Haman before him, Mordechai issued his decree in the political center — it was *"given out in Shushan the citadel"* (ch. 8, v. 14). When Mordechai went out in royal apparel, the whole city was happy (ch. 8, v. 15).

Ch. 9, vs. 6, 11, and 12 concern the killing on the first day, which took place in *"the citadel."*

Ch. 9, vs. 13, 14, 15, and 18 talk of Shushan, the city, where a second day of fighting occurred, and so *"the citadel"* is omitted. (Ed.)

Shushan *the city* and to hang Haman's ten sons. Then, no one would dare threaten the Jews.

יד   וַיֹּ֤אמֶר הַמֶּ֙לֶךְ֙ לְהֵעָשׂ֣וֹת כֵּ֔ן וַתִּנָּתֵ֥ן דָּ֖ת בְּשׁוּשָׁ֑ן
וְאֵ֛ת עֲשֶׂ֥רֶת בְּנֵֽי־הָמָ֖ן תָּלֽוּ: טו   וַיִּקָּהֲל֣וּ הַיְּהוּדִ֣יִים
אֲשֶׁר־בְּשׁוּשָׁ֗ן גַּ֚ם בְּי֣וֹם אַרְבָּעָ֣ה עָשָׂר֙ לְחֹ֣דֶשׁ אֲדָ֔ר
וַיַּֽהַרְג֣וּ בְשׁוּשָׁ֔ן שְׁלֹ֥שׁ מֵא֖וֹת אִ֑ישׁ וּבַ֨בִּזָּ֔ה לֹ֥א שָֽׁלְח֖וּ
אֶת־יָדָֽם:

14 The king ordered this to be done. A decree was given out in Shushan, and they hanged the ten sons of Haman.

15 The Jews that were in Shushan also assembled on the fourteenth of the month of Adar. They killed three hundred men in Shushan, but did not touch the spoils.

טז   וּשְׁאָ֣ר הַיְּהוּדִ֡ים אֲשֶׁר֩ בִּמְדִינ֨וֹת הַמֶּ֜לֶךְ נִקְהֲל֣וּ ׀
וְעָמֹ֤ד עַל־נַפְשָׁם֙ וְנ֙וֹחַ֙ מֵאֹ֣יְבֵיהֶ֔ם וְהָרֹג֙ בְּשֹׂנְאֵיהֶ֔ם
חֲמִשָּׁ֥ה וְשִׁבְעִ֖ים אָ֑לֶף וּבַ֨בִּזָּ֔ה לֹ֥א שָֽׁלְח֖וּ אֶת־יָדָֽם:

16 The other Jews, who were in the king's provinces, assembled and stood for their lives. They had rest from their enemies and killed fifty-seven thousand of those that hated them, but they did not touch the spoils.

QUESTIONS

THIS entire verse, describing the anihilation of enemies outside of Shushan, is apparently superfluous. Apart from the number of those killed, it seems to tell us very little we do not already know from verses 2, 3, and 5.

FURTHERMORE, there seems to be a contradiction between this verse and verse 2. In verse 2, we learned that *"no man stood up to them."* Here, though, we read that the Jews *"assembled and stood for their lives,"* implying that they were forced to fight.

WHY, in this verse, are we told that the Jews *"had rest from their enemies and killed...those that hated them,"* whereas in verse 5 we read that they *"smote all their enemies with the sword... and they did as they wanted with those who hated them"*?

COMMENTARY

In verse 2[1] we were told what happened in the large, walled cities, where the ministers lived and where regiments of the army were based. These were able to protect the Jews, ensuring that *"no man stood up to them."* The Jews there had no need to fight for their survival.

This verse, though, describes what happened in the un-walled cities — the small towns and villages where there were no ministers to take the side of the Jews and no army to defend them. There, the Jews were attacked by their enemies.

Therefore, **the other Jews, who were in the king's provinces,** and not in the walled cities, **assembled and stood for their lives,** in armed combat, until **they had rest from their enemies,** finally overcoming them. In the heat of battle they had the pretext to annihilate Amalekites and successfully **killed fifty-seven**

---

1. The Hebrew text of the Malbim's commentary refers to this as being בפסוק ג. This should really be verse 2, not 3.

thousand of those that hated them. In the walled cities, where *"no man stood up to them,"*[1] there was no battle and no justification for killing them. Instead, they merely *"did as they wanted with those who hated them,"* humiliating and shaming them.

יז   בְּיוֹם־שְׁלוֹשָׁה עָשָׂר לְחֹדֶשׁ אֲדָר וְנוֹחַ בְּאַרְבָּעָה עָשָׂר בּוֹ וְעָשֹׂה אֹתוֹ יוֹם מִשְׁתֶּה וְשִׂמְחָה:
יח   וְהַיְּהוּדִיים אֲשֶׁר־בְּשׁוּשָׁן נִקְהֲלוּ בִּשְׁלוֹשָׁה עָשָׂר בּוֹ וּבְאַרְבָּעָה עָשָׂר בּוֹ וְנוֹחַ בַּחֲמִשָּׁה עָשָׂר בּוֹ וְעָשֹׂה אֹתוֹ יוֹם מִשְׁתֶּה וְשִׂמְחָה:

17 This happened on the thirteenth and they rested on the fourteenth, making it a day of feasting and happiness. 18 But the Jews in Shushan assembled on both the thirteenth and fourteenth, resting on the fifteenth and making it a day of feasting and happiness.

יט   עַל־כֵּן הַיְּהוּדִים הַפְּרָזִים הַיֹּשְׁבִים בְּעָרֵי הַפְּרָזוֹת עֹשִׂים אֵת יוֹם אַרְבָּעָה עָשָׂר לְחֹדֶשׁ אֲדָר שִׂמְחָה וּמִשְׁתֶּה וְיוֹם טוֹב וּמִשְׁלֹחַ מָנוֹת אִישׁ לְרֵעֵהוּ:

19 Therefore, the "open city Jews" — those who live in unwalled cities — made the fourteenth day of the month of Adar one of happiness and feasting, a holiday with sending portions to one another.

---

1. Verse 2.

QUESTIONS

FROM this verse it appears that only those in unwalled cities accepted upon themselves to make a day of *"happiness and feasting,"* and not those in walled cities. Why should this have been so?

WHY did they initially adopt just the fourteenth, whereas Mordechai told them[1] to keep both the fourteenth and fifteenth?[2]

THEY originally kept the day as a *Yom Tov* (יום טוב) — *"a holiday,"* but Mordechai did not institute that it should become a *Yom Tov.*[3] Why?

COMMENTARY

That same year, only those in unwalled cities celebrated with *"happiness and feasting."* This was because the sealed letters that Haman sent, ordering the extermination of the Jews, were never publicized by the governors and officials.[4] No one besides the officials ever knew that the Jews' enemies had been given authorization to annihilate the Jewish people.

The Jews thought one of two possibilities was true. Either that the report that a royal decree had been issued to kill the Jews was entirely false, spread about by the evil Haman. Or that the report was true but the king had rescinded this first decree, replacing it with the second.

Whichever of these was true, there did not seem to be anything miraculous about the fourteenth of Adar. According to the Jews' perception, it was through royal decree that they *"dominated*

---

1. Verse 21.
2. This question and the next are answered by the commentary on this verse in conjunction with that on verse 21.
3. Verse 22 mentions *"feasting and happiness,"* and *"sending portions,"* but not *"holiday."*
4. See commentary on verse 3.

those who hated them." There was no danger that they would be attacked because the army was ready and prepared to protect them. Consequently, they never made days of *"feasting and happiness."*

The Jews in the unwalled cities, though, had been in real danger. Their enemies had attacked them, and there were no army regiments to protect them. Therefore, only **those who live in unwalled cities** made a day **of happiness and feasting.** They even made it **a holiday** — a *Yom Tov* with a prohibition of work. The Jewish people is not allowed to institute new "holidays" with such a prohibition, because of the command against adding to the Torah, בל תוסיף.[1] Here, though, since it applied only to the Jews of unwalled cities, they were considered as "individuals," who are allowed to institute such a holiday for themselves.[2]

---

1. See Devarim 4:2 and 13:1. Many commentators, including Rashi, learn that this prohibition only includes tampering with an existing Torah law. For example, saying that *tzitzis* are to be placed on a garment with *five* and not four corners would be a transgression of this prohibition. However, the institution of a new observance would not.

   Others, though, include a new observance, purporting to be Torah law, under the prohibition. See, for example, *Aderes Eliyahu* of the Vilna Gaon, which explains that Devarim 4:2 prohibits tampering with existing Torah laws, while 13:1 forbids new additions.

   See also Ramban on Devarim 4:2, who writes that Yerovom, in making a festival *"in the month which he had devised of his own heart"* (Melachim I 12:33), transgressed the prohibition against adding to Torah law.

2. This distinction, between the Jewish people as a whole and individuals, does not seem to appear in the sources that discuss the prohibition of adding to Torah law. It may be that the Malbim's intent is clarified by what he wrote in his commentary to ch. 9, v. 31. There he explains that if a new observance is regarded as though it originated from Sinai, then the prohibition is transgressed. If it is undertaken as a "vow," a voluntarily accepted commitment, then it is permissible.

   If all the Jewish people were to accept the festival, then there might be a danger that they would regard it as having the authority of a commandment stemming from Sinai. However, if only certain

כ וַיִּכְתֹּב מָרְדֳּכַי אֶת־הַדְּבָרִים הָאֵלֶּה וַיִּשְׁלַח
סְפָרִים אֶל־כָּל־הַיְּהוּדִים אֲשֶׁר בְּכָל־מְדִינוֹת הַמֶּלֶךְ
אֲחַשְׁוֵרוֹשׁ הַקְּרוֹבִים וְהָרְחוֹקִים:

20 **Mordechai wrote these things and sent
letters to all the Jews in all the provinces
of King Achashverosh, both near and far,**

QUESTIONS

*"MORDECHAI wrote **these things**"* — what things?

COMMENTARY

Mordechai saw that the Jews in the walled cities had not
celebrated days of Purim, due to their lack of awareness of how
gravely dangerous their situation had been and how extraordinary their deliverance. Haman's decree had never been revoked
and remained in full force, permitting the Jews' slaughter. It was
only the miracle that the fear of Mordechai had fallen upon the
king's officials which made them hide Haman's sealed letters.

Mordechai realized that he needed to write **to all the Jews
in all the provinces,** telling them **these things,** that is, the matters explained in verses 24 and 25. Then they would know that
Haman's decree had been in force all the time and would understand that they had been in serious, mortal danger.

---

communities adopted the observance, there would be no such risk.

Ultimately, all the Jews accepted Purim. However, as we see
from the commentary on verse 31, Esther went to considerable
lengths to emphasize that the observance was not equivalent to
laws commanded at Sinai. (Ed.)

כא לְקַיֵּם עֲלֵיהֶם לִהְיוֹת עֹשִׂים אֵת יוֹם אַרְבָּעָה
עָשָׂר לְחֹדֶשׁ אֲדָר וְאֵת יוֹם־חֲמִשָּׁה עָשָׂר בּוֹ בְּכָל־
שָׁנָה וְשָׁנָה:

21 to establish the annual observance of the fourteenth and fifteenth days of the month of Adar,

QUESTIONS

WHY did Mordechai order that both the fourteenth and fifteenth of Adar should be celebrated?

WHY, merely because the inhabitants of Shushan did not have rest until the fifteenth, did Mordechai institute that *all* walled cities should observe the fifteenth? What was their connection to Shushan?

IF the reason was to honor the capital city, why did Mordechai not establish that all Jews should celebrate the fifteenth? Furthermore, what honor would this confer upon Shushan?

COMMENTARY

Following what we have learned, we can understand why Mordechai distinguished between walled and unwalled cities, the latter to observe the fourteenth and the former the fifteenth.

Haman's decree had ordered *"all the king's provinces to destroy, kill, and eradicate all the Jews...on one day."*[1] It is clear that this decree was not strictly limited to one day — forbidding the murder, after the thirteenth of Adar, of those Jews who had so far escaped their enemies. Haman's aim was to totally obliterate any

---

1. Ch. 3, v. 13.

memory of the Jewish people, and he definitely intended that it was only the start of the annihilation that should take place on the thirteenth. Any Jews found after this day were obviously meant to be killed as well. If, in any city, there were too many Jews to exterminate on one day, the decree clearly directed that they should be killed after the thirteenth.

When Achashverosh sent out the second set of letters, the Jews were given authority to kill their enemies, but *only* on the thirteenth of Adar. It was evident that Achashverosh did not want a never-ending carnage. This can be clearly seen from the fact that Esther had to plead with the king to make an exception and allow the Jews of Shushan an extra day.[1] To achieve this, a special edict had to be issued in Shushan,[2] since Achashverosh's decree only permitted one day.

The consequence of this was that on the fourteenth the Jews were actually in mortal danger. Haman's decree was still in force, not limited to the thirteenth, whereas the Jews were no longer allowed to kill their enemies, their mandate having expired at the end of the thirteenth. If the foes of the Jews would have attacked then, the governors could not save them or support them in their struggle. The extermination of the Jews would be legitimate, with the Jews having no authority to fight back.

Only after the fourteenth had passed did it become clear that officials had concealed the first sealed letters; the Jews' enemies would receive no sanction to harm them. Now the Jews could discern the extent of the miracle. Thus, in all walled cities, the Jews only truly had respite from their enemies on the fifteenth, being under threat on the fourteenth. Therefore, Mordechai ordered all walled cities to observe the fifteenth as Purim. This was not because the Jews of Shushan were still involved in eliminating their enemies on the fourteenth, but because Jews in all walled cities had really been in such grave danger on the fourteenth.

---

1. Verse 13.
2. Verse 14.

In the unwalled cities, however, there were no governors or army regiments. The Jews, themselves, fought and overcame their enemies. By the end of the thirteenth they knew that they were out of danger. Therefore, Mordechai told them to observe the fourteenth.

כב כַּיָּמִים אֲשֶׁר־נָחוּ בָהֶם הַיְּהוּדִים מֵאֹיְבֵיהֶם וְהַחֹדֶשׁ אֲשֶׁר נֶהְפַּךְ לָהֶם מִיָּגוֹן לְשִׂמְחָה וּמֵאֵבֶל לְיוֹם טוֹב לַעֲשׂוֹת אוֹתָם יְמֵי מִשְׁתֶּה וְשִׂמְחָה וּמִשְׁלֹחַ מָנוֹת אִישׁ לְרֵעֵהוּ וּמַתָּנוֹת לָאֶבְיֹנִים:

22 as the days when the Jews had rest from their enemies, and the month which was transformed for them from sorrow to happiness and from mourning to holiday; they were to make them days of feasting and happiness, sending portions to one another and gifts to the poor.

COMMENTARY

The phrase **as the days when the Jews had rest from their enemies** means that the observance of each community should correspond to the day when it had respite from its enemies, in unwalled cities on the fourteenth and in walled cities on the fifteenth.

We are now told why Mordechai instituted that the Jews should make Purim days of feasting and sending portions to one another.

It was **the month which was transformed for them** in two different ways. First, **from sorrow to happiness** and second,

from mourning to holiday. Corresponding to the *"happiness,"* the Jews were to make **days of feasting and happiness.** With regard to *"holiday,"* Mordechai could not institute a holiday, a *Yom Tov.* It is forbidden to institute a new *Yom Tov,* on which work is forbidden, for the entire Jewish people.[1] Instead, Mordechai instituted **gifts to the poor,** something that the unwalled cities had not yet undertaken by themselves. Just as the purpose of a *Yom Tov* is to separate oneself from the pursuit of the material and to concentrate on the spiritual, so, too, giving *tzedakah,* financial support to the poor, is a separation from the material in pursuit of the spiritual.

כג וְקִבֵּל הַיְּהוּדִים אֵת אֲשֶׁר־הֵחֵלּוּ לַעֲשׂוֹת וְאֵת
אֲשֶׁר־כָּתַב מָרְדֳּכַי אֲלֵיהֶם:

23 **The Jews undertook to continue what they had begun to practice, and what Mordechai wrote to them.**

QUESTIONS

IT seems from this verse that the Jews undertook two different observances — *"what they had begun to practice"* and *"what Mordechai wrote to them."* Surely these are identical — both being the celebration of days of *"feasting and happiness"*!

COMMENTARY

The Jews all **undertook** to observe Purim. With some this was **to continue what they had begun to practice** — those of

---

1. See verse 19 with commentary and footnotes.

unwalled cities who already celebrated on the fourteenth, based on their own initiative. Those of walled cities, though, had not begun to observe Purim on their own, and they accepted **what Mordechai wrote to them** — to observe the fifteenth.

כד   כִּי הָמָן בֶּן־הַמְּדָתָא הָאֲגָגִי צֹרֵר כָּל־הַיְּהוּדִים חָשַׁב עַל־הַיְּהוּדִים לְאַבְּדָם וְהִפִּיל פּוּר הוּא הַגּוֹרָל לְהֻמָּם וּלְאַבְּדָם:

24 **That Haman, the son of Hamdatha, the Agagite, the oppressor of all the Jews, had schemed against the Jews to eradicate them, and had cast a *pur*, which is a lot, to crush them and to eradicate them;**

QUESTIONS

WHY are we again told Haman's lineage, which we already know?[1]

WHY are we told that Haman originally *"schemed against the Jews to eradicate them"* whereas the lot was cast *"to crush them and to eradicate them"*?

WHY is the casting of *"a pur"* mentioned here?

COMMENTARY

We are now told what Mordechai wrote to the Jews. This verse is the continuation of verse 20, which recounted that *"Mor-*

---

1. See ch. 3, vs. 1 and 10; ch. 8, v. 5.

dechai wrote these things" without telling us what they were.[1]

He informed them about the true nature and magnitude of their miraculous deliverance.

No one should imagine that Haman's hatred was a personal vendetta against Mordechai for not bowing down to him. **Haman**, because he was an **Agagite** and descended from Amalek, nurtured within himself the rabid hatred of the Jews that had been the hallmark of his ancestors. This was the reason for his being **the oppressor of *all* the Jews**, wanting to see them all annihilated.

The reprieve of the Jews had been especially remarkable because the time was not propitious for the the Jewish people, but one that favored their enemies. Originally, Haman only **schemed** to **eradicate** the Jews — to wipe out their identity as a nation and their religion,[2] without actually killing them. However, after he **cast a *pur***, the constellations that prevailed on the day which the **lot** determined encouraged Haman **to crush them and to eradicate them**, a total extermination of all Jews.[3]

---

1. Many commentaries and translations understand this verse as follows: *"**Because Haman**...had schemed against the Jews,"* i.e., as an explanation of *why* the Jews undertook to do as Mordechai wrote to them.

    The Malbim, though, translates the word כי as *"that"* and not *"because."* The purpose of the verse, according to this translation, is to inform us what are *"these things"* which verse 20 tells us Mordechai wrote.

2. See commentary on ch. 3, v. 9, where the Malbim explains that לאבד, as well as connoting destruction, can mean to obliterate the old form, making something new.

3. This paragraph of the commentary seems to require further thought. In ch. 3, v. 6, we read that after Mordechai had refused to bow, *"Haman wanted to exterminate all the Jews"* — i.e., death. This was already before the lot was cast in verse 7, clearly implying that his desire to physically annihilate the Jews had not been influenced by the *pur*. The distinction that the Malbim makes here, between removing the Jews' national identity and religion, and annihilat-

כה וּבְבֹאָהּ֮ לִפְנֵ֣י הַמֶּ֒לֶךְ֒ אָמַ֣ר עִם־הַסֵּ֔פֶר יָשׁ֞וּב
מַחֲשַׁבְתּ֧וֹ הָרָעָ֛ה אֲשֶׁר־חָשַׁ֥ב עַל־הַיְּהוּדִ֖ים עַל־רֹאשׁ֑וֹ
וְתָל֥וּ אֹת֛וֹ וְאֶת־בָּנָ֖יו עַל־הָעֵֽץ׃

25 but when it came before the king, he
ordered, with the letter, that his
[Haman's] evil scheme, which he had
plotted against the Jews, should rebound
on his own head; and they hanged him
and his sons on the gallows.

QUESTIONS

THE commentators have been greatly challenged in their attempts to explain the meaning of the word ובבאה, which we have
translated as *"but when it came."* What came before the king?

WHAT is the meaning of the puzzling phrase *"with the letter"*?

COMMENTARY

In addition to the fact that the miracle was extraordinary for
having gone against the tide of fortune, it was also remarkable for
having been clearly evident on the day of the decree itself.

For **when it came** — the scheme of Haman referred to in the
previous verse[1] — **before the king**, that is, when the king was in-

---

ing them, was mentioned above, in the commentary on ch. 3, vs. 9
and 13. There, though, the idea of merely removing the identity of
the Jewish people was not Haman's real intention, but merely Haman's way of deceiving the king into sanctioning his decree. (Ed.)

1. The word ובבאה can mean *"and when she came"* (literally *"and with
her coming"*) or *"and when it came,"* where the *"it"* is a feminine
noun. Many commentators, including Rashi, follow the first mean-

formed of how Haman planned to harm the Jews, he did not revoke the first letters. Instead, the sealed letter that Haman had
written would be the instrument to ensure his downfall. The result was that **he ordered, with the letter** — the king's order was
necessitated by Haman's letter. Thereby, because of the letter, it
was inevitable **that his [Haman's] evil scheme...should rebound on his own head.**[1] Since the king could not recall the first
set of letters, and could only send an additional set, he was compelled to hang Haman. Only then would the officials in all provinces ignore the first letters, fearing to meet the same end as Haman. Thus Haman's letters, and the fact that they were still in

---

ing and explain that the *"she"* refers to Esther. The difficulty with
this explanantion is that Esther was last mentioned in verse 13,
twelve verses previously. The use of the feminine possessive suffix
in connection with a person not just mentioned is not straightforward. This is very possibly the reason that the Malbim preferred to
interpret the word according to the second meaning, where the *"it"*
refers to the scheme of Haman referred to in the previous verse.

The question might be asked on the Malbim's interpretation
that the previous verse never referred to Haman's scheme as a
noun, but in a verbal form — *"had schemed against the Jews."* However, our verse does mention the *"scheme"* as a noun and thus,
though the Malbim does not mention this, the possessive suffix
can relate to the noun written later in the same verse. (Ed.)

1. The phrase *"with the letter"* is usually interpreted as a continuation
of *"he ordered,"* describing how Achashverosh conveyed his order.
A difficulty with this interpretation is that the use of the definite article implies that the letter is one we have already encountered.
Since it is a new letter this use of the definite article seems inappropriate.

The Malbim, however, explains that the phrase introduces
"that his evil scheme... should rebound on his own head," and it teaches
why this had to be so. According to this interpretation, the letter in
question is the sealed letter which Haman wrote, and so the use of
the definite article is in place. (Ed.)

force, were the very cause of Haman's execution.[1]

This execution clearly demonstrated that the first letters had not been rescinded. Now the Jews realized that on the thirteenth of Adar they had still been in mortal danger and that the miracle had been at its peak at that time.

כו   עַל־כֵּן קָרְאוּ לַיָּמִים הָאֵלֶּה פוּרִים עַל־שֵׁם
הַפּוּר עַל־כֵּן עַל־כָּל־דִּבְרֵי הָאִגֶּרֶת הַזֹּאת וּמָה־רָאוּ
עַל־כָּכָה וּמָה הִגִּיעַ אֲלֵיהֶם:

26 **Therefore, they called these days "Purim" after the word** *"pur."* **Therefore, because of all the words of this letter, and of what they had seen of this matter and what had happened to them,**

QUESTIONS

WHAT is the significance of the name *"Purim"*?

WHAT is the reason for two clauses in this verse, both starting with *"therefore"*? What is the meaning of the second clause?[2]

COMMENTARY

The name **Purim**, which was called **after the word** *"pur,"* is to remind us of the enormity of the miracle. It is the plural form

---

1.   See ch. 8, vs. 7 and 8, with commentary.

2.   Our translation follows the commentary of the Malbim, and thus, makes it clear that the second *"therefore"* continues into the next verse. This would not be quite so apparent from an initial reading of the Hebrew text.

of *"pur,"* and hints at the fact that the *"pur"* of Haman, the prediction of his success and good fortune, was totally turned around to be *our "pur."*

The second *"therefore"* continues into the next verse. **Therefore, because of all the words of this letter**, which informed the Jews, in great detail, about the full extent of the miracle and how they had been in such great peril even on the thirteenth of Adar itself....

כז   קִיְּמ֣וּ וְקִבֵּ֣ל הַיְּהוּדִים֩ ׀ עֲלֵיהֶ֨ם ׀ וְעַל־זַרְעָ֜ם וְעַ֣ל
כָּל־הַנִּלְוִ֣ים עֲלֵיהֶם֮ וְלֹ֣א יַעֲבֹור֒ לִהְי֣וֹת עֹשִׂ֗ים אֵת־
שְׁנֵ֤י הַיָּמִים֙ הָאֵ֔לֶּה כִּכְתָבָ֖ם וְכִזְמַנָּ֑ם בְּכָל־שָׁנָ֖ה וְשָׁנָֽה׃

27 **the Jews established and accepted upon themselves, upon their offspring, and upon all who would join them, not to lapse, to keep these two days according to their writing, and at their appointed time every year;**

QUESTIONS

WHAT is the meaning of *"not to lapse"*? Surely every enactment is meant to be observed without it lapsing!

WHAT is the meaning of *"according to their writing"* and of *"at their appointed time"*?

COMMENTARY

...In consequence, **the Jews established and accepted upon themselves** several commitments.

First, that the undertaking to celebrate Purim would include both **themselves** and **their offspring.**

Second, that Purim was **not to lapse.** Generally, a Rabbinic enactment passed by a *Beis Din* (Rabbinic legislative body) can be overturned by a subsequent *Beis Din,* if it is both more learned and has more members than that which passed the legislation.[1] In the case of the observance of Purim, though, an exception was made, and it was stipulated that it was *"not to lapse"* under any circumstances.

Third, that the days of Purim were to be **according to their writing,** with public reading of the Megillah — the written account of the Purim story.

Fourth, that the days of Purim were to be kept **at their appointed time every year** — on the fourteenth in unwalled cities and on the fifteenth in walled cities.

כח   וְהַיָּמִים הָאֵלֶּה נִזְכָּרִים וְנַעֲשִׂים בְּכָל־דּוֹר וָדוֹר מִשְׁפָּחָה וּמִשְׁפָּחָה מְדִינָה וּמְדִינָה וְעִיר וָעִיר וִימֵי הַפּוּרִים הָאֵלֶּה לֹא יַעַבְרוּ מִתּוֹךְ הַיְּהוּדִים וְזִכְרָם לֹא־יָסוּף מִזַּרְעָם:

28 and that these days should be remembered and observed in every generation by every family, every province, and every city; and that these days of Purim should not pass from among the Jews, and their memory should not cease from their offspring.

---

1. See Rambam, *Mishneh Torah, Hilchos Mamrim* 2:2.

COMMENTARY

The **days should be remembered** by the reading the Megillah[1] **and observed** with *"feasting and happiness, sending portions to one another and gifts to the poor."*[2]

כט °וַתִּכְתֹּב אֶסְתֵּר הַמַּלְכָּה בַת־אֲבִיחַיִל וּמָרְדֳּכַי הַיְּהוּדִי אֶת־כָּל־ תֹּקֶף לְקַיֵּם אֵת אִגֶּרֶת הַפּוּרִים הַזֹּאת הַשֵּׁנִית:

29 **Esther the queen, the daughter of Avichayil, and Mordechai the Jew wrote, with all power, to confirm this second letter of Purim.**

QUESTIONS

WHY did Esther write a *"second letter of Purim"*?

WHAT is *"with all power"*?

WHAT was the *"second letter of Purim"* and what did it add to the first?

COMMENTARY

Esther wanted the Megillah to be included as one of the books of the Holy Writings (כתובים). An argument ensued between the Sages, since it is forbidden to add to the Holy Writings.

---

1. See *Yerushalmi Megillah* 1:1, which explains this verse as the Malbim does.
2. Verse 22.

The Talmud[1] recounts that Esther sent a request to the Sages that she should be commemorated for future generations. Initially the Sages did not agree. There was also opposition to the institution of the days of Purim as a permanent addition to the Jewish calendar, since it is forbidden to add to Torah law.[2]

Therefore, Esther joined forces with Mordechai and, **with all** the power of the throne behind them, wrote **to confirm this second letter of Purim**, that is, to establish the letter itself. This second letter was the text of the Megillah as we have it, from the words *"And it came to pass in the days of Achashverosh"* to *"all its offspring."* Esther wrote to the Sages, telling them that this letter, the Megillah, should become part of the Holy Writings.

לْ וַיִּשְׁלַח סְפָרִים אֶל־כָּל־הַיְּהוּדִים אֶל־שֶׁבַע
וְעֶשְׂרִים וּמֵאָה מְדִינָה מַלְכוּת אֲחַשְׁוֵרוֹשׁ דִּבְרֵי
שָׁלוֹם וֶאֱמֶת:

30 **He sent letters to all the Jews, to all one hundred and twenty-seven provinces of Achashverosh's kingdom, containing words of peace and truth,**

Questions

WHAT were *"words of peace and truth"*?

Commentary

Since there had been argument between the Sages, Esther[3]

---

1. *Megillah* 7a.
2. See commentary on verses 19 and 22.
3. The verb used in the previous verse is ותכתב — literally "and *she* wrote." The verb used in this verse is וישלח — literally "and *he* sent."

wrote **words of peace**, persuading them to come to agreement, and requested **truth**, convinced that the *halachah*, the correct Torah position, was as she said.

לֹא   לְקַיֵּם אֶת־יְמֵי הַפֻּרִים הָאֵלֶּה בִּזְמַנֵּיהֶם כַּאֲשֶׁר
קִיַּם עֲלֵיהֶם מָרְדֳּכַי הַיְּהוּדִי וְאֶסְתֵּר הַמַּלְכָּה וְכַאֲשֶׁר
קִיְּמוּ עַל־ נַפְשָׁם וְעַל־זַרְעָם דִּבְרֵי הַצּוֹמוֹת
וְזַעֲקָתָם:

31 **to establish these days of Purim in their appointed time, as Mordechai the Jew and Esther the queen had ordained for them, and as they had accepted, upon themselves and upon their offspring, edicts of fasts with lamentation.**

QUESTIONS

WHAT are the *"edicts of fasts with lamentation"*? There seems to be no indication what these fasts were?

SINCE we already know that *"the Jews established and accepted upon themselves,"*[1] why was there a further need *"to establish these days of Purim"*?

The Malbim in his commentary stresses that Esther was the main author of the letter, following the use of the feminine singular verb in verse 29.

It would seem that Mordechai was the main executant of the distribution of the letters, from the use of the masculine singular in this verse. (Ed.)

1. Verse 27.

COMMENTARY

To refute the argument that it was impossible to institute a festival as a permanent addition to the Jewish calendar, Esther responded that this would only be forbidden if it was accepted as being a Torah law, with equal status to the commandments received at Sinai. However, if it had the status of a vow, a commitment undertaken voluntarily and not regarded as stemming from any Divine imperative, it would be permissible.[1]

Esther maintained that the days would not be accepted as Torah law, but **as Mordechai the Jew and Esther the queen had ordained for them**, and then there would be no problem with the introduction of the festival. She adduced proof from the fact that the Jews **had accepted, upon themselves and upon their offspring, edicts of fasts** — the four fasts: the seventeenth of Tammuz, the ninth of Av, the fast of Gedaliah, and the tenth of Teves.[2] These were not commanded at Sinai, but are derived from

---

1. See Rambam, *Mishneh Torah, Hilchos Mamrim* 2:9.
2. Many commentaries explain that *"the edicts of fasts"* were the three days of fasting that Esther requested of the Jews in Shushan (ch. 4, v. 16).

    An advantage to learning the Malbim's interpretation is that the four fasts have been accepted by the entire Jewish people, and thus can be compared with the institution of the festival of Purim, which was also for the entire Jewish nation.

    Furthermore, there seems to be a textual inference supporting the Malbim's interpretation. We are told that the Jews accepted the fast *"upon themselves and upon their offspring."* The three days of fasting were a one-time observance and not a permanent institution. The phrase *"upon their offspring,"* however, seems to imply that the fasts would continue into the future. One can, perhaps, answer that the phrase teaches us that the children were also obliged to fast. This is not a straightforward answer. Children are not obliged to fast, and even on *Yom Kippur* they are not required to fast the entire fast. A three-day fast would have been even more inappropriate for children.

    If, though, the fasts referred to are the four fasts alluded to in

a verse in the book of Zechariah:[1] "The fast of the fourth (month, i.e., Tammuz), the fast of the fifth (Av), the fast of the seventh (Tishrei, when the fast of Gedaliah is observed), and the fast of the tenth (Teves) shall become times of joy and happiness."

Just as these had been accepted by the Jewish people, without transgressing the prohibition of adding to Torah law, so one could also introduce the festival of Purim.

לב   וּמַאֲמַר אֶסְתֵּר קִיַּם דִּבְרֵי הַפֻּרִים הָאֵלֶּה וְנִכְתָּב בַּסֵּפֶר:

32 The declaration of Esther established these words of Purim, and it was written in the book.

QUESTIONS

WHAT is the meaning of *"the declaration of Esther established"*?

COMMENTARY

The result of **the declaration of Esther** — the arguments for introducing Purim as a festival which she wrote to the Sages — was that she **established these words of Purim**, the Sages agreeing to enforce Purim and establish it as a permanent fixture in the Jewish year.

In addition, **it was written in the book**. Although there had been opposition to including the Megillah in the book of Holy Writings, eventually all Sages agreed to Esther's request.

---

the book of Zechariah, then these were destined to apply for generations to come, and the phrase *"upon their offspring"* is apt.

1.   Zechariah 8:19.

CHAPTER 10

י א   וַיָּשֶׂם הַמֶּלֶךְ אֲחַשְׁרֹשׁ ׀ מַס עַל־הָאָרֶץ וְאִיֵּי
הַיָּם: ב   וְכָל־מַעֲשֵׂה תָקְפּוֹ וּגְבוּרָתוֹ וּפָרָשַׁת גְּדֻלַּת
מָרְדֳּכַי אֲשֶׁר גִּדְּלוֹ הַמֶּלֶךְ הֲלוֹא־הֵם כְּתוּבִים עַל־
סֵפֶר דִּבְרֵי הַיָּמִים לְמַלְכֵי מָדַי וּפָרָס:

1 King Achashverosh placed a tax upon the land and upon the islands of the sea.
2 And all the acts of his power and his might, and the account of the greatness of Mordechai and how the king promoted him, are recorded in the book of chronicles of the kings of Persia and Media.

QUESTIONS

WHY did Achashverosh levy a tax, and why are we told about it?

WHAT is the relevance of the *"power"* and *"might"* of Achashverosh to the Megillah?

COMMENTARY

Mordechai was so successful in governing the affairs of the empire that he managed to conquer many foreign countries with the king's army.[1] This enabled Achashverosh to collect the tribute of a **tax** both from countries that had shared a **land** border with his empire and also from distant **islands of the sea**.

To give honor to the king, this success was attributed to him. In truth, it was Mordechai's achievement.

And all the acts of his power and his might which were brought about through Mordechai's accomplishments, and how, as a result, **the king** further **promoted him**, are **recorded in the book of chronicles.**

ג   כִּי ׀ מָרְדֳּכַי הַיְּהוּדִי מִשְׁנֶה לַמֶּלֶךְ אֲחַשְׁוֵרוֹשׁ
וְגָדוֹל לַיְּהוּדִים וְרָצוּי לְרֹב אֶחָיו דֹּרֵשׁ טוֹב לְעַמּוֹ
וְדֹבֵר שָׁלוֹם לְכָל־זַרְעוֹ:

3 **For Mordechai the Jew was second-in-command to King Achashverosh, was great among the Jews, popular with most of his brethren; he sought the good of his people and spoke peace to all its offspring.**

---

1. See commentary on ch. 9, v. 4.

Commentary

Mordechai remained at the pinnacle of political power with unceasing success. Even though he was **second-in-command to King Achashverosh**, and **great among the Jews**, administering their affairs, he was still **popular with most of his brethren.** This was because **he sought the good of his people**[1] and did not act in an overbearing manner, but with peace and honesty.

---

1. Although the Malbim mentions, in his commentary, the phrase *"he sought the good of his people,"* he does not mention *"and spoke peace to all its offspring."* This final phrase of the Megillah is ambiguous. The word זרעו can be translated as *"his offspring,"* in which case it would refer to the offspring of Mordechai. Many commentators explain it this way.

    It can also mean *"its offspring,"* referring to the offspring of Mordechai's *"people."* Rashi is one of the commentators who follows this interpretation.

    Since the Malbim does not mention the phrase, there would not seem to be any evidence as to how he would have translated these words. Perhaps a slight indication might be that, in explaining how Mordechai dealt with his people, the Malbim uses the phrase "with peace and honesty." The word "peace" echoes the word used in the phrase *"and spoke **peace** to all its offspring."* This may imply that the Malbim understood that this phrase also concerns the people, describing how Mordechai treated its offspring. Therefore, we followed Rashi s interpretation and used the translation *"its offspring."* (Ed.)

Appendix

Achashverosh —Innocent or Guilty?

The Coexistence of Pshat and Drash

A surprise which many readers encounter when studying the Malbim's commentary on Megillas Esther is the portrait of Achashverosh that emerges. According to the Malbim, he is an innocent man, with no evil designs against the Jewish nation, who was deceived by the scheming Haman.

To those acquainted with the way the Sages of the Talmud describe Achashverosh, this comes as a shock. In *Maseches Megillah* 11a, we are taught that the apparently superfluous phrase *"he was the Achashverosh"* in the opening verse of the Megillah teaches us that he was the same *evil* man from the start of the narrative until its conclusion. His wicked rule is compared to that of Nevuchadnetzar.

More specifically, Achashverosh's attitude to Haman's plot to destroy the Jewish people is described by our Sages[1] with a parable: There were two men, one of whom had a mound of earth in his field, while the other had a ditch in his field. The owner of the ditch was willing to offer money to obtain the mound of earth to fill his ditch. The other was willing to pay to dispose of his mound in the ditch. When they met each other, the owner of the

---

1. *Megillah* 14a.

ditch asked the owner of the mound to sell it to him. The response was "Take it for free." Similarly, Achashverosh was only too happy to have Haman rid him of the Jews.

How is the Malbim's commentary to be reconciled with these teachings of our Sages? An answer may be found in a fascinating explanation by Rav Yaakov Kamenetsky, *zt"l*, in the collection of his insights on the weekly Torah reading, *Emess LeYaakov*.

In the narrative of Yosef and his brothers, Yosef frames his brother Binyamin and accuses him of stealing his silver goblet. He allows the other brothers to go free, retaining only Binyamin as his slave. Yehudah, unaware that the man in front of him is really his brother Yosef, approaches him to plead for Binyamin's release. His opening words are: "Please, my master, let your servant speak a word in the ears of my master, and do not be angry with your servant, for you are like Pharaoh."[1]

This seems to be an expression of great respect and deference. Rashi in his commentary, however, quotes our Sages who explain it differently:

> *For you are like Pharaoh.* The straightforward meaning is that "I regard you as important as a king." The Midrashic explanation is, "You will be punished for this with *tzora'as*[2] just as Pharaoh was afflicted with *tzora'as* for retaining my great-grandmother against her will for one night." Another explanation is, "Just as Pharaoh decrees and does not abide by his decrees, and promises without keeping his word, so do you. Is this the fulfillment of your assurance that you merely wished to set eyes on him [Binyamin]?" Another explanation is, "For you are like Pharaoh — if you provoke

---

1. Bereishis 44:18.
2. A type of skin disease meted out as Divine punishment.

me, I will kill both you and your master [Pharaoh]."

Rashi explains the *pshat* — the straightforward meaning of the text — that Yehudah is speaking to Yosef with great respect. Then Rashi brings three explanations of *drash* — Rabbinic interpretations — which teach us that Yehudah is insulting Yosef and even threatening him. These are totally inconsistent with the *pshat*. How is this to be understood?

Rav Yaakov taught that just as there are various types of explanation of the Torah — *pshat*, *drash*, *remez*, and *sod* — so, too, there are corresponding levels in every person.[1] We know that every person has many levels of consciousness. When Yehudah spoke with Tzofnas Paneach (Yosef), a bystander would have seen Yehudah speaking with great respect, just like the *pshat* in his words. However, below the surface Yehudah felt different emotions that ranged from holding Tzofnas Paneach in contempt to a desire to kill him. Thus both the *pshat* and *drash* are true.[2]

Returning to Megillas Esther, we can now understand that the Malbim wrote his commentary according to the *pshat*, which is what an onlooker would have seen if he had been with Achashverosh in his palace. Achashverosh was not consciously aware that Haman planned the destruction of the Jewish people. However, our Sages, using the techniques of *drash*, reveal that in

1. Rav Yaakov Kamenetsky, *zt"l*, develops this idea in his explanation of Bereishis 13:10. Rav Yitzchak Hutner, *zt"l*, in the volume of *Pachad Yitzchok* about Pesach, gives a somewhat similar though more esoteric explanation. See *Ma'amar 52*, paragraph 6.
2. This approach is used by Rav Kamenetsky to explain the apparent contradiction between the *pshat* of Yaakov's message to Esav and the *drash* which Rashi brings in his commentary to Bereishis 33:10. Another example where this idea resolves such a contradiction is the reaction of Yisro on hearing of the deaths of Egyptians at the Reed Sea (Shemos 18:9). According to the *pshat* he was happy, whereas according to the *drash* quoted in Rashi's commentary, he was greatly upset.

deeper levels of consciousness, perhaps in his subconscious mind, he was aware and approved of Haman's plan.

This idea is fundamental to appreciating the depth of Midrashic teaching and to understanding that *pshat* and *drash* do not contradict each other, but shed light on different facets and levels of the truth.

ברכות המגילה

בָּרוּךְ אַתָּה יְהֹוָה אֱלֹהֵינוּ מֶלֶךְ הָעוֹלָם. אֲשֶׁר קִדְּשָׁנוּ בְּמִצְוֹתָיו וְצִוָּנוּ עַל
מִקְרָא מְגִלָּה:
בָּרוּךְ אַתָּה יְהֹוָה אֱלֹהֵינוּ מֶלֶךְ הָעוֹלָם. שֶׁעָשָׂה נִסִּים לַאֲבוֹתֵינוּ בַּיָּמִים הָהֵם
בַּזְּמַן הַזֶּה:
בָּרוּךְ אַתָּה יְהֹוָה אֱלֹהֵינוּ מֶלֶךְ הָעוֹלָם. שֶׁהֶחֱיָנוּ וְקִיְּמָנוּ וְהִגִּיעָנוּ לַזְּמַן הַזֶּה:

א א וַיְהִי בִּימֵי אֲחַשְׁוֵרוֹשׁ הוּא אֲחַשְׁוֵרוֹשׁ הַמֹּלֵךְ מֵהֹדּוּ וְעַד־כּוּשׁ שֶׁבַע
וְעֶשְׂרִים וּמֵאָה מְדִינָה: ב בַּיָּמִים הָהֵם כְּשֶׁבֶת | הַמֶּלֶךְ אֲחַשְׁוֵרוֹשׁ עַל כִּסֵּא
מַלְכוּתוֹ אֲשֶׁר בְּשׁוּשַׁן הַבִּירָה: ג בִּשְׁנַת שָׁלוֹשׁ לְמָלְכוֹ עָשָׂה מִשְׁתֶּה
לְכָל־שָׂרָיו וַעֲבָדָיו חֵיל | פָּרַס וּמָדַי הַפַּרְתְּמִים וְשָׂרֵי הַמְּדִינוֹת לְפָנָיו:
ד בְּהַרְאֹתוֹ אֶת־עֹשֶׁר כְּבוֹד מַלְכוּתוֹ וְאֶת־יְקָר תִּפְאֶרֶת גְּדוּלָּתוֹ יָמִים רַבִּים
שְׁמוֹנִים וּמְאַת יוֹם: ה וּבִמְלוֹאת | הַיָּמִים הָאֵלֶּה עָשָׂה הַמֶּלֶךְ לְכָל־הָעָם
הַנִּמְצְאִים בְּשׁוּשַׁן הַבִּירָה לְמִגָּדוֹל וְעַד־קָטָן מִשְׁתֶּה שִׁבְעַת יָמִים בַּחֲצַר גִּנַּת
בִּיתַן הַמֶּלֶךְ: ו חוּר | כַּרְפַּס וּתְכֵלֶת אָחוּז בְּחַבְלֵי־בוּץ וְאַרְגָּמָן עַל־גְּלִילֵי
כֶסֶף וְעַמּוּדֵי שֵׁשׁ מִטּוֹת | זָהָב וָכֶסֶף עַל רִצְפַת בַּהַט־ וָשֵׁשׁ וְדַר וְסֹחָרֶת:
ז וְהַשְׁקוֹת בִּכְלֵי זָהָב וְכֵלִים מִכֵּלִים שׁוֹנִים וְיַיִן מַלְכוּת רָב כְּיַד הַמֶּלֶךְ:
ח וְהַשְּׁתִיָּה כַדָּת אֵין אֹנֵס כִּי־כֵן | יִסַּד הַמֶּלֶךְ עַל כָּל־רַב בֵּיתוֹ לַעֲשׂוֹת כִּרְצוֹן
אִישׁ־וָאִישׁ: ט גַּם וַשְׁתִּי הַמַּלְכָּה עָשְׂתָה מִשְׁתֵּה נָשִׁים בֵּית הַמַּלְכוּת אֲשֶׁר
לַמֶּלֶךְ אֲחַשְׁוֵרוֹשׁ: י בַּיּוֹם הַשְּׁבִיעִי כְּטוֹב לֵב־הַמֶּלֶךְ בַּיָּיִן אָמַר לִמְהוּמָן בִּזְּתָא
חַרְבוֹנָא בִּגְתָא וַאֲבַגְתָא זֵתַר וְכַרְכַּס שִׁבְעַת הַסָּרִיסִים הַמְשָׁרְתִים אֶת־פְּנֵי
הַמֶּלֶךְ אֲחַשְׁוֵרוֹשׁ: יא לְהָבִיא אֶת־וַשְׁתִּי הַמַּלְכָּה לִפְנֵי הַמֶּלֶךְ בְּכֶתֶר מַלְכוּת
לְהַרְאוֹת הָעַמִּים וְהַשָּׂרִים אֶת־יָפְיָהּ כִּי־טוֹבַת מַרְאֶה הִיא: יב וַתְּמָאֵן הַמַּלְכָּה
וַשְׁתִּי לָבוֹא בִּדְבַר הַמֶּלֶךְ אֲשֶׁר בְּיַד הַסָּרִיסִים וַיִּקְצֹף הַמֶּלֶךְ מְאֹד וַחֲמָתוֹ

בְּעָרָה בֽוֹ: יג וַיֹּאמֶר הַמֶּלֶךְ לַחֲכָמִים יֹדְעֵי הָעִתִּים כִּי־כֵן דְּבַר הַמֶּלֶךְ לִפְנֵי כָּל־יֹדְעֵי דָּת וָדִין: יד וְהַקָּרֹב אֵלָיו כַּרְשְׁנָא שֵׁתָר אַדְמָתָא תַרְשִׁישׁ מֶרֶס מַרְסְנָא מְמוּכָן שִׁבְעַת שָׂרֵי ׀ פָּרַס וּמָדַי רֹאֵי פְּנֵי הַמֶּלֶךְ הַיֹּשְׁבִים רִאשֹׁנָה בַּמַּלְכֽוּת: טו כְּדָת מַה־לַּעֲשֹׂות בַּמַּלְכָּה וַשְׁתִּי עַל ׀ אֲשֶׁר לֹא־עָשְׂתָה אֶת־מַאֲמַר הַמֶּלֶךְ אֲחַשְׁוֵרֹושׁ בְּיַד הַסָּרִיסִֽים: טז וַיֹּאמֶר מְמוּכָן לִפְנֵי הַמֶּלֶךְ וְהַשָּׂרִים לֹא עַל־הַמֶּלֶךְ לְבַדֹּו עָוְתָה וַשְׁתִּי הַמַּלְכָּה כִּי עַל־כָּל־הַשָּׂרִים וְעַל־כָּל־הָעַמִּים אֲשֶׁר בְּכָל־מְדִינֹות הַמֶּלֶךְ אֲחַשְׁוֵרֹֽושׁ: יז כִּי־יֵצֵא דְבַר־ הַמַּלְכָּה עַל־כָּל־הַנָּשִׁים לְהַבְזֹות בַּעְלֵיהֶן בְּעֵינֵיהֶן בְּאָמְרָם הַמֶּלֶךְ אֲחַשְׁוֵרֹושׁ אָמַר לְהָבִיא אֶת־וַשְׁתִּי הַמַּלְכָּה לְפָנָיו וְלֹא־בָֽאָה: יח וְֽהַיֹּום הַזֶּה תֹּאמַרְנָה ׀ שָׂרֹות פָּרַס־וּמָדַי אֲשֶׁר שָׁמְעוּ אֶת־דְּבַר הַמַּלְכָּה לְכֹל שָׂרֵי הַמֶּלֶךְ וּכְדַי בִּזָּיֹון וָקָֽצֶף: יט אִם־עַל־הַמֶּלֶךְ טֹוב יֵצֵא דְבַר־מַלְכוּת מִלְּפָנָיו וְיִכָּתֵב בְּדָתֵי פָרַס־וּמָדַי וְלֹא יַעֲבֹור אֲשֶׁר לֹא־תָבֹוא וַשְׁתִּי לִפְנֵי הַמֶּלֶךְ אֲחַשְׁוֵרֹושׁ וּמַלְכוּתָהּ יִתֵּן הַמֶּלֶךְ לִרְעוּתָהּ הַטֹּובָה מִמֶּֽנָּה: כ וְנִשְׁמַע פִּתְגָם הַמֶּלֶךְ אֲשֶׁר־יַעֲשֶׂה בְּכָל־מַלְכוּתֹו כִּי רַבָּה הִיא וְכָל־הַנָּשִׁים יִתְּנוּ יְקָר לְבַעְלֵיהֶן לְמִגָּדֹול וְעַד־קָטָֽן: כא וַיִּיטַב הַדָּבָר בְּעֵינֵי הַמֶּלֶךְ וְהַשָּׂרִים וַיַּעַשׂ הַמֶּלֶךְ כִּדְבַר מְמוּכָֽן: כב וַיִּשְׁלַח סְפָרִים אֶל־כָּל־מְדִינֹות הַמֶּלֶךְ אֶל־מְדִינָה וּמְדִינָה כִּכְתָבָהּ וְאֶל־עַם וָעָם כִּלְשֹׁנֹו לִהְיֹות כָּל־אִישׁ שֹׂרֵר בְּבֵיתֹו וּמְדַבֵּר כִּלְשֹׁון עַמֹּֽו: ב א אַחַר הַדְּבָרִים הָאֵלֶּה כְּשֹׁךְ חֲמַת הַמֶּלֶךְ אֲחַשְׁוֵרֹושׁ זָכַר אֶת־וַשְׁתִּי וְאֵת אֲשֶׁר־עָשָׂתָה וְאֵת אֲשֶׁר־נִגְזַר עָלֶֽיהָ: ב וַיֹּאמְרוּ נַעֲרֵי־הַמֶּלֶךְ מְשָׁרְתָיו יְבַקְשׁוּ לַמֶּלֶךְ נְעָרֹות בְּתוּלֹות טֹובֹות מַרְאֶֽה: ג וְיַפְקֵד הַמֶּלֶךְ פְּקִידִים בְּכָל־מְדִינֹות מַלְכוּתֹו וְיִקְבְּצוּ אֶת־כָּל־נַעֲרָה־בְתוּלָה טֹובַת מַרְאֶה אֶל־שׁוּשַׁן הַבִּירָה אֶל־בֵּית הַנָּשִׁים אֶל־יַד הֵגֶא סְרִיס הַמֶּלֶךְ שֹׁמֵר הַנָּשִׁים וְנָתֹון תַּמְרֻקֵיהֶֽן: ד וְהַנַּעֲרָה אֲשֶׁר תִּיטַב בְּעֵינֵי הַמֶּלֶךְ תִּמְלֹךְ תַּחַת וַשְׁתִּי וַיִּיטַב הַדָּבָר בְּעֵינֵי הַמֶּלֶךְ וַיַּֽעַשׂ כֵּֽן: ה אִישׁ יְהוּדִי הָיָה בְּשׁוּשַׁן הַבִּירָה וּשְׁמֹו מָרְדֳּכַי בֶּן יָאִיר בֶּן־שִׁמְעִי בֶּן־קִישׁ אִישׁ יְמִינִֽי: ו אֲשֶׁר הָגְלָה מִירוּשָׁלַיִם עִם־הַגֹּלָה אֲשֶׁר הָגְלְתָה עִם יְכָנְיָה מֶֽלֶךְ־יְהוּדָה אֲשֶׁר הֶגְלָה נְבוּכַדְנֶצַּר מֶלֶךְ בָּבֶֽל: ז וַיְהִי אֹמֵן אֶת־הֲדַסָּה הִיא אֶסְתֵּר בַּת־דֹּדֹו כִּי אֵין לָהּ אָב וָאֵם וְהַנַּעֲרָה יְפַת־תֹּאַר וְטֹובַת מַרְאֶה וּבְמֹות אָבִיהָ וְאִמָּהּ לְקָחָהּ מָרְדֳּכַי לֹו לְבַֽת: ח וַיְהִי בְּהִשָּׁמַע דְּבַר־הַמֶּלֶךְ וְדָתֹו וּֽבְהִקָּבֵץ נְעָרֹות רַבֹּות אֶל־שׁוּשַׁן הַבִּירָה אֶל־יַד הֵגָי וַתִּלָּקַח אֶסְתֵּר אֶל־בֵּית הַמֶּלֶךְ אֶל־יַד הֵגַי שֹׁמֵר הַנָּשִֽׁים: ט וַתִּיטַב הַנַּעֲרָה בְעֵינָיו וַתִּשָּׂא חֶסֶד לְפָנָיו וַיְבַהֵל אֶת־תַּמְרוּקֶיהָ וְאֶת־מָנֹותֶהָ לָתֵת לָהּ וְאֵת שֶׁבַע הַנְּעָרֹות הָרְאֻיֹות לָֽתֶת־לָהּ מִבֵּית הַמֶּלֶךְ וַיְשַׁנֶּהָ וְאֶת־נַעֲרֹותֶיהָ

לְטוֹב בֵּית הַנָּשִׁים: י לֹא־הִגִּידָה אֶסְתֵּר אֶת־עַמָּהּ וְאֶת־מוֹלַדְתָּהּ כִּי מָרְדֳּכַי
צִוָּה עָלֶיהָ אֲשֶׁר לֹא־תַגִּיד: יא וּבְכָל־יוֹם וָיוֹם מָרְדֳּכַי מִתְהַלֵּךְ לִפְנֵי חֲצַר
בֵּית־הַנָּשִׁים לָדַעַת אֶת־שְׁלוֹם אֶסְתֵּר וּמַה־יֵּעָשֶׂה בָּהּ: יב וּבְהַגִּיעַ תֹּר נַעֲרָה
וְנַעֲרָה לָבוֹא ׀ אֶל־הַמֶּלֶךְ אֲחַשְׁוֵרוֹשׁ מִקֵּץ הֱיוֹת לָהּ כְּדָת הַנָּשִׁים שְׁנֵים עָשָׂר
חֹדֶשׁ כִּי כֵּן יִמְלְאוּ יְמֵי מְרוּקֵיהֶן שִׁשָּׁה חֳדָשִׁים בְּשֶׁמֶן הַמֹּר וְשִׁשָּׁה חֳדָשִׁים
בַּבְּשָׂמִים וּבְתַמְרוּקֵי הַנָּשִׁים: יג וּבָזֶה הַנַּעֲרָה בָּאָה אֶל־הַמֶּלֶךְ אֵת כָּל־אֲשֶׁר
תֹּאמַר יִנָּתֵן לָהּ לָבוֹא עִמָּהּ מִבֵּית הַנָּשִׁים עַד־בֵּית הַמֶּלֶךְ: יד בָּעֶרֶב ׀ הִיא
בָאָה וּבַבֹּקֶר הִיא שָׁבָה אֶל־בֵּית הַנָּשִׁים שֵׁנִי אֶל־יַד שַׁעַשְׁגַז סְרִיס הַמֶּלֶךְ
שֹׁמֵר הַפִּילַגְשִׁים לֹא־תָבוֹא עוֹד אֶל־הַמֶּלֶךְ כִּי אִם־חָפֵץ בָּהּ הַמֶּלֶךְ וְנִקְרְאָה
בְשֵׁם: טו וּבְהַגִּיעַ תֹּר־ אֶסְתֵּר בַּת־אֲבִיחַיִל ׀ דֹּד מָרְדֳּכַי אֲשֶׁר לָקַח־לוֹ לְבַת
לָבוֹא אֶל־הַמֶּלֶךְ לֹא בִקְשָׁה דָּבָר כִּי אִם אֶת־אֲשֶׁר יֹאמַר הֵגַי סְרִיס־הַמֶּלֶךְ
שֹׁמֵר הַנָּשִׁים וַתְּהִי אֶסְתֵּר נֹשֵׂאת חֵן בְּעֵינֵי כָּל־רֹאֶיהָ: טז וַתִּלָּקַח אֶסְתֵּר
אֶל־הַמֶּלֶךְ אֲחַשְׁוֵרוֹשׁ אֶל־בֵּית מַלְכוּתוֹ בַּחֹדֶשׁ הָעֲשִׂירִי הוּא־ חֹדֶשׁ טֵבֵת
בִּשְׁנַת־שֶׁבַע לְמַלְכוּתוֹ: יז וַיֶּאֱהַב הַמֶּלֶךְ אֶת־אֶסְתֵּר מִכָּל־הַנָּשִׁים וַתִּשָּׂא־חֵן
וָחֶסֶד לְפָנָיו מִכָּל־הַבְּתוּלוֹת וַיָּשֶׂם כֶּתֶר־מַלְכוּת בְּרֹאשָׁהּ וַיַּמְלִיכֶהָ תַּחַת
וַשְׁתִּי: יח וַיַּעַשׂ הַמֶּלֶךְ מִשְׁתֶּה גָדוֹל לְכָל־שָׂרָיו וַעֲבָדָיו אֵת מִשְׁתֵּה אֶסְתֵּר
וַהֲנָחָה לַמְּדִינוֹת עָשָׂה וַיִּתֵּן מַשְׂאֵת כְּיַד הַמֶּלֶךְ: יט וּבְהִקָּבֵץ בְּתוּלוֹת שֵׁנִית
וּמָרְדֳּכַי יֹשֵׁב בְּשַׁעַר־הַמֶּלֶךְ: כ אֵין אֶסְתֵּר מַגֶּדֶת מוֹלַדְתָּהּ וְאֶת־עַמָּהּ כַּאֲשֶׁר
צִוָּה עָלֶיהָ מָרְדֳּכָי וְאֶת־ מַאֲמַר מָרְדֳּכַי אֶסְתֵּר עֹשָׂה כַּאֲשֶׁר הָיְתָה בְאָמְנָה
אִתּוֹ: כא בַּיָּמִים הָהֵם וּמָרְדֳּכַי יוֹשֵׁב בְּשַׁעַר־הַמֶּלֶךְ קָצַף בִּגְתָן וָתֶרֶשׁ
שְׁנֵי־סָרִיסֵי הַמֶּלֶךְ מִשֹּׁמְרֵי הַסַּף וַיְבַקְשׁוּ לִשְׁלֹחַ יָד בַּמֶּלֶךְ אֲחַשְׁוֵרֹשׁ:
כב וַיִּוָּדַע הַדָּבָר לְמָרְדֳּכַי וַיַּגֵּד לְאֶסְתֵּר הַמַּלְכָּה וַתֹּאמֶר אֶסְתֵּר לַמֶּלֶךְ בְּשֵׁם
מָרְדֳּכָי: כג וַיְבֻקַּשׁ הַדָּבָר וַיִּמָּצֵא וַיִּתָּלוּ שְׁנֵיהֶם עַל־עֵץ וַיִּכָּתֵב בְּסֵפֶר דִּבְרֵי
הַיָּמִים לִפְנֵי הַמֶּלֶךְ: ג א אַחַר ׀ הַדְּבָרִים הָאֵלֶּה גִּדַּל הַמֶּלֶךְ אֲחַשְׁוֵרוֹשׁ
אֶת־הָמָן בֶּן־הַמְּדָתָא הָאֲגָגִי וַיְנַשְּׂאֵהוּ וַיָּשֶׂם אֶת־כִּסְאוֹ מֵעַל כָּל־הַשָּׂרִים אֲשֶׁר
אִתּוֹ: ב וְכָל־עַבְדֵי הַמֶּלֶךְ אֲשֶׁר־בְּשַׁעַר הַמֶּלֶךְ כֹּרְעִים וּמִשְׁתַּחֲוִים לְהָמָן
כִּי־כֵן צִוָּה־לוֹ הַמֶּלֶךְ וּמָרְדֳּכַי לֹא יִכְרַע וְלֹא יִשְׁתַּחֲוֶה: ג וַיֹּאמְרוּ עַבְדֵי
הַמֶּלֶךְ אֲשֶׁר־ בְּשַׁעַר הַמֶּלֶךְ לְמָרְדֳּכָי מַדּוּעַ אַתָּה עוֹבֵר אֵת מִצְוַת הַמֶּלֶךְ:
ד וַיְהִי בְּאָמְרָם אֵלָיו יוֹם וָיוֹם וְלֹא שָׁמַע אֲלֵיהֶם וַיַּגִּידוּ לְהָמָן לִרְאוֹת הֲיַעַמְדוּ
דִּבְרֵי מָרְדֳּכַי כִּי־הִגִּיד לָהֶם אֲשֶׁר־הוּא יְהוּדִי: ה וַיַּרְא הָמָן כִּי־אֵין מָרְדֳּכַי
כֹּרֵעַ וּמִשְׁתַּחֲוֶה לוֹ וַיִּמָּלֵא הָמָן חֵמָה: ו וַיִּבֶז בְּעֵינָיו לִשְׁלֹחַ יָד בְּמָרְדֳּכַי לְבַדּוֹ
כִּי־הִגִּידוּ לוֹ אֶת־עַם מָרְדֳּכָי וַיְבַקֵּשׁ הָמָן לְהַשְׁמִיד אֶת־כָּל־הַיְּהוּדִים אֲשֶׁר

בְּכָל־מַלְכוּת אֲחַשְׁוֵרוֹשׁ עַם מָרְדֳּכָי: ז בַּחֹדֶשׁ הָרִאשׁוֹן הוּא־חֹדֶשׁ נִיסָן בִּשְׁנַת
שְׁתֵּים עֶשְׂרֵה לַמֶּלֶךְ אֲחַשְׁוֵרוֹשׁ הִפִּיל פּוּר הוּא הַגּוֹרָל לִפְנֵי הָמָן מִיּוֹם | לְיוֹם
וּמֵחֹדֶשׁ לְחֹדֶשׁ שְׁנֵים־עָשָׂר הוּא־חֹדֶשׁ אֲדָר: ח וַיֹּאמֶר הָמָן לַמֶּלֶךְ אֲחַשְׁוֵרוֹשׁ
יֶשְׁנוֹ עַם־אֶחָד מְפֻזָּר וּמְפֹרָד בֵּין הָעַמִּים בְּכֹל מְדִינוֹת מַלְכוּתֶךָ וְדָתֵיהֶם
שֹׁנוֹת מִכָּל־עָם וְאֶת־דָּתֵי הַמֶּלֶךְ אֵינָם עֹשִׂים וְלַמֶּלֶךְ אֵין־שֹׁוֶה לְהַנִּיחָם:
ט אִם־עַל־הַמֶּלֶךְ טוֹב יִכָּתֵב לְאַבְּדָם וַעֲשֶׂרֶת אֲלָפִים כִּכַּר־כֶּסֶף אֶשְׁקוֹל
עַל־יְדֵי עֹשֵׂי הַמְּלָאכָה לְהָבִיא אֶל־גִּנְזֵי הַמֶּלֶךְ: י וַיָּסַר הַמֶּלֶךְ אֶת־טַבַּעְתּוֹ
מֵעַל יָדוֹ וַיִּתְּנָהּ לְהָמָן בֶּן־הַמְּדָתָא הָאֲגָגִי צֹרֵר הַיְּהוּדִים: יא וַיֹּאמֶר הַמֶּלֶךְ
לְהָמָן הַכֶּסֶף נָתוּן לָךְ וְהָעָם לַעֲשׂוֹת בּוֹ כַּטּוֹב בְּעֵינֶיךָ: יב וַיִּקָּרְאוּ סֹפְרֵי
הַמֶּלֶךְ בַּחֹדֶשׁ הָרִאשׁוֹן בִּשְׁלוֹשָׁה עָשָׂר יוֹם בּוֹ וַיִּכָּתֵב כְּכָל־אֲשֶׁר־צִוָּה הָמָן
אֶל אֲחַשְׁדַּרְפְּנֵי־הַמֶּלֶךְ וְאֶל־הַפַּחוֹת אֲשֶׁר | עַל־מְדִינָה וּמְדִינָה וְאֶל־שָׂרֵי עַם
וָעָם מְדִינָה וּמְדִינָה כִּכְתָבָהּ וְעַם וָעָם כִּלְשׁוֹנוֹ בְּשֵׁם הַמֶּלֶךְ אֲחַשְׁוֵרֹשׁ נִכְתָּב
וְנֶחְתָּם בְּטַבַּעַת הַמֶּלֶךְ: יג וְנִשְׁלוֹחַ סְפָרִים בְּיַד הָרָצִים אֶל־כָּל־מְדִינוֹת
הַמֶּלֶךְ לְהַשְׁמִיד לַהֲרֹג וּלְאַבֵּד אֶת־כָּל־הַיְּהוּדִים מִנַּעַר וְעַד־זָקֵן טַף וְנָשִׁים
בְּיוֹם אֶחָד בִּשְׁלוֹשָׁה עָשָׂר לְחֹדֶשׁ שְׁנֵים־עָשָׂר הוּא־חֹדֶשׁ אֲדָר וּשְׁלָלָם לָבוֹז:
יד פַּתְשֶׁגֶן הַכְּתָב לְהִנָּתֵן דָּת בְּכָל־מְדִינָה וּמְדִינָה גָּלוּי לְכָל־הָעַמִּים לִהְיוֹת
עֲתִדִים לַיּוֹם הַזֶּה: טו הָרָצִים יָצְאוּ דְחוּפִים בִּדְבַר הַמֶּלֶךְ וְהַדָּת נִתְּנָה בְּשׁוּשַׁן
הַבִּירָה וְהַמֶּלֶךְ וְהָמָן יָשְׁבוּ לִשְׁתּוֹת וְהָעִיר שׁוּשָׁן נָבוֹכָה: ד א וּמָרְדֳּכַי יָדַע
אֶת־כָּל־אֲשֶׁר נַעֲשָׂה וַיִּקְרַע מָרְדֳּכַי אֶת־בְּגָדָיו וַיִּלְבַּשׁ שַׂק וָאֵפֶר וַיֵּצֵא בְּתוֹךְ
הָעִיר וַיִּזְעַק זְעָקָה גְדוֹלָה וּמָרָה: ב וַיָּבוֹא עַד לִפְנֵי שַׁעַר־הַמֶּלֶךְ כִּי אֵין
לָבוֹא אֶל־שַׁעַר הַמֶּלֶךְ בִּלְבוּשׁ שָׂק: ג וּבְכָל־מְדִינָה וּמְדִינָה מְקוֹם אֲשֶׁר
דְּבַר־הַמֶּלֶךְ וְדָתוֹ מַגִּיעַ אֵבֶל גָּדוֹל לַיְּהוּדִים וְצוֹם וּבְכִי וּמִסְפֵּד שַׂק וָאֵפֶר
יֻצַּע לָרַבִּים: ד וַתָּבוֹאינָה נַעֲרוֹת אֶסְתֵּר וְסָרִיסֶיהָ וַיַּגִּידוּ לָהּ וַתִּתְחַלְחַל
הַמַּלְכָּה מְאֹד וַתִּשְׁלַח בְּגָדִים לְהַלְבִּישׁ אֶת־מָרְדֳּכַי וּלְהָסִיר שַׂקּוֹ מֵעָלָיו וְלֹא
קִבֵּל: ה וַתִּקְרָא אֶסְתֵּר לַהֲתָךְ מִסָּרִיסֵי הַמֶּלֶךְ אֲשֶׁר הֶעֱמִיד לְפָנֶיהָ וַתְּצַוֵּהוּ
עַל־מָרְדֳּכָי לָדַעַת מַה־זֶּה וְעַל־מַה־זֶּה: ו וַיֵּצֵא הֲתָךְ אֶל־מָרְדֳּכָי אֶל־רְחוֹב
הָעִיר אֲשֶׁר לִפְנֵי שַׁעַר־הַמֶּלֶךְ: ז וַיַּגֶּד־לוֹ מָרְדֳּכַי אֵת כָּל־אֲשֶׁר קָרָהוּ וְאֵת |
פָּרָשַׁת הַכֶּסֶף אֲשֶׁר אָמַר הָמָן לִשְׁקוֹל עַל־גִּנְזֵי הַמֶּלֶךְ בַּיְּהוּדִיים לְאַבְּדָם:
ח וְאֶת־פַּתְשֶׁגֶן כְּתָב־הַדָּת אֲשֶׁר־נִתַּן בְּשׁוּשָׁן לְהַשְׁמִידָם נָתַן לוֹ לְהַרְאוֹת
אֶת־אֶסְתֵּר וּלְהַגִּיד לָהּ וּלְצַוּוֹת עָלֶיהָ לָבוֹא אֶל־הַמֶּלֶךְ לְהִתְחַנֶּן־לוֹ וּלְבַקֵּשׁ
מִלְּפָנָיו עַל־עַמָּהּ: ט וַיָּבוֹא הֲתָךְ וַיַּגֵּד לְאֶסְתֵּר אֵת דִּבְרֵי מָרְדֳּכָי: י וַתֹּאמֶר
אֶסְתֵּר לַהֲתָךְ וַתְּצַוֵּהוּ אֶל־מָרְדֳּכָי: יא כָּל־עַבְדֵי הַמֶּלֶךְ וְעַם־מְדִינוֹת הַמֶּלֶךְ

יֹדְעִים אֲשֶׁר כָּל־אִישׁ וְאִשָּׁה אֲשֶׁר יָבוֹא־אֶל־הַמֶּלֶךְ אֶל־הֶחָצֵר הַפְּנִימִית אֲשֶׁר
לֹא־יִקָּרֵא אַחַת דָּתוֹ לְהָמִית לְבַד מֵאֲשֶׁר יוֹשִׁיט־לוֹ הַמֶּלֶךְ אֶת־שַׁרְבִיט הַזָּהָב
וְחָיָה וַאֲנִי לֹא נִקְרֵאתִי לָבוֹא אֶל־הַמֶּלֶךְ זֶה שְׁלוֹשִׁים יוֹם: יב וַיַּגִּידוּ לְמָרְדֳּכָי
אֵת דִּבְרֵי אֶסְתֵּר: יג וַיֹּאמֶר מָרְדֳּכַי לְהָשִׁיב אֶל־אֶסְתֵּר אַל־תְּדַמִּי בְנַפְשֵׁךְ
לְהִמָּלֵט בֵּית־הַמֶּלֶךְ מִכָּל־הַיְּהוּדִים: יד כִּי אִם־הַחֲרֵשׁ תַּחֲרִישִׁי בָּעֵת הַזֹּאת
רֶוַח וְהַצָּלָה יַעֲמוֹד לַיְּהוּדִים מִמָּקוֹם אַחֵר וְאַתְּ וּבֵית־אָבִיךְ תֹּאבֵדוּ וּמִי יוֹדֵעַ
אִם־לְעֵת כָּזֹאת הִגַּעַתְּ לַמַּלְכוּת: טו וַתֹּאמֶר אֶסְתֵּר לְהָשִׁיב אֶל־מָרְדֳּכָי:
טז לֵךְ כְּנוֹס אֶת־כָּל־ הַיְּהוּדִים הַנִּמְצְאִים בְּשׁוּשָׁן וְצוּמוּ עָלַי וְאַל־תֹּאכְלוּ
וְאַל־תִּשְׁתּוּ שְׁלֹשֶׁת יָמִים לַיְלָה וָיוֹם גַּם־אֲנִי וְנַעֲרֹתַי אָצוּם כֵּן וּבְכֵן אָבוֹא
אֶל־הַמֶּלֶךְ אֲשֶׁר לֹא־כַדָּת וְכַאֲשֶׁר אָבַדְתִּי אָבָדְתִּי: יז וַיַּעֲבֹר מָרְדֳּכָי וַיַּעַשׂ
כְּכֹל אֲשֶׁר־צִוְּתָה עָלָיו אֶסְתֵּר: ה א וַיְהִי ׀ בַּיּוֹם הַשְּׁלִישִׁי וַתִּלְבַּשׁ אֶסְתֵּר
מַלְכוּת וַתַּעֲמֹד בַּחֲצַר בֵּית־הַמֶּלֶךְ הַפְּנִימִית נֹכַח בֵּית הַמֶּלֶךְ וְהַמֶּלֶךְ יוֹשֵׁב
עַל־כִּסֵּא מַלְכוּתוֹ בְּבֵית הַמַּלְכוּת נֹכַח פֶּתַח הַבָּיִת: ב וַיְהִי כִרְאוֹת הַמֶּלֶךְ
אֶת־אֶסְתֵּר הַמַּלְכָּה עֹמֶדֶת בֶּחָצֵר נָשְׂאָה חֵן בְּעֵינָיו וַיּוֹשֶׁט הַמֶּלֶךְ לְאֶסְתֵּר
אֶת־שַׁרְבִיט הַזָּהָב אֲשֶׁר בְּיָדוֹ וַתִּקְרַב אֶסְתֵּר וַתִּגַּע בְּרֹאשׁ הַשַּׁרְבִיט: ג וַיֹּאמֶר
לָהּ הַמֶּלֶךְ מַה־לָּךְ אֶסְתֵּר הַמַּלְכָּה וּמַה־בַּקָּשָׁתֵךְ עַד־חֲצִי הַמַּלְכוּת וְיִנָּתֵן לָךְ:
ד וַתֹּאמֶר אֶסְתֵּר אִם־עַל־הַמֶּלֶךְ טוֹב יָבוֹא הַמֶּלֶךְ וְהָמָן הַיּוֹם אֶל־הַמִּשְׁתֶּה
אֲשֶׁר־עָשִׂיתִי לוֹ: ה וַיֹּאמֶר הַמֶּלֶךְ מַהֲרוּ אֶת־הָמָן לַעֲשׂוֹת אֶת־דְּבַר אֶסְתֵּר
וַיָּבֹא הַמֶּלֶךְ וְהָמָן אֶל־הַמִּשְׁתֶּה אֲשֶׁר־עָשְׂתָה אֶסְתֵּר: ו וַיֹּאמֶר הַמֶּלֶךְ לְאֶסְתֵּר
בְּמִשְׁתֵּה הַיַּיִן מַה־שְּׁאֵלָתֵךְ וְיִנָּתֵן לָךְ וּמַה־בַּקָּשָׁתֵךְ עַד־חֲצִי הַמַּלְכוּת וְתֵעָשׂ:
ז וַתַּעַן אֶסְתֵּר וַתֹּאמַר שְׁאֵלָתִי וּבַקָּשָׁתִי: ח אִם־מָצָאתִי חֵן בְּעֵינֵי הַמֶּלֶךְ
וְאִם־עַל־הַמֶּלֶךְ טוֹב לָתֵת אֶת־ שְׁאֵלָתִי וְלַעֲשׂוֹת אֶת־בַּקָּשָׁתִי יָבוֹא הַמֶּלֶךְ
וְהָמָן אֶל־ הַמִּשְׁתֶּה אֲשֶׁר אֶעֱשֶׂה לָהֶם וּמָחָר אֶעֱשֶׂה כִּדְבַר הַמֶּלֶךְ: ט וַיֵּצֵא
הָמָן בַּיּוֹם הַהוּא שָׂמֵחַ וְטוֹב לֵב וְכִרְאוֹת הָמָן אֶת־מָרְדֳּכַי בְּשַׁעַר הַמֶּלֶךְ
וְלֹא־קָם וְלֹא־זָע מִמֶּנּוּ וַיִּמָּלֵא הָמָן עַל־מָרְדֳּכַי חֵמָה: י וַיִּתְאַפַּק הָמָן וַיָּבוֹא
אֶל־בֵּיתוֹ וַיִּשְׁלַח וַיָּבֵא אֶת־אֹהֲבָיו וְאֶת־ זֶרֶשׁ אִשְׁתּוֹ: יא וַיְסַפֵּר לָהֶם הָמָן
אֶת־כְּבוֹד עָשְׁרוֹ וְרֹב בָּנָיו וְאֵת כָּל־אֲשֶׁר גִּדְּלוֹ הַמֶּלֶךְ וְאֵת אֲשֶׁר נִשְּׂאוֹ
עַל־הַשָּׂרִים וְעַבְדֵי הַמֶּלֶךְ: יב וַיֹּאמֶר הָמָן אַף לֹא־ הֵבִיאָה אֶסְתֵּר הַמַּלְכָּה
עִם־הַמֶּלֶךְ אֶל־הַמִּשְׁתֶּה אֲשֶׁר־ עָשָׂתָה כִּי אִם־אוֹתִי וְגַם־לְמָחָר אֲנִי קָרוּא־
לָהּ עִם־ הַמֶּלֶךְ: יג וְכָל־זֶה אֵינֶנּוּ שֹׁוֶה לִי בְּכָל־עֵת אֲשֶׁר אֲנִי רֹאֶה
אֶת־מָרְדֳּכַי הַיְּהוּדִי יוֹשֵׁב בְּשַׁעַר הַמֶּלֶךְ: יד וַתֹּאמֶר לוֹ זֶרֶשׁ אִשְׁתּוֹ וְכָל־
אֹהֲבָיו יַעֲשׂוּ־עֵץ גָּבֹהַּ חֲמִשִּׁים אַמָּה וּבַבֹּקֶר ׀ אֱמֹר לַמֶּלֶךְ וְיִתְלוּ אֶת־מָרְדֳּכַי

עָלָיו וּבָא עִם־הַמֶּלֶךְ אֶל־הַמִּשְׁתֶּה שָׂמֵחַ וְטוֹב לֵב וַיִּיטַב הַדָּבָר לִפְנֵי הָמָן וַיַּעַשׂ הָעֵץ:

ו א בַּלַּיְלָה הַהוּא נָדְדָה שְׁנַת הַמֶּלֶךְ וַיֹּאמֶר לְהָבִיא אֶת־סֵפֶר הַזִּכְרֹנוֹת דִּבְרֵי הַיָּמִים וַיִּהְיוּ נִקְרָאִים לִפְנֵי הַמֶּלֶךְ: ב וַיִּמָּצֵא כָתוּב אֲשֶׁר הִגִּיד מָרְדֳּכַי עַל־בִּגְתָנָא וָתֶרֶשׁ שְׁנֵי סָרִיסֵי הַמֶּלֶךְ מִשֹּׁמְרֵי הַסַּף אֲשֶׁר בִּקְשׁוּ לִשְׁלֹחַ יָד בַּמֶּלֶךְ אֲחַשְׁוֵרוֹשׁ: ג וַיֹּאמֶר הַמֶּלֶךְ מַה־נַּעֲשָׂה יְקָר וּגְדוּלָּה לְמָרְדֳּכַי עַל־זֶה וַיֹּאמְרוּ נַעֲרֵי הַמֶּלֶךְ מְשָׁרְתָיו לֹא־נַעֲשָׂה עִמּוֹ דָּבָר: ד וַיֹּאמֶר הַמֶּלֶךְ מִי בֶחָצֵר וְהָמָן בָּא לַחֲצַר בֵּית־הַמֶּלֶךְ הַחִיצוֹנָה לֵאמֹר לַמֶּלֶךְ לִתְלוֹת אֶת־מָרְדֳּכַי עַל־הָעֵץ אֲשֶׁר־הֵכִין לוֹ: ה וַיֹּאמְרוּ נַעֲרֵי הַמֶּלֶךְ אֵלָיו הִנֵּה הָמָן עֹמֵד בֶּחָצֵר וַיֹּאמֶר הַמֶּלֶךְ יָבוֹא: ו וַיָּבוֹא הָמָן וַיֹּאמֶר לוֹ הַמֶּלֶךְ מַה־לַעֲשׂוֹת בָּאִישׁ אֲשֶׁר הַמֶּלֶךְ חָפֵץ בִּיקָרוֹ וַיֹּאמֶר הָמָן בְּלִבּוֹ לְמִי יַחְפֹּץ הַמֶּלֶךְ לַעֲשׂוֹת יְקָר יוֹתֵר מִמֶּנִּי: ז וַיֹּאמֶר הָמָן אֶל־הַמֶּלֶךְ אִישׁ אֲשֶׁר הַמֶּלֶךְ חָפֵץ בִּיקָרוֹ: ח יָבִיאוּ לְבוּשׁ מַלְכוּת אֲשֶׁר לָבַשׁ־בּוֹ הַמֶּלֶךְ וְסוּס אֲשֶׁר רָכַב עָלָיו הַמֶּלֶךְ וַאֲשֶׁר נִתַּן כֶּתֶר מַלְכוּת בְּרֹאשׁוֹ: ט וְנָתוֹן הַלְּבוּשׁ וְהַסּוּס עַל־יַד־אִישׁ מִשָּׂרֵי הַמֶּלֶךְ הַפַּרְתְּמִים וְהִלְבִּישׁוּ אֶת־הָאִישׁ אֲשֶׁר הַמֶּלֶךְ חָפֵץ בִּיקָרוֹ וְהִרְכִּיבֻהוּ עַל־הַסּוּס בִּרְחוֹב הָעִיר וְקָרְאוּ לְפָנָיו כָּכָה יֵעָשֶׂה לָאִישׁ אֲשֶׁר הַמֶּלֶךְ חָפֵץ בִּיקָרוֹ: י וַיֹּאמֶר הַמֶּלֶךְ לְהָמָן מַהֵר קַח אֶת־הַלְּבוּשׁ וְאֶת־הַסּוּס כַּאֲשֶׁר דִּבַּרְתָּ וַעֲשֵׂה־כֵן לְמָרְדֳּכַי הַיְּהוּדִי הַיּוֹשֵׁב בְּשַׁעַר הַמֶּלֶךְ אַל־תַּפֵּל דָּבָר מִכֹּל אֲשֶׁר דִּבַּרְתָּ: יא וַיִּקַּח הָמָן אֶת־הַלְּבוּשׁ וְאֶת־הַסּוּס וַיַּלְבֵּשׁ אֶת־מָרְדֳּכַי וַיַּרְכִּיבֵהוּ בִּרְחוֹב הָעִיר וַיִּקְרָא לְפָנָיו כָּכָה יֵעָשֶׂה לָאִישׁ אֲשֶׁר הַמֶּלֶךְ חָפֵץ בִּיקָרוֹ: יב וַיָּשָׁב מָרְדֳּכַי אֶל־שַׁעַר הַמֶּלֶךְ וְהָמָן נִדְחַף אֶל־בֵּיתוֹ אָבֵל וַחֲפוּי רֹאשׁ: יג וַיְסַפֵּר הָמָן לְזֶרֶשׁ אִשְׁתּוֹ וּלְכָל־אֹהֲבָיו אֵת כָּל־אֲשֶׁר קָרָהוּ וַיֹּאמְרוּ לוֹ חֲכָמָיו וְזֶרֶשׁ אִשְׁתּוֹ אִם מִזֶּרַע הַיְּהוּדִים מָרְדֳּכַי אֲשֶׁר הַחִלּוֹתָ לִנְפֹּל לְפָנָיו לֹא־תוּכַל לוֹ כִּי־נָפוֹל תִּפּוֹל לְפָנָיו: יד עוֹדָם מְדַבְּרִים עִמּוֹ וְסָרִיסֵי הַמֶּלֶךְ הִגִּיעוּ וַיַּבְהִלוּ לְהָבִיא אֶת־הָמָן אֶל־הַמִּשְׁתֶּה אֲשֶׁר־עָשְׂתָה אֶסְתֵּר: ז א וַיָּבֹא הַמֶּלֶךְ וְהָמָן לִשְׁתּוֹת עִם־אֶסְתֵּר הַמַּלְכָּה: ב וַיֹּאמֶר הַמֶּלֶךְ לְאֶסְתֵּר גַּם בַּיּוֹם הַשֵּׁנִי בְּמִשְׁתֵּה הַיַּיִן מַה־שְּׁאֵלָתֵךְ אֶסְתֵּר הַמַּלְכָּה וְתִנָּתֵן לָךְ וּמַה־בַּקָּשָׁתֵךְ עַד־חֲצִי הַמַּלְכוּת וְתֵעָשׂ: ג וַתַּעַן אֶסְתֵּר הַמַּלְכָּה וַתֹּאמַר אִם־מָצָאתִי חֵן בְּעֵינֶיךָ הַמֶּלֶךְ וְאִם־עַל־הַמֶּלֶךְ טוֹב תִּנָּתֶן־לִי נַפְשִׁי בִּשְׁאֵלָתִי וְעַמִּי בְּבַקָּשָׁתִי: ד כִּי נִמְכַּרְנוּ אֲנִי וְעַמִּי לְהַשְׁמִיד לַהֲרוֹג וּלְאַבֵּד וְאִלּוּ לַעֲבָדִים וְלִשְׁפָחוֹת נִמְכַּרְנוּ הֶחֱרַשְׁתִּי כִּי אֵין הַצָּר שֹׁוֶה בְּנֵזֶק הַמֶּלֶךְ: ה וַיֹּאמֶר הַמֶּלֶךְ אֲחַשְׁוֵרוֹשׁ וַיֹּאמֶר לְאֶסְתֵּר הַמַּלְכָּה מִי הוּא זֶה וְאֵי־זֶה הוּא אֲשֶׁר־מְלָאוֹ לִבּוֹ לַעֲשׂוֹת כֵּן: ו וַתֹּאמֶר אֶסְתֵּר אִישׁ צַר וְאוֹיֵב הָמָן הָרַע הַזֶּה וְהָמָן נִבְעַת

מִלִּפְנֵי הַמֶּלֶךְ וְהַמַּלְכָּה: ז וְהַמֶּלֶךְ קָם בַּחֲמָתוֹ מִמִּשְׁתֵּה הַיַּיִן אֶל־גִּנַּת הַבִּיתָן וְהָמָן עָמַד לְבַקֵּשׁ עַל־נַפְשׁוֹ מֵאֶסְתֵּר הַמַּלְכָּה כִּי רָאָה כִּי־כָלְתָה אֵלָיו הָרָעָה מֵאֵת הַמֶּלֶךְ: ח וְהַמֶּלֶךְ שָׁב מִגִּנַּת הַבִּיתָן אֶל־בֵּית | מִשְׁתֵּה הַיַּיִן וְהָמָן נֹפֵל עַל־הַמִּטָּה אֲשֶׁר אֶסְתֵּר עָלֶיהָ וַיֹּאמֶר הַמֶּלֶךְ הֲגַם לִכְבּוֹשׁ אֶת־הַמַּלְכָּה עִמִּי בַּבָּיִת הַדָּבָר יָצָא מִפִּי הַמֶּלֶךְ וּפְנֵי הָמָן חָפוּ: ט וַיֹּאמֶר חַרְבוֹנָה אֶחָד מִן־הַסָּרִיסִים לִפְנֵי הַמֶּלֶךְ גַּם הִנֵּה־הָעֵץ אֲשֶׁר־עָשָׂה הָמָן לְמָרְדֳּכַי אֲשֶׁר דִּבֶּר־טוֹב עַל־הַמֶּלֶךְ עֹמֵד בְּבֵית הָמָן גָּבֹהַּ חֲמִשִּׁים אַמָּה וַיֹּאמֶר הַמֶּלֶךְ תְּלֻהוּ עָלָיו: י וַיִּתְלוּ אֶת־הָמָן עַל־הָעֵץ אֲשֶׁר־הֵכִין לְמָרְדֳּכָי וַחֲמַת הַמֶּלֶךְ שָׁכָכָה: ח א בַּיּוֹם הַהוּא נָתַן הַמֶּלֶךְ אֲחַשְׁוֵרוֹשׁ לְאֶסְתֵּר הַמַּלְכָּה אֶת־בֵּית הָמָן צֹרֵר הַיְּהוּדִיים וּמָרְדֳּכַי בָּא לִפְנֵי הַמֶּלֶךְ כִּי־הִגִּידָה אֶסְתֵּר מָה הוּא־לָהּ: ב וַיָּסַר הַמֶּלֶךְ אֶת־טַבַּעְתּוֹ אֲשֶׁר הֶעֱבִיר מֵהָמָן וַיִּתְּנָהּ לְמָרְדֳּכָי וַתָּשֶׂם אֶסְתֵּר אֶת־מָרְדֳּכַי עַל־בֵּית הָמָן: ג וַתּוֹסֶף אֶסְתֵּר וַתְּדַבֵּר לִפְנֵי הַמֶּלֶךְ וַתִּפֹּל לִפְנֵי רַגְלָיו וַתֵּבְךְּ וַתִּתְחַנֶּן־לוֹ לְהַעֲבִיר אֶת־רָעַת הָמָן הָאֲגָגִי וְאֵת מַחֲשַׁבְתּוֹ אֲשֶׁר חָשַׁב עַל־הַיְּהוּדִים: ד וַיּוֹשֶׁט הַמֶּלֶךְ לְאֶסְתֵּר אֵת שַׁרְבִט הַזָּהָב וַתָּקָם אֶסְתֵּר וַתַּעֲמֹד לִפְנֵי הַמֶּלֶךְ: ה וַתֹּאמֶר אִם־עַל־הַמֶּלֶךְ טוֹב וְאִם־מָצָאתִי חֵן לְפָנָיו וְכָשֵׁר הַדָּבָר לִפְנֵי הַמֶּלֶךְ וְטוֹבָה אֲנִי בְּעֵינָיו יִכָּתֵב לְהָשִׁיב אֶת־הַסְּפָרִים מַחֲשֶׁבֶת הָמָן בֶּן־הַמְּדָתָא הָאֲגָגִי אֲשֶׁר כָּתַב לְאַבֵּד אֶת־הַיְּהוּדִים אֲשֶׁר בְּכָל־מְדִינוֹת הַמֶּלֶךְ: ו כִּי אֵיכָכָה אוּכַל וְרָאִיתִי בָּרָעָה אֲשֶׁר־יִמְצָא אֶת־עַמִּי וְאֵיכָכָה אוּכַל וְרָאִיתִי בְּאָבְדַן מוֹלַדְתִּי: ז וַיֹּאמֶר הַמֶּלֶךְ אֲחַשְׁוֵרֹשׁ לְאֶסְתֵּר הַמַּלְכָּה וּלְמָרְדֳּכַי הַיְּהוּדִי הִנֵּה בֵית־הָמָן נָתַתִּי לְאֶסְתֵּר וְאֹתוֹ תָּלוּ עַל־הָעֵץ עַל אֲשֶׁר־שָׁלַח יָדוֹ בַּיְּהוּדִיים: ח וְאַתֶּם כִּתְבוּ עַל־הַיְּהוּדִים כַּטּוֹב בְּעֵינֵיכֶם בְּשֵׁם הַמֶּלֶךְ וְחִתְמוּ בְּטַבַּעַת הַמֶּלֶךְ כִּי־כְתָב אֲשֶׁר־נִכְתָּב בְּשֵׁם־הַמֶּלֶךְ וְנַחְתּוֹם בְּטַבַּעַת הַמֶּלֶךְ אֵין לְהָשִׁיב: ט וַיִּקָּרְאוּ סֹפְרֵי־הַמֶּלֶךְ בָּעֵת־הַהִיא בַּחֹדֶשׁ הַשְּׁלִישִׁי הוּא־חֹדֶשׁ סִיוָן בִּשְׁלוֹשָׁה וְעֶשְׂרִים בּוֹ וַיִּכָּתֵב כְּכָל־אֲשֶׁר־צִוָּה מָרְדֳּכַי אֶל־הַיְּהוּדִים וְאֶל הָאֲחַשְׁדַּרְפְּנִים־וְהַפַּחוֹת וְשָׂרֵי הַמְּדִינוֹת אֲשֶׁר | מֵהֹדּוּ וְעַד־כּוּשׁ שֶׁבַע וְעֶשְׂרִים וּמֵאָה מְדִינָה מְדִינָה וּמְדִינָה כִּכְתָבָהּ וְעַם וָעָם כִּלְשֹׁנוֹ וְאֶל־הַיְּהוּדִים כִּכְתָבָם וְכִלְשׁוֹנָם: י וַיִּכְתֹּב בְּשֵׁם הַמֶּלֶךְ אֲחַשְׁוֵרֹשׁ וַיַּחְתֹּם בְּטַבַּעַת הַמֶּלֶךְ וַיִּשְׁלַח סְפָרִים בְּיַד הָרָצִים בַּסּוּסִים רֹכְבֵי הָרֶכֶשׁ הָאֲחַשְׁתְּרָנִים בְּנֵי הָרַמָּכִים: יא אֲשֶׁר נָתַן הַמֶּלֶךְ לַיְּהוּדִים | אֲשֶׁר בְּכָל־עִיר־וָעִיר לְהִקָּהֵל וְלַעֲמֹד עַל־נַפְשָׁם לְהַשְׁמִיד וְלַהֲרֹג וּלְאַבֵּד אֶת־כָּל־חֵיל עַם וּמְדִינָה הַצָּרִים אֹתָם טַף וְנָשִׁים וּשְׁלָלָם לָבוֹז: יב בְּיוֹם אֶחָד בְּכָל־מְדִינוֹת הַמֶּלֶךְ אֲחַשְׁוֵרֹשׁ בִּשְׁלוֹשָׁה עָשָׂר לְחֹדֶשׁ שְׁנֵים־עָשָׂר הוּא־חֹדֶשׁ אֲדָר:

יג פַּתְשֶׁגֶן הַכְּתָב לְהִנָּתֵן דָּת בְּכָל־מְדִינָה וּמְדִינָה גָּלוּי לְכָל־הָעַמִּים וְלִהְיוֹת
הַיְּהוּדִיים עֲתוּדִים לַיּוֹם הַזֶּה לְהִנָּקֵם מֵאֹיְבֵיהֶם: יד הָרָצִים רֹכְבֵי הָרֶכֶשׁ
הָאֲחַשְׁתְּרָנִים יָצְאוּ מְבֹהָלִים וּדְחוּפִים בִּדְבַר הַמֶּלֶךְ וְהַדָּת נִתְּנָה בְּשׁוּשַׁן
הַבִּירָה: טו וּמָרְדֳּכַי יָצָא | מִלִּפְנֵי הַמֶּלֶךְ בִּלְבוּשׁ מַלְכוּת תְּכֵלֶת וָחוּר וַעֲטֶרֶת
זָהָב גְּדוֹלָה וְתַכְרִיךְ בּוּץ וְאַרְגָּמָן וְהָעִיר שׁוּשָׁן צָהֲלָה וְשָׂמֵחָה: טז לַיְּהוּדִים
הָיְתָה אוֹרָה וְשִׂמְחָה וְשָׂשֹׂן וִיקָר: יז וּבְכָל־ מְדִינָה וּמְדִינָה וּבְכָל־עִיר וָעִיר
מְקוֹם אֲשֶׁר דְּבַר־ הַמֶּלֶךְ וְדָתוֹ מַגִּיעַ שִׂמְחָה וְשָׂשֹׂן לַיְּהוּדִים מִשְׁתֶּה וְיוֹם
טוֹב וְרַבִּים מֵעַמֵּי הָאָרֶץ מִתְיַהֲדִים כִּי־נָפַל פַּחַד־ הַיְּהוּדִים עֲלֵיהֶם: **ט**
א וּבִשְׁנֵים עָשָׂר חֹדֶשׁ הוּא־חֹדֶשׁ אֲדָר בִּשְׁלוֹשָׁה עָשָׂר יוֹם בּוֹ אֲשֶׁר הִגִּיעַ
דְּבַר הַמֶּלֶךְ וְדָתוֹ לְהֵעָשׂוֹת בַּיּוֹם אֲשֶׁר שִׂבְּרוּ אֹיְבֵי הַיְּהוּדִים לִשְׁלוֹט בָּהֶם
וְנַהֲפוֹךְ הוּא אֲשֶׁר יִשְׁלְטוּ הַיְּהוּדִים הֵמָּה בְּשֹׂנְאֵיהֶם: ב נִקְהֲלוּ הַיְּהוּדִים
בְּעָרֵיהֶם בְּכָל־מְדִינוֹת הַמֶּלֶךְ אֲחַשְׁוֵרוֹשׁ לִשְׁלֹחַ יָד בִּמְבַקְשֵׁי רָעָתָם וְאִישׁ
לֹא־עָמַד לִפְנֵיהֶם כִּי־נָפַל פַּחְדָּם עַל־כָּל־הָעַמִּים: ג וְכָל־שָׂרֵי הַמְּדִינוֹת
וְהָאֲחַשְׁדַּרְפְּנִים וְהַפַּחוֹת וְעֹשֵׂי הַמְּלָאכָה אֲשֶׁר לַמֶּלֶךְ מְנַשְּׂאִים אֶת־הַיְּהוּדִים
כִּי־נָפַל פַּחַד־מָרְדֳּכַי עֲלֵיהֶם: ד כִּי־גָדוֹל מָרְדֳּכַי בְּבֵית הַמֶּלֶךְ וְשָׁמְעוֹ הוֹלֵךְ
בְּכָל־הַמְּדִינוֹת כִּי־הָאִישׁ מָרְדֳּכַי הוֹלֵךְ וְגָדוֹל: ה וַיַּכּוּ הַיְּהוּדִים בְּכָל־
אֹיְבֵיהֶם מַכַּת־חֶרֶב וְהֶרֶג וְאַבְדָן וַיַּעֲשׂוּ בְשֹׂנְאֵיהֶם כִּרְצוֹנָם: ו וּבְשׁוּשַׁן
הַבִּירָה הָרְגוּ הַיְּהוּדִים וְאַבֵּד חֲמֵשׁ מֵאוֹת אִישׁ: ז וְאֵת | פַּרְשַׁנְדָּתָא וְאֵת |
דַּלְפוֹן וְאֵת | אַסְפָּתָא: ח וְאֵת | פּוֹרָתָא וְאֵת | אֲדַלְיָא וְאֵת | אֲרִידָתָא: ט וְאֵת
| פַּרְמַשְׁתָּא וְאֵת | אֲרִיסַי וְאֵת | אֲרִדַי וְאֵת | וַיְזָתָא: י עֲשֶׂרֶת בְּנֵי הָמָן
בֶּן־הַמְּדָתָא צֹרֵר הַיְּהוּדִים הָרָגוּ וּבַבִּזָּה לֹא שָׁלְחוּ אֶת־יָדָם: יא בַּיּוֹם הַהוּא
בָּא מִסְפַּר הַהֲרוּגִים בְּשׁוּשַׁן הַבִּירָה לִפְנֵי הַמֶּלֶךְ: יב וַיֹּאמֶר הַמֶּלֶךְ לְאֶסְתֵּר
הַמַּלְכָּה בְּשׁוּשַׁן הַבִּירָה הָרְגוּ הַיְּהוּדִים וְאַבֵּד חֲמֵשׁ מֵאוֹת אִישׁ וְאֵת עֲשֶׂרֶת
בְּנֵי־הָמָן בִּשְׁאָר מְדִינוֹת הַמֶּלֶךְ מֶה עָשׂוּ וּמַה־שְּׁאֵלָתֵךְ וְיִנָּתֵן לָךְ וּמַה־
בַּקָּשָׁתֵךְ עוֹד וְתֵעָשׂ: יג וַתֹּאמֶר אֶסְתֵּר אִם־עַל־ הַמֶּלֶךְ טוֹב יִנָּתֵן גַּם־מָחָר
לַיְּהוּדִים אֲשֶׁר בְּשׁוּשָׁן לַעֲשׂוֹת כְּדָת הַיּוֹם וְאֵת עֲשֶׂרֶת בְּנֵי־הָמָן יִתְלוּ
עַל־הָעֵץ: יד וַיֹּאמֶר הַמֶּלֶךְ לְהֵעָשׂוֹת כֵּן וַתִּנָּתֵן דָּת בְּשׁוּשָׁן וְאֵת עֲשֶׂרֶת
בְּנֵי־הָמָן תָּלוּ: טו וַיִּקָּהֲלוּ הַיְּהוּדִים אֲשֶׁר־בְּשׁוּשָׁן גַּם בְּיוֹם אַרְבָּעָה עָשָׂר
לְחֹדֶשׁ אֲדָר וַיַּהַרְגוּ בְשׁוּשָׁן שְׁלֹשׁ מֵאוֹת אִישׁ וּבַבִּזָּה לֹא שָׁלְחוּ אֶת־יָדָם:
טז וּשְׁאָר הַיְּהוּדִים אֲשֶׁר בִּמְדִינוֹת הַמֶּלֶךְ נִקְהֲלוּ | וְעָמֹד עַל־נַפְשָׁם וְנוֹחַ
מֵאֹיְבֵיהֶם וְהָרוֹג בְּשֹׂנְאֵיהֶם חֲמִשָּׁה וְשִׁבְעִים אָלֶף וּבַבִּזָּה לֹא שָׁלְחוּ אֶת־יָדָם:
יז בְּיוֹם־שְׁלוֹשָׁה עָשָׂר לְחֹדֶשׁ אֲדָר וְנוֹחַ בְּאַרְבָּעָה עָשָׂר בּוֹ וְעָשֹׂה אֹתוֹ יוֹם

מִשְׁתֶּה וְשִׂמְחָה: יח וְהַיְּהוּדִים אֲשֶׁר־בְּשׁוּשָׁן נִקְהֲלוּ בִּשְׁלוֹשָׁה עָשָׂר בּוֹ
וּבְאַרְבָּעָה עָשָׂר בּוֹ וְנוֹחַ בַּחֲמִשָּׁה עָשָׂר בּוֹ וְעָשֹׂה אֹתוֹ יוֹם מִשְׁתֶּה וְשִׂמְחָה:
יט עַל־כֵּן הַיְּהוּדִים הַפְּרָזִים הַיֹּשְׁבִים בְּעָרֵי הַפְּרָזוֹת עֹשִׂים אֵת יוֹם אַרְבָּעָה
עָשָׂר לְחֹדֶשׁ אֲדָר שִׂמְחָה וּמִשְׁתֶּה וְיוֹם טוֹב וּמִשְׁלֹחַ מָנוֹת אִישׁ לְרֵעֵהוּ:
כ וַיִּכְתֹּב מָרְדֳּכַי אֶת־הַדְּבָרִים הָאֵלֶּה וַיִּשְׁלַח סְפָרִים אֶל־כָּל־הַיְּהוּדִים אֲשֶׁר
בְּכָל־מְדִינוֹת הַמֶּלֶךְ אֲחַשְׁוֵרוֹשׁ הַקְּרוֹבִים וְהָרְחוֹקִים: כא לְקַיֵּם עֲלֵיהֶם
לִהְיוֹת עֹשִׂים אֵת יוֹם אַרְבָּעָה עָשָׂר לְחֹדֶשׁ אֲדָר וְאֵת יוֹם־חֲמִשָּׁה עָשָׂר בּוֹ
בְּכָל־שָׁנָה וְשָׁנָה: כב כַּיָּמִים אֲשֶׁר־נָחוּ בָהֶם הַיְּהוּדִים מֵאֹיְבֵיהֶם וְהַחֹדֶשׁ
אֲשֶׁר נֶהְפַּךְ לָהֶם מִיָּגוֹן לְשִׂמְחָה וּמֵאֵבֶל לְיוֹם טוֹב לַעֲשׂוֹת אוֹתָם יְמֵי מִשְׁתֶּה
וְשִׂמְחָה וּמִשְׁלֹחַ מָנוֹת אִישׁ לְרֵעֵהוּ וּמַתָּנוֹת לָאֶבְיֹנִים: כג וְקִבֵּל הַיְּהוּדִים אֵת
אֲשֶׁר־הֵחֵלּוּ לַעֲשׂוֹת וְאֵת אֲשֶׁר־כָּתַב מָרְדֳּכַי אֲלֵיהֶם: כד כִּי הָמָן בֶּן־הַמְּדָתָא
הָאֲגָגִי צֹרֵר כָּל־הַיְּהוּדִים חָשַׁב עַל־הַיְּהוּדִים לְאַבְּדָם וְהִפִּיל פּוּר הוּא הַגּוֹרָל
לְהֻמָּם וּלְאַבְּדָם: כה וּבְבֹאָהּ לִפְנֵי הַמֶּלֶךְ אָמַר עִם־הַסֵּפֶר יָשׁוּב מַחֲשַׁבְתּוֹ
הָרָעָה אֲשֶׁר־חָשַׁב עַל־הַיְּהוּדִים עַל־רֹאשׁוֹ וְתָלוּ אֹתוֹ וְאֶת־בָּנָיו עַל־הָעֵץ:
כו עַל־כֵּן קָרְאוּ לַיָּמִים הָאֵלֶּה פוּרִים עַל־שֵׁם הַפּוּר עַל־כֵּן עַל־כָּל־דִּבְרֵי
הָאִגֶּרֶת הַזֹּאת וּמָה־רָאוּ עַל־כָּכָה וּמָה הִגִּיעַ אֲלֵיהֶם: כז קִיְּמוּ וְקִבְּלוּ הַיְּהוּדִים
עֲלֵיהֶם | וְעַל־זַרְעָם וְעַל כָּל־הַנִּלְוִים עֲלֵיהֶם וְלֹא יַעֲבוֹר לִהְיוֹת עֹשִׂים
אֵת־שְׁנֵי הַיָּמִים הָאֵלֶּה כִּכְתָבָם וְכִזְמַנָּם בְּכָל־שָׁנָה וְשָׁנָה: כח וְהַיָּמִים הָאֵלֶּה
נִזְכָּרִים וְנַעֲשִׂים בְּכָל־דּוֹר וָדוֹר מִשְׁפָּחָה וּמִשְׁפָּחָה מְדִינָה וּמְדִינָה וְעִיר וָעִיר
וִימֵי הַפּוּרִים הָאֵלֶּה לֹא יַעַבְרוּ מִתּוֹךְ הַיְּהוּדִים וְזִכְרָם לֹא־יָסוּף מִזַּרְעָם:
כט וַתִּכְתֹּב אֶסְתֵּר הַמַּלְכָּה בַת־אֲבִיחַיִל וּמָרְדֳּכַי הַיְּהוּדִי אֶת־כָּל־תֹּקֶף לְקַיֵּם
אֵת אִגֶּרֶת הַפּוּרִים הַזֹּאת הַשֵּׁנִית: ל וַיִּשְׁלַח סְפָרִים אֶל־כָּל־הַיְּהוּדִים
אֶל־שֶׁבַע וְעֶשְׂרִים וּמֵאָה מְדִינָה מַלְכוּת אֲחַשְׁוֵרוֹשׁ דִּבְרֵי שָׁלוֹם וֶאֱמֶת:
לא לְקַיֵּם אֶת־יְמֵי הַפֻּרִים הָאֵלֶּה בִּזְמַנֵּיהֶם כַּאֲשֶׁר קִיַּם עֲלֵיהֶם מָרְדֳּכַי
הַיְּהוּדִי וְאֶסְתֵּר הַמַּלְכָּה וְכַאֲשֶׁר קִיְּמוּ עַל־נַפְשָׁם וְעַל־זַרְעָם דִּבְרֵי הַצֹּמוֹת
וְזַעֲקָתָם: לב וּמַאֲמַר אֶסְתֵּר קִיַּם דִּבְרֵי הַפֻּרִים הָאֵלֶּה וְנִכְתָּב בַּסֵּפֶר: י
א וַיָּשֶׂם הַמֶּלֶךְ אֲחַשְׁרֹשׁ | מַס עַל־הָאָרֶץ וְאִיֵּי הַיָּם: ב וְכָל־מַעֲשֵׂה תָקְפּוֹ
וּגְבוּרָתוֹ וּפָרָשַׁת גְּדֻלַּת מָרְדֳּכַי אֲשֶׁר גִּדְּלוֹ הַמֶּלֶךְ הֲלוֹא־הֵם כְּתוּבִים עַל־סֵפֶר
דִּבְרֵי הַיָּמִים לְמַלְכֵי מָדַי וּפָרָס: ג כִּי | מָרְדֳּכַי הַיְּהוּדִי מִשְׁנֶה לַמֶּלֶךְ
אֲחַשְׁוֵרוֹשׁ וְגָדוֹל לַיְּהוּדִים וְרָצוּי לְרֹב אֶחָיו דֹּרֵשׁ טוֹב לְעַמּוֹ וְדֹבֵר שָׁלוֹם
לְכָל־זַרְעוֹ:

ברכה אחר קריאת המגילה

בָּרוּךְ אַתָּה יְהֹוָה אֱלֹהֵינוּ מֶלֶךְ הָעוֹלָם. הָרָב אֶת רִיבֵנוּ. וְהַדָּן אֶת דִּינֵנוּ. וְהַנּוֹקֵם אֶת נִקְמָתֵנוּ. וְהַמְשַׁלֵּם גְּמוּל לְכָל אוֹיְבֵי נַפְשֵׁנוּ. וְהַנִּפְרָע לָנוּ מִצָּרֵינוּ. בָּרוּךְ אַתָּה יְהֹוָה. הַנִּפְרָע לְעַמּוֹ יִשְׂרָאֵל מִכָּל צָרֵיהֶם. הָאֵל הַמּוֹשִׁיעַ:

אֲשֶׁר הֵנִיא עֲצַת גּוֹיִם וַיָּפֶר מַחְשְׁבוֹת עֲרוּמִים: בְּקוּם עָלֵינוּ אָדָם רָשָׁע. נֵצֶר זָדוֹן מִזֶּרַע עֲמָלֵק: גָּאָה בְעָשְׁרוֹ וְכָרָה לוֹ בוֹר. וּגְדֻלָּתוֹ יָקְשָׁה לוֹ לָכֶד: דִּמָּה בְנַפְשׁוֹ לִלְכֹּד וְנִלְכָּד. בִּקֵּשׁ לְהַשְׁמִיד וְנִשְׁמַד מְהֵרָה: הָמָן הוֹדִיעַ אֵיבַת אֲבוֹתָיו וְעוֹרֵר שִׂנְאַת אַחִים לַבָּנִים: וְלֹא זָכַר רַחֲמֵי שָׁאוּל. כִּי בְחֶמְלָתוֹ עַל אֲגָג נוֹלַד אוֹיֵב: זָמַם רָשָׁע לְהַכְרִית צַדִּיק. וְנִלְכַּד טָמֵא בִּידֵי טָהוֹר: חֶסֶד גָּבַר עַל שִׁגְגַת אָב. וְרָשָׁע הוֹסִיף חֵטְא עַל חֲטָאָיו: טָמַן בְּלִבּוֹ מַחְשְׁבוֹת עֲרוּמָיו. וַיִּתְמַכֵּר לַעֲשׂוֹת רָעָה: יָדוֹ שָׁלַח בִּקְדוֹשֵׁי אֵל. כַּסְפּוֹ נָתַן לְהַכְרִית זִכְרָם: כִּרְאוֹת מָרְדְּכַי כִּי יָצָא קֶצֶף וְדָתֵי הָמָן נִתְּנוּ בְשׁוּשָׁן: לָבַשׁ שַׂק וְקָשַׁר מִסְפֵּד וְגָזַר צוֹם וַיֵּשֶׁב עַל הָאֵפֶר: מִי זֶה יַעֲמֹד לְכַפֵּר שְׁגָגָה וְלִמְחֹל חַטַּאת עֲוֹן אֲבוֹתֵינוּ: נֵץ פָּרַח מִלּוּלָב. הֵן הֲדַסָּה עָמְדָה לְעוֹרֵר יְשֵׁנִים: סָרִיסֶיהָ הִבְהִילוּ לְהָמָן לְהַשְׁקוֹתוֹ יֵין חֲמַת תַּנִּינִים: עָמַד בְּעָשְׁרוֹ וְנָפַל בְּרִשְׁעוֹ. עָשָׂה לוֹ עֵץ וְנִתְלָה עָלָיו: פִּיהֶם פָּתְחוּ כָל יוֹשְׁבֵי תֵבֵל. כִּי פוּר הָמָן נֶהְפַּךְ לְפוּרֵנוּ: צַדִּיק נֶחֱלַץ מִיַּד רָשָׁע. אוֹיֵב נִתַּן תַּחַת נַפְשׁוֹ: קִימוּ עֲלֵיהֶם לַעֲשׂוֹת פּוּרִים וְלִשְׂמֹחַ בְּכָל שָׁנָה וְשָׁנָה: רָאִיתָ אֶת תְּפִלַּת מָרְדְּכַי וְאֶסְתֵּר. הָמָן וּבָנָיו עַל הָעֵץ תָּלִיתָ:

שׁוֹשַׁנַּת יַעֲקֹב צָהֲלָה וְשָׂמֵחָה בִּרְאוֹתָם יַחַד תְּכֵלֶת מָרְדְּכַי תְּשׁוּעָתָם הָיִיתָ לָנֶצַח. וְתִקְוָתָם בְּכָל דּוֹר וָדוֹר. לְהוֹדִיעַ שֶׁכָּל קֹוֶיךָ לֹא יֵבֹשׁוּ. וְלֹא יִכָּלְמוּ לָנֶצַח כָּל הַחוֹסִים בָּךְ. אָרוּר הָמָן אֲשֶׁר בִּקֵּשׁ לְאַבְּדִי. בָּרוּךְ מָרְדְּכַי הַיְּהוּדִי. אֲרוּרָה זֶרֶשׁ אֵשֶׁת מַפְחִידִי. בְּרוּכָה אֶסְתֵּר בַּעֲדִי. אֲרוּרִים כָּל הָרְשָׁעִים. בְּרוּכִים כָּל הַצַּדִּיקִים. וְגַם חַרְבוֹנָה זָכוּר לַטּוֹב: